Questions
& Answers
about
Building

Fine Homebuilding®

Questions & Answers about Building

The Taunton Press

Library of Congress Cataloging-in-Publication Data

Fine homebuilding questions/answers about building,
    p.   cm.
    Cover title: Fine homebuilding questions & answers about building.
    "A Fine homebuilding book"—Verso of t.p.
    Includes index.
    ISBN 0-942391-29-2; $9.95
    1. House construction—Miscellanea. 2. Dwellings—Remodeling—
Miscellanea. I. Fine homebuilding. II. Title: Fine homebuilding
questions & answers about building. III. Title: Fine homebuilding
questions and answers about building. IV. Title: Questions/answers
about building.
TH4812.F56   1989
643'.7—dc20   89-50671
                                                                   CIP

TAUNTON
BOOKS&VIDEOS

...by fellow enthusiasts

First printing: September 1989
Second printing: April 1990
Printed in the United States of America

A FINE HOMEBUILDING Book

FINE HOMEBUILDING® is a trademark of The Taunton Press, Inc.,
registered in the U.S. Patent and Trademark Office.

The Taunton Press, Inc.
63 South Main Street
Box 5506
Newtown, Connecticut 06470-5506

Introduction

During the eight years that *Fine Homebuilding* has been published, no aspect of the magazine's life has been more vigorous than that of the Questions & Answers column. That's because it's the place where readers come to put their problems to the experts. And it's because the column's editors have taken such unusual delight in putting readers in touch with the right information. Whatever the question, they tried to find a practicing professional builder to answer it. We published in the magazine the best and most instructive of these questions and answers.

Here you'll find, in one volume, the best of the best—a miniature text on residential construction techniques. It's organized according to topics and indexed for handy reference. We hope you find this little book as informative and helpful as we found it fun to put together.

—*John Lively, editor*

Table of Contents

Chapter 1:

Foundations and Basements

Foundation drain retrofit

My six-year-old frame house sits on a concrete-block foundation. The footing is no more than a foot below grade. The ground is very rocky and drainage is good. So far, there are no cracks in the foundation. The house is on a slope, though, and every spring, melting snow comes under the footing on the north side of the house and floods the crawl space on its way downhill.

I've considered digging a trench 4 ft. deep beside the house, pouring a concrete wall in the trench next to the footing and placing a drain pipe and crushed stone next to the wall. Would this help? Or would I be better off digging a trench a few feet away from the foundation and putting in a drain pipe and crushed stone?

—*Michael Weinberg, Andes, N. Y.*

Kenneth Hughes, a consulting structural and civil engineer in Lafayette, Calif., replies: The concrete wall you are proposing would be effective only if it were securely anchored to your footing. Without careful detailing, however, it could do more harm than good.

By installing an underground, perforated drain pipe and surrounding it with rock, you can intercept the water before it seeps under the footing. A slightly sloping drain pipe gives the water an easy path in which to continue downhill. I suggest using drain rock, which is rounded, instead of crushed rock, which is angular. It is also good practice to wrap the drain rock with a filter fabric so fine particles of soil can't pass through it.

Place the pipe 6 in. to 12 in. below the bottom of the foundation and run it downhill until the pipe emerges from below grade. However, don't excavate straight down alongside the foundation because you might undermine it. A safe rule of thumb is not to excavate below an imaginary line projected at a 45° angle down and away from the bottom edge of the foundation (drawing below). While doing this work, you should also install a waterproof

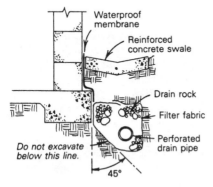

membrane on the surface of the concrete block below grade.

Another line of defense can be achieved by diverting the surface water before it soaks into the ground. Do this by building a concrete swale on the ground surface and slope it in such a way that water is directed around and away from the house.

Plaster pop-off

The brick foundation on my 75-year-old two-story house is crumbling away. The 3½ ft. above grade has been plastered over with mortar several times, but after a few years the mortar falls off again, taking some more of the brick with it. In some spots the brick has eroded as much as 1½ in. Aside from raising the house up and rebuilding the entire foundation, is there any way to repair and preserve what is left of the foundation? —*William N. Marske, Michigan City, Ind.*

Dick Kreh, a mason and author in Maryland, replies: First, try to determine what is causing the mortar plaster to come off. The answer is usually excess moisture. Check to make sure that soffits or downspouts aren't dripping water onto the wall. Excess humidity inside your house may also be sweating through to the exterior, creating constant dampness. Use a humidifier to remove most of this moisture from the air inside the house.

Excess moisture or not, you will need a mortar mix that will bond to the old work so that the parging you do now will still be on the wall in a few years. You don't want a superhard mortar; in fact, that would be the worst mix to use. Just as in repointing old brick, the inner mortar joints are soft, and a high lime mortar should be used. A high concentration of lime will cut down slightly on strength, but the mix will adhere well to the old wall surface. I would use one part Type 1 portland cement to two parts mason's hydrated lime to eight parts washed building sand. Type S hydrated lime is a little better, if you can get it in your area, because of its fineness. However, regular mason's hydrated lime will work fine. This mortar will cure to a compression strength of about 375 psi— plenty strong enough, and waterproof as well.

There are two methods of patching the eroded brick in preparation for parging the wall. If the brick is still solid on its eroded surfaces, it can be built out with the parging. Apply several coats, and allow them to dry before putting on more. If the brick is crumbling, you can nail metal lath over the eroded areas, and then parge over the reinforcing. This will create a much better bonding patch than regular parging. Ask for 3.4 diamond-mesh copper-bearing metal lath. It will resist rusting longer than other types.

To prepare the wall for parging, remove any loose material on the wall—mortar or old paint—by rubbing briskly with a wire brush. If sections of old parging still remain, try to chip or scrape off as much as you can. Next, dampen the area to be parged with a tank-type garden sprayer, using a fine mist. Don't soak the wall, just dampen it. Work a small area so that your wall does not dry out too fast.

Now trowel on the mortar about ⅜ in. thick using a plastering trowel. After the first coat is on, scratch the surface with an old broom, or use a special scratching tool, which you can buy at a masonry-supply or building-supply house. Let the mortar cure overnight, and trowel on the final coat the next day.

Underground utilities

I want to run my house utility lines—water, electricity, natural gas—under my driveway to the garage. I've heard a lot of conflicting information about how to separate these utilities into different trenches. How deep should they be buried? Also, how should I prepare the bed for these lines, and what materials should I use for pipe and conduit?
—Jeffrey A. Katz, New Bedford, Mass.

Consulting editor Bob Syvanen replies: You should dig more than one trench. A trencher rented for about $90 a day will save your back, and won't break your budget. The hazard in burying everything together is not that something will happen underground, but that problems will come up when digging down to repair or reroute one of these lines sometime in the future. A misdirected shovel that cuts a power line while you're searching for a gas leak could be a disaster. So for safety's sake, electrical lines should be in a separate trench, which is enough to one side that it won't be in the way when you dig up utilities in an adjacent trench. Power should be run in plastic-covered cable that's rated for underground use. If the line is to be in or under concrete, metal conduit must be used.

The reason you are getting different stories is that burying utilities is affected a great deal by local conditions, both climatic and political. This is particularly true for how deep the trench should be and what materials should be used for carrying the utilities. The two biggest issues here are whether the ground freezes in winter, and whether your community has accepted plastic pipe.

Where I live in Cape Cod, water lines need to be buried 48 in. deep so they won't freeze, and plastic pipe is the accepted material. In most areas, natural gas is run in black iron pipe wrapped with asphalt-coated paper or plastic to prevent corrosion. High-pressure gas lines are typically buried 24 in. deep, and low-pressure lines as little as 12 in. to 18 in. deep. Water and gas are often allowed in the same trench, but it's not really a good idea. If you are having to follow out a water line to repair a break, you don't want a pressurized natural gas line in the same trench, particularly if it comes as a surprise. Often, though, these utilities come from different locations and need to be buried at different depths, so there's little temptation to run them in the same trench.

The Massachusetts code (2118.4), which prevails where you live unless the local code is more stringent, requires that the piping be protected against physical damage and be laid in a solid bed. The code does not specify what the bed should be composed of, but sand is often used. It provides an easily leveled surface that offers support for pipe, good drainage, and gives future backhoe operators or laborers an indication that they're in the vicinity of utility runs.

Winter foundation protection

I am building two houses, and for reasons of time and finances their basements must be completed during the summer with an intervening winter before they are framed and finished. The houses are located in Schenectady, N. Y., and Mt. Vernon, Ohio. If the basement walls are capped with the first-floor deck, what other measures should be taken, such as sealing and heating, in order to protect the new foundations from winter damage?
—Walter Kaufmann,
Mt. Vernon, Ohio

Consulting editor Tom Law replies: The chief enemy of building in a cold climate is frost heave. Treat an unattended basement like any

other house to protect it from freezing below the footings. The upper floor should be on and water shed with plastic or builder's felt. Drain tile should be in place and walls backfilled, with finish grade sloping away from the wall in every direction. Close off any openings and monitor the temperature. In extreme cold, introduce heat if required. Even though the earth mass outside is sufficient to prevent freezing at footing level, the floor and walls can get cold enough to cause the earth below the footings to freeze.

Siting a septic system

My house site is densely wooded with spruce and aspen. Although I would like to keep as many trees as possible, I'm worried about their roots damaging my septic system. How close to the trees can I put the septic field?
—Mike Walsh, Willowdale, Ont.

David Bird, a soils engineer in Plymouth, Mich., replies: You're wise to anticipate the problem before you put in your septic system. Keep the leach lines at least 10 ft. away from the drip line (the outer tip of the tree branches) of the nearest trees. Even then, you should take some extra precautions.

One of the best things you can do is to use lots of crushed stone or aggregate beneath and around the leach-line tile. Roots seek out the areas with the greatest moisture. Since the moisture from the tile will accumulate at the bottom of the gravel layer, the roots will grow under the lines, causing little disturbance. Put 12 in. of gravel beneath the leach line, and 3 in. above the pipe. You can use gravel anywhere from ½ in. to 2½ in. in size, as long as it's free of silt, clay and other fine soils.

There are also some important considerations for the connection between the sewer pipe and the septic tank, and the connection between the tank and the distribution box. When these points are poorly attached, roots can enter the sewer line itself. Avoid this by using lead-caulked cast-iron pipe, a sulfur-base or bituminous pipe-joint compound, copper rings over pipe joints, or lump copper sulfate in the pipe trenches.

One last line of defense, which is especially helpful in installations that receive only seasonal use such as summer cabins, is treating the septic system with 2 lb. or 3 lb. of copper-sulfate crystals once a year. You can do this by flushing the copper sulfate down the toilet bowl. Do this in the late evening hours so that it will get the maximum contact time in the lines before being diluted by further flushing. The copper sulfate will destroy any roots it comes in contact with in the sewer line and trenches. However, copper sulfate will also corrode chrome, iron and brass, so be very careful. Cast iron is normally not affected by this kind of copper-sulfate treatment, nor should it interrupt the septic tank's biological breaking down of waste when used in this kind of moderate dosage.

Drainage for a wet backyard

My house sits on a flat shelf that was bulldozed in the hillside. Behind the house, the ground is sloped in the shape of a saucer.

This area collects water, which makes the backyard unusable during rainy winters (last year we got a record 65 in.). Because I have done extensive landscaping over the years, regrading the area is impractical. I am concerned about the possibility of landslides, since this surface water eventually is absorbed by the ground behind the house. I am thinking of installing a drain system. How should I spec pipe size, depth, slope, gravel size, etc.?

—W. A. Ruhland, Orinda, Calif.

David Bird, a soils engineer in Plymouth, Mich., replies: Although I don't have the specific information about things like soil type and the grade of the slope that I need in order to make a thorough study of the situation, your concerns about a landslide are probably unfounded. The bulldozer work on the hill that created the site for your house actually reduced the danger of a slope failure. Although you are technically correct in your worries about the water that pools in your backyard, in practical fact, one of the best reasons for providing proper drainage is to make the yard more usable.

The drawing on the facing page shows a typical drainage system that works well in most situations. Either rigid or flexible 4-in. perforated PVC pipe could be used. With rigid pipe you can use a 1% slope. The slope should be increased to 4% for flexible pipe since it is more difficult to keep this material headed in a straight line downhill. Use at least 2 in. of clean (less than 5% silt and clay), well-graded granular soil under the drainage pipe in the trench. Backfill the trench with this same

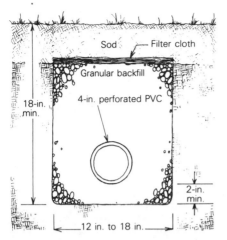

Sod — Filter cloth

Granular backfill

4-in. perforated PVC

18-in. min.

2-in. min.

12 in. to 18 in.

material once you have installed the pipe. Pea gravel, washed sand or crushed aggregate can also be used in most situations. Be careful if you are covering the ground with sod over the drainage area. If the sod is supported by a topsoil that erodes easily into fine silts, you will need to use a filter cloth where the topsoil and the granular backfill meet. You may also need a filter cloth if you use very porous backfill with large voids.

Pinning foundations to rock

I am designing a house for a wooded site with many rock outcroppings. Typical trench foundations don't seem appropriate, but pinning the foundation walls to rock might be the way to go. The home will be two stories (typical construction), possibly with an adjacent pool. Could you tell me how best to design foundation details? Also, what method of investigation would be appropriate in lieu of soil borings, which appear unfeasible?
—Paul Scott, Garden City, Mich.

Structural engineer Kenneth Hughes replies: Pinning foundations to surface rock is usually not recommended because of the uncertainties involved in designing a suitable foundation. Although the rock may appear to be strong and part of a large formation, its actual strength and embedment would be difficult to evaluate by someone other than a competent soils engineer. Even if the rock is substantial enough to tie a foundation wall to, there would be cause for concern regarding differential support where the foundation bears on soil. Differential settlement could be mitigated by extending concrete piers through the soil down to bedrock.

A conventional foundation set into an excavated trench has a natural ability to resist lateral forces through passive soil resistance and friction against the sides of the foundation. When a foundation wall is being anchored to surface rock, an alternate means of lateral support is needed. This would most likely take the form of drilled holes in the rock with reinforcing dowels set and grouted into place and projecting up into the foundation concrete.

If deep soil borings are not feasible, other evaluation procedures, such as shallow exploratory pits in the soil between or above the rock, can reveal the necessary information for developing appropriate foundation criteria. Additionally, rock should be evaluated for strength, ability to support various types of anchors and general compatibility with different types of foundations. Retaining a soils engineer is a good idea, especially when irregular conditions are involved.

Insulating fieldstone

How should I insulate an exposed fieldstone foundation? Can I take advantage of the foundation's mass? —*Chris Hall, Bath, Maine*

Peter Mann, who teaches passive-solar house design at Mohawk College in Hamilton, Ont., replies: The only way I know to insulate a fieldstone wall is to construct a cavity wall and fill it with loose insulation. This kind of wall is not nearly as strong as a solid foundation, and requires careful engineering. Also, this method is not very effective. With a 4-in. cavity totally filled with loose insulation (an unlikely event because it settles), the maximum value would be about R-12. Also, if the foundation wall doesn't get direct sunlight, it won't be useful for thermal storage. To achieve the aesthetics you want, you may have to compromise. Build a well-insulated concrete foundation wall and apply a stone veneer.

Gravity-type retaining walls

My brick home is about 100 years old. Part of the house, a one-story attached room addition on grade, was built with a foundation of laid stone over a crawl space. When the previous owners had a central-heating system put in, they dug the crawl space to provide a cellar with enough clearance to install a furnace and ductwork. However, the foundation was not extended down at the same time, and for years it has rested only on a small ledge of clay subsoil.

To provide lateral bracing for the addition, I recently built a con-crete-block wall within the existing excavation to the height of the bottom of the old foundation. A gap of approximately 1 ft. exists between this new wall and the excavated soil wall. What material should I use to fill the gap for optimum lateral and vertical support? I should also tell you that I'm planning to raise the roof on this addition and add a second story in the near future.
—*David R. Morris, Sunbury, Ohio*

David Bird, a soils engineer in Plymouth, Mich., replies: It's difficult to make specific recommendations without the benefit of an on-site inspection, coupled with some information about your soil and the dimensions of your foundation. Considering the consequences of a foundation failure though, getting an engineer out to inspect your site could be dollars well spent.

However, I can give you some general suggestions. Provided the existing single-story structure doesn't show significant diagonal cracks radiating from the windows, sagging floors or out-of-square door frames, it is pretty safe to assume that the clay soil supporting the existing foundation is relatively hard. A softer clay soil would probably have crept and bulged laterally into the basement by now, with the obvious signs of structural distress mentioned above.

Constructing the block wall was a step in the right direction. The next step, providing it meets with the code requirements in your area, would be to incorporate your new block wall into a gravity-type retaining wall. This type of wall, shown on the facing page, resists lateral load by its weight alone. It is designed to reduce the risk of a sudden failure of the soil supporting the existing footings. This failure could be caused by additional load on the footing, cracking of the soil due to drying out, or a long-term creep movement of the soil.

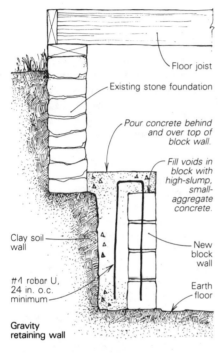

Floor joist

Existing stone foundation

Pour concrete behind and over top of block wall.

Fill voids in block with high-slump, small-aggregate concrete.

Clay soil wall

New block wall

#4 rebar U, 24 in. o.c. minimum

Earth floor

Gravity retaining wall

To make a gravity-type retaining wall, you should fill the voids in your block wall with high-slump, small-size aggregate concrete or mortar grout mix. Reduce the size of air voids in the concrete as much as possible by using a pencil-type concrete vibrator.

The space between the soil wall supporting the existing foundation and the new block wall should be filled and capped with concrete. This can be a standard mix, but should be poured monolithically (no cold joints) and vibrated. U-shaped steel reinforcing rods should be added before pouring the concrete to connect the block wall and the concrete behind it, improving the bending strength of the wall. In addition, take care that you provide sufficient lateral bracing of the block wall when pouring behind it, since the wet concrete could force the block wall out of plumb. The lateral bracing can be removed after the concrete has cured.

It's not prudent to add any more load to the existing foundation with a second-story addition. This extra weight could cause some settling, and increase the lateral pressure on the new block wall. With the advice of an engineer who could make an on-site inspection and provide you with drawings, you could underpin the existing single-story wall footings, or permanently brace the new block wall to restrict this lateral movement, allowing you to add another story.

Concrete ills

The foundation of my home and my garage slab, built in the late 1930s, have the appearance of exposed aggregate. We are always cleaning up dislodged pebbles and cement-like powder around the outside of the house. The interior side of the foundation is less affected. However, I have had occasion to drill through the foundation, and the interior of the concrete is hard and stable. Any suggestions?   —Gary Olson, Walnut Creek, Calif.

William C. Panarese, a construction specialist with the Portland Cement Association, replies: It sounds like the concrete is suffering from old age. The typical residential foundation isn't subjected to tremendous loads, so unless the walls have worn down to a cross section much thinner than the original, the problem probably isn't very serious.

The powdering of your slab could be slowed substantially or stopped completely by applying a sealer or hardener. The most effective sealers are penetrating epoxy resins. Hardeners should contain zinc or magnesium silicofluorides as the primary ingredient. They are used extensively on concrete-slab floors to remedy dusting problems.

Where the problem is more severe than dusting but the underlying concrete is sound, the surface of the foundation walls could be scarified (abraded) or sandblasted to remove loose material, then plastered with a conventional cement-stucco mixture. A bonding agent applied first will help ensure that the stucco sticks permanently to the concrete.

Different repair procedures should be followed for the garage floor because of the greater amount of loading and abrasion it will need to withstand. If scarifying or chipping the weak, friable surface layer reveals a sound concrete layer underneath, then one option is thin-bonded resurfacing, using a cement grout between the newly cleaned concrete slab and a new topping of concrete.

Slabs are best cleaned dry using machines that grind the concrete or sandblast it. Once all the loose material is removed down to sound concrete, the 1:1:½ cement/sand/water grout should be scrubbed in, and a minimum 1-in. topping of high-strength concrete using pea-gravel (⅜-in.) aggregate placed on top.

Make sure that the grout is still damp when the overlay concrete is poured. Complete details of this procedure are given in the Portland Cement Association pamphlet IS144.04T, "Resurfacing Concrete Floors" (5420 Old Orchard Rd., Skokie, Ill. 60077).

Spalling foundation

I am in the process of renovating the foundation of a house built in 1920 which was poured with what we call "native gravel." The sand and gravel particles contain a large amount of clay.

Exposure to moisture over the years has resulted in sloughing (spalling) up to 1½ in. in some places, on both the interior and exterior. Although the walls are still structurally sound, a few more years will render them nonfunctional. Is there anything that can be done to restore these surfaces short of pouring new walls?
—Ted Birdsall, Chadron, Neb.

David Bird, a soils engineer in Plymouth, Mich., replies: I'm afraid the news isn't good as far as coming up with an economical solution to the problem. Several factors are probably causing the deterioration of your basement walls, and almost all of them have to do with the quality of the concrete. To start, there's the aggregate. Deterioration and spalling often occur if non-durable aggregates (shale, soft sandstone, mudstone, etc.) are used. If the aggregate wasn't washed and was coated with soil, the effect is the same.

Second, there may not have been enough cement used in the concrete, or the cement may not have been of very good quality. The type of cement is also important. In modern-day concrete for cold climates, air-entraining cement is used to resist freeze-thaw deterioration. The tiny air bubbles in the concrete are resilient and tolerate the expansion and contraction of this cycle. This would apply only to the exterior of the wall.

Probably the single most damaging factor in this case is moisture. Over the years the concrete has become saturated with moisture from the ground. The continual movement of the moisture from the wall's exterior toward the basement's interior coupled with the other factors caused the concrete to weaken and gradually spall apart.

If there is a sound core to the existing wall and the wall could be thoroughly dried out, then an epoxy bonding agent and a latex concrete overlay could be used to restore the integrity of the wall. To dry out the wall this thoroughly, however, would require the complete removal of all of the soil around the wall perimeter as well as an elaborate heating system to take the moisture out of the wall. This type of treatment would undoubtedly be very expensive, and would have a high risk of failure. But any lesser attempt would almost certainly fail.

If there is a reasonable solution short of replacing the existing walls, it is constructing a new wall just inside the existing wall. The new wall would be supported on the existing floor slab or, in the case of a basement without a floor slab, on a new foundation constructed at the same level as the existing basement-wall foundation. Some special structural details may be required to support the existing wall loads on the new wall, since the new wall will be located inside of the existing sill plates. If the exterior stud walls were constructed on top of the first-floor deck, then it may be possible to wedge the existing floor joists on top of the new wall and transfer the vertical loads a short distance along the joists to the new basement wall.

The only problem then would be to cover the original foundation wall on the exterior. You could rely on an architectural treatment to conceal the spalling wall or just stucco over it with a latex concrete parging. Because the surrounding moisture will continue to work on the old wall and cause it to spall, the parging would have to be replaced every couple of years to keep it looking nice.

Footings for brick veneer

I own a 25-year-old concrete-block home that I would like to dress up on the exterior with brick veneer. How should I go about pouring new footings to support the weight of the veneer?
—Daryl Bensinger, Narvon, Pa.

Dick Kreh, an author and mason in Maryland, replies: First excavate around the foundation to determine if your original footings are wide enough to carry the new brick veneer, which will total about 4½ in. The extra weight of the veneer usually doesn't cause any problems.

If the footings are not wide enough to support the veneer, they will have to be widened by pouring additional concrete. The two footings can be tied together by drilling into the original masonry foundation just above the original footing and

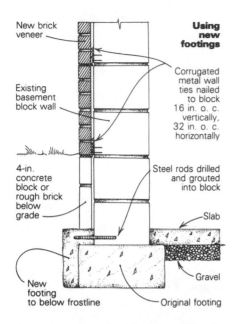

New brick veneer

Existing basement block wall

4-in. concrete block or rough brick below grade

New footing to below frostline

Using new footings

Corrugated metal wall ties nailed to block 16 in. o. c. vertically, 32 in. o. c. horizontally

Steel rods drilled and grouted into block

Slab

Gravel

Original footing

inserting short lengths of steel rod, as shown above. These should be grouted into the old wall with cement. The new footing should then be poured about 4 in. higher than the top of the original, resting on it at the bottom and extending outward to support the new brickwork. If you only butt the new footing against the existing one, in all probability it will crack at that point. In any case, the earth around the footing must be tamped firm.

The part of the foundation wall below finished grade line (usually 4-in. concrete block) should be built with Type M mortar. This is available premixed from building suppliers or it can be mixed on site with 1 part portland cement to ¼ part hydrated lime to 3 parts sand. The brickwork above grade should be laid with Type N masonry cement mortar or a comparable mix using 1 part portland cement to 1 part hydrated lime to 6 parts sand.

Another way to support brick veneer is to bolt continuous corrosion-resistant steel angle irons to the existing foundation wall at or slightly below the finished grade line. The drawing below shows this method in use where brick veneer has been used to cover existing conventional wood siding on a frame house. This method keeps excavation and masonry below grade to a minimum. Do not bolt into wood plates or any of the framing members but to the masonry foundation itself to carry the load safely.

This method is recommended only for a one-story structure (the wall height shouldn't exceed 14 ft.). Make sure the irons will carry the weight. Consider the size and spacing of the bolts that anchor the angle iron as well, not only for the dead load to be carried, but also for the bearing value of the foundation wall itself. To be on the safe side, run

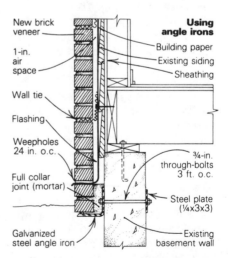

New brick veneer

1-in. air space

Wall tie

Flashing

Weepholes 24 in. o.c.

Full collar joint (mortar)

Galvanized steel angle iron

Using angle irons

Building paper

Existing siding

Sheathing

¾-in. through-bolts 3 ft. o.c.

Steel plate (¼x3x3)

Existing basement wall

your calculations past an engineer in your area.

Coat the hot-dipped galvanized angle iron with a bituminous material to protect it from rust. To install the angle irons, measure down with a bricklayer's modular-scale rule to a level that will keep full courses at window sills and at the top of the wall.

Guarding against frost heave

I'm going to need to put a frost footing under a timber-frame building I'm remodeling, which is currently supported by spot footings. My idea is to ditch-witch on either side of the sill plate, then join the footings with concrete slab just under the plate. Would this protect the building against frost heave?
—*Mark Korzeniewski, Fairfield, Iowa*

David Bird, a soils engineer in Plymouth, Mich., replies: Although joined spot footings under the existing sill could be made to support the structure, it wouldn't be any protection against frost heaving. If there is a likelihood of frost heave, then the footings must be extended below the normal depth of seasonal frost penetration, or frost line. This depth varies with the locale; you can find out what it is from your local building department.

Understanding how frost heave happens will help in designing to prevent it. Three conditions set the stage for heaving: an extended period of cold weather; a source of water—usually rising by capillary attraction through soil voids from the water table below, but sometimes percolating from a surface source; and a sufficiently permeable soil to permit the transmission of water. When this moisture freezes, it forms an ice lens, which will continue to

grow in thickness and diameter as long as the soil remains frozen and there is a supply of water. The result is that everything above the lens is forced upward.

Not all soils are susceptible to frost heave. It generally occurs in silt, fine sand and silty sand-size soils. These soils permit moisture to rise above the water table, even in winter. Although clean medium-to-coarse clays and silty clays have very high capillary rise heights,

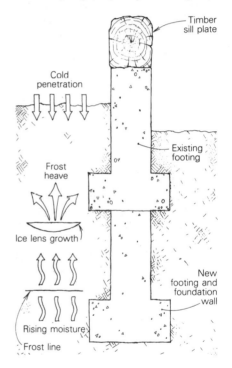

they are so impermeable that it takes longer than the length of a normal winter for the water to form an ice lens.

You could have your building's footings extended to frost depth as an underpinning operation. A portion of each footing would be undermined to the required depth, and a new footing poured at this level. A new foundation wall could then be formed and poured to sit on top of the new footing, and support the existing footing above it. This work has to be done in short sections so as not to undermine too much of the existing footings at any one time, which could cause extensive damage to the house. The process is tricky and is best done by an underpinning contractor who has both the experience and the right tools. Even then, you should expect the building to settle some—exactly how much will depend on the care taken and the soil conditions.

One of the biggest drawbacks of this procedure is its expense, and you could leave the existing footings as they are and use one of several quicker, less expensive solutions, if there hasn't been a history of serious frost-heave problems with your building. These alternatives include burying permanent insulation, or using temporary surface insulation that is placed each fall and removed each spring. Reducing the depth of frost penetration with insulation doesn't guarantee that frost heaving won't happen. It simply reduces its likelihood. An unusually long and cold winter without much snow may heave buildings that have never had problems before.

Rigid extruded polystyrene insulation is the best material for burying. It should slope away from the existing footings a little and extend at least 2 ft. away from the building. Cover each panel with enough topsoil to support plant growth. A temporary insulation could be hay, straw or even snow, if it fell early enough and was piled against the building's walls.

Wood foundations

I have read several articles on using salt-treated lumber in the construction of all-weather wood foundations (AWWF). The advantages of this type of construction for basements or earth-bermed houses are obvious: ease of construction, insulation, wiring and interior wall treatment. Proper drainage is a must, but I haven't seen any other drawbacks mentioned. Just how feasible is an AWWF, and approximately how long will it last?
—John Bower, Lafayette. Ind.

John Rose, project manager for construction markets at the American Plywood Association, replies: All-weather wood foundations are constructed from framing lumber and plywood that has been pressure treated with special waterborne preservatives (either ammoniacal copper arsenate or chromated copper arsenate). During the pressure-treating process, these compounds are forced into the wood fibers under hear and pressure. Treated lumber and plywood can be bought and assembled at the site by the builder, although some lumber dealers or wood-foundation contractors will prefabricate entire foundation sections that are trucked to the site.

As far as permanence is concerned, tests conducted by the U.S. Department of Agriculture indicate a long-term service life for such materials. Samples put in the ground more than 30 years ago have remained in good condition in spite of severe exposure to the elements.

Care is needed during AWWF construction to ensure proper fabrication and installation. Securing the wall to the footing and building adequate structural support into the wall (correct size and spacing of studs) are the two areas where mistakes can be made. Proper drainage is also important, since continued exposure to water would shorten the life of the wood wall and cause leakage. Pressure-treated wood foundations, originally developed in Canada, have come into use in the U.S. only in the last decade. During this time, an estimated 40,000 houses have been built using wood foundations. Perhaps as energy and concrete construction costs rise, more builders will take an interest in all-weather wood foundations.

Comprehensive information about building and installing all-weather wood foundations is available from the American Plywood Association, P.O. Box 11700, Tacoma, Wash. 98411; (206) 565-6600. For general information about pressure-treated lumber and plywood, you can contact either the American Wood Preservers' Institute (1651 Old Meadow Rd., McLean, Va. 22101; [703] 893-4005) or the Society of American Wood Preservers (1401 Wilson Blvd., Suite 205, Arlington, VA. 22209 [703] 841-1500).

Wood-preservative worries

Presently, we are involved in the design of some totally underground residential buildings. We are considering using an all-weather wood foundation but are concerned about the toxicity of the chromated copper arsenate (CCA) employed in the preservative treatment of these wood materials.
—*Eugene Wukasch, Austin, Tex.*

Terry Amburgey, of the Forest Products Utilization Laboratory at Mississippi State University, replies: Chromated copper arsenate (CCA) is a water-borne formulation that is one of the best wood preservatives that has been developed. Three types of CCA are produced (types A, B and C); type C is currently the most widely used in the U.S. (see American Wood Preservers' Association Standard P-5). Wood treated with CCA is greyish-green in color but is otherwise clean, paintable and free of objectionable odors. While it is toxic to wood-inhabiting insects and fungi, CCA-treated wood presents no significant health risks to humans or animals. As wood is being treated with CCA, the components of the formulation interact with one another and with the wood cells to form a complex mixture of insoluble chromates that are "fixed" within the wood. During this fixation reaction, the chromium and arsenic are converted to relatively non-toxic forms. Fixation is virtually complete when CCA-treated wood has dried.

While I know of no data that deal directly with the use of CCA-treated material in underground residential construction, CCA-treated wood is considered safe for use in fabricating picnic tables, playground equipment, park benches, house foundations and structural supports. It is safe for decks on houses, around swimming pools, and on piers. Some log homes are made entirely of CCA-treated material, as are stick-built homes in some tropical areas.

The exposed surfaces of picnic tables, benches and playground equipment usually are washed with detergent to remove possible surface deposits of chemicals prior to use. Otherwise, no special precautions need to be taken when using CCA-treated wood for products that may come in contact with bare skin. I would be more concerned with the safety of applying chlorinated hydrocarbon insecticides (e.g., chlordane, heptachlor) outside the walls of underground structures to control subterranean termites than with possible health effects of using CCA-treated wood. Termites cannot feed on treated wood, but they can pass through cracks or joints in treated wood to reach untreated materials inside of the structure. I suggest that Dursban (Dow Chemical Co.) be used to control subterranean termites in regions of high hazard. While this product, to my knowledge, has not been tested in underground structures, it has been labeled (at least in some states) for use in houses with subfloor air plenums. Of course, insecticides should always be applied according to approved procedures by qualified pest-control operators.

Wine-cellar temperature

I want to build a wine cellar in my basement to take advantage of the constant coolness there. However, after monitoring the temperature for a year, I was distressed to learn that it ranged from 68°F to 80°F during the summer, far in excess of the 55°F recommended for wine storage. My basement is concrete block, with a slab floor and a 9-ft. ceiling. About 6 ft. of the basement is actually in the ground, with small casement windows above grade. What kind of construction do you recommend for my wine cellar? Is there some sort of small refrigeration unit, air-conditioning or heat-exchanger that I can use to keep the temperature close to the ideal for the wine grape?
—*Richard Yeskoo, Summit, N. J.*

Malcolm Wells, of Brewster, Mass., architect, author and consultant on earth-sheltered housing, replies: I'm not surprised to hear about New Jersey basement temperatures of 68°F to 80°F. The "constantly cool earth" myth, which I'm afraid I helped spread a few years back, dies very slowly. Even at depths of 5 ft. to 6 ft., the temperature of the earth in the temperate zone will range from 30°F to 65°F during the course of a year. Although this is not the ideal 55°F, there is very little heating or cooling to do to get there.

I'd build a wine cellar in the corner of the basement where there aren't any windows, and where I could take the most advantage of the moderating influence of the earth outside. The foundation walls wouldn't require insulation, but some serious waterproofing would have to be done if the walls or floor were contributing to a moisture problem. The two stud walls that would separate the wine cellar from the basement could be filled with 3 in. of fiberglass with a good continuous vapor barrier on the warm (basement) side. The ceiling would also require at least 3 in. of insulation with a vapor barrier placed on the upper (house) side of the batts. Try this for a year, monitoring it all the while with a maximum-minimum temperature recording thermometer to see if you can do without any machinery other than a very small circulating fan. Even if the temperature doesn't stay within the acceptable range, you'll know a lot more the next year about the temperature ranges you have to modify.

Underground waterproofing

I am refurbishing an old grain cellar that is built into a slope and extends about eight feet into the ground at its deepest point. The walls are stone, and in the springtime, water seeps through them. I don't want to cover up the walls inside because they're beautiful. And it is impossible to parge them from the outside because the outside layer is rubble. It occurred to me that I might bury sheets of plywood in the ground around the perimeter of the cellar, with a drain at the bottom, and divert ground water away from the building. Do you think this would work?
—John Jacobs, Highland, N. Y.

Architect Alex Wade replies: Using plywood as a waterproofing membrane in this case would be more trouble than it's worth. It would be extremely difficult to seal the sheets together and virtually impossible to keep them sealed. But this is a common problem and well worth a discussion.

First of all, use gutters and downspouts to make sure that water from the roof of the building is diverted away from the foundation. Second, surface grading around the building should do the same thing. If necessary a surface drain system may have to be installed at the uphill side of the building to divert water. These steps alone might clear up the problem.

If you do install a sub-grade waterproofing membrane, digging a ditch with a drain at the bottom is a good start; it's just the use of plywood that's faulty. The solution used in commercial construction would be to use bentonite clay, a highly expansive dense clay used as a waterproofing membrane. It's packed between sheets of biodegradable kraft paper and sold in panel form. One supplier is the American Colloid Company (Building Materials Department, 1500 West Shure Drive, Arlington Heights, Ill. 60004). However, bentonite is relatively expensive. A heavy (10-mil) continuous plastic sheet would also work, and I have used this technique with good results.

For historic structures whose foundations require special care, there is an English technique known as electro-osmosis. In this technique, anodes are inserted into the wall at intervals and connected with copper wire. Cathodes are driven into the ground at intervals a short distance from the wall. When the soil is wet, a charge is created in the earth surrounding the building that prevents the flow of water. These systems are guaranteed for 20 years. Patents for this system are held by Electro Damp-Proofing, Ltd. Moorside Road, Winnall, Winchester, Hampshire, England. This firm manufactures all the equipment for these installations and licenses installers.

The electro-osmotic dampproofing method is described in detail in the book, *Dampness in Buildings* by R. T. Gratwick, (Crosby, Lockwood, Staples, London, Second Edition, 1974). This book contains a wealth of information on the physical causes and effects of dampness and an intriguing variety of methods for controlling the problem.

A fan for excess humidity

I recently purchased a summer home and am converting it to year-round use. It is a ranch house with a 4½-ft. crawl space that has access to outside air through two small vents. I have added 4 in. of insulation between the joists. The soil is well covered with thick plastic sheeting to hold down moisture. A sump pump runs frequently during the spring rains. There is also a hot-water heater and a floor space heater.

Recently I have noticed a white mold or mildew on the floor joists, although they don't appear to be wet. The north side of the crawl space is the worst. Should I be worried about this?
—*Bruce D. Smith, Maynard, Mass.*

Dan Desmond, an energy consultant in Lancaster, Pa., replies: Your problem may have been aggravated by the new floor insulation retarding vapor transfer to the living area. This doesn't mean you shouldn't have insulated, but you do need to pay attention to the excess humidity in your crawl space. Ground covering notwithstanding, your high water table is creating moisture in excess of the capacity of your vents.

The problem is complicated by the presence of the space heater and the hot-water heater. Without a sufficient supply of direct combustion air, their burners can't draft properly and can contribute substantial quantities of water vapor to the interior air as a by-product of combustion.

This is to say nothing of the dangers of carbon monoxide.

I'd suggest supplying an outside source of combustion air for the heaters, and installing a humidistat-controlled fan in one of the vents to control air moisture levels.

Crawl-space moisture

I own a single-story brick home, built in 1951. My house has 4-in. cinder-block walls with a brick face and uses a post-and-beam support structure. The windows are old steel casements. We have been using window air conditioners to cool the house during the summer months.

When we bought the house, the floor above the crawl space had already been insulated with fiberglass insulation between the beams, and the ground was entirely covered with plastic. Earlier this year I had occasion to go into the crawl space and discovered that the insulation was soaking wet underneath the two bedrooms with air conditioners. Some of the insulation was so heavy with water, it had dropped out from between the joists. The wood was wet, and there was mold growing. This had to come from condensation of moisture caused by the air-conditioned rooms, and I know I should do something to prevent this in the future.

One suggestion is to staple a layer of polyethylene plastic to the underside of the floor above any new insulation, but water might then condense in the wood subflooring. The only other solution I can think of is to pull up the car-

pets and cover the floor with an oil-based varnish, which might act as a vapor barrier. Do you have a better solution?
—*Henry J. Stock Jr., Bethesda, Md.*

David Kaufman, a residential energy consultant in Waldoboro, Maine, replies: The moisture you describe is probably coming from underneath your floor, not above it, unless condensation from the air-conditioning units is leaking down to the crawl space. In either case, adding varnish or polyethylene to the floors won't solve your problem.

In the summer, the underside of the air-conditioned rooms is the coldest spot in the crawl space. Moisture is somehow entering the area and condensing there, much as water condenses on the outside of a cold can of beer on a hot summer day. The plastic ground cover makes it unlikely that the ground is the source of moisture, so I suspect the culprit is humid summer air entering through the ventilation of the crawl space.

Ventilation of crawl spaces has long been standard practice, but lately it has come under increasing fire. It's helpful in drying out cellars plagued by annual interior spring floods, but it may be that introducing warm, humid summer air into an otherwise dry crawl space can actually increase moisture levels.

I recommend temporarily removing the fiberglass in the areas with moisture problems (to facilitate drying) and ventilating through the fall or taking other steps to get the wood dry. Then reinsulate and close the crawl space off—no more ventilation. Some authorities even recommend winter ventilation to reduce

moisture levels, but due to the impact on heating bills, I'd suggest it only as a last resort. You might also try extending the polyethylene ground cover up onto the walls and installing an air barrier (such as Dupont's Tyvek or Reemay's Typar) across the bottom of the joists to curtail air flow into the insulation. Polyethylene would work a bit better for this, but it would act as a wrong-side vapor barrier in the winter and once again trap moisture in the insulation.

A word of caution: Before closing off the crawl space, you should test for radon. If you do have a radon problem, then you'll have to deal with that separately. You probably won't be able to eliminate the crawl-space ventilation because that could result in a dangerous build-up of the gas.

Venting crawl spaces

Could you explain the purpose of vents along the band joist above the foundation walls? My home has a 48-in. high crawl space consisting of concrete walls and concrete slab. Running through this area are the hot-water pipes (insulated) below the insulated floor. Is it necessary to leave these vents open all year, and would closing them further prevent heat loss from the pipes?
—*Andrew Ludmar, Syosset, N. Y.*

Consulting editor Bob Syvanen replies: Crawl spaces are vented to prevent moisture damage. Because most of the moisture in a crawl space is drawn up from the ground by capillary action, keep crawl spaces dry by covering the ground with a continuous vapor barrier.

If you can't install a vapor barrier, you'll have to ventilate the area. Here are four basic rules on ventilating crawl spaces. The ventilation area should equal 2 sq. ft. per 100 lin. ft. of building perimeter plus 5% of the crawl-space ground area. Use at least four vents, with one near each corner. Vents should be placed no higher than the bottom of floor joists. Vents should remain open all year.

I have known people who have closed their crawl-space vents for the cold weather and their houses suffered no moisture damage, but these crawl spaces had always been dry. I have seen others suffer pretty bad damage from mildew and rot. Chances are that the concrete floor will help keep your crawl space dry, but if it doesn't, it's safer to leave the vents open and add more insulation to your pipes.

Drying out a humid basement

My house is L-shaped in plan, with a full basement built into a moderate slope. Although the glass doors at the south and west ends of the basement can be opened for ventilation, I find that I have to run two dehumidifiers in order to keep up with the moisture that accumulates down there. These machines are noisy and hot. People who design and live in underground houses must have come up with some solutions to this problem.   —*Michael B. Corbett, Fall River, Mass.*

Charles Lane, an underground-construction consultant in St. Paul, Minn., replies: Uninsulated basement walls lose a large amount of heat to the surrounding soil,

which increases the relative humidity in the basement air. This combination of cool walls and high relative humidity lowers the dew point (the temperature at which water vapor in the air condenses into droplets), and results in increased condensation on the walls. This is much of the reason for the musty smell of many uninsulated basements.

You ought to consider insulating your basement walls on the inside (R-5 insulation is the minimum for this). Insulating the basement wall will warm up the inner surface of the wall. This will not only cut down on the musty smell, but also retain more heat in the basement. This warm air will hold more moisture without increasing the relative humidity, and will feel more comfortable.

Running one dehumidifier will also help. This will release about 1,000 Btus of heat into the basement air for each pint of water removed. A 20-pint-a-day dehumidifier adds about 20,000 Btus to the air per day. This may sound like a lot, but most of this heat just replaces what is lost to the soil through the walls.

Moving air through the basement will also help considerably to re-evaporate moisture that has condensed, drying the basement and reducing mold growth. You should run one or two oscillating fans on foggy or cool days. On warmer, dry days, open the glass doors on the south and west for cross-ventilation.

On warm and windless days where cross-ventilation will not work, you can open all of the windows and light a hot fire in the basement fireplace. The draft through the chimney will pull in warm outside air to give the basement a good drying out.

Greenhouse-mildew effect

We are currently in the process of building a timber-framed saltbox with a greenhouse for passive-solar heat. We have heard of problems arising from mildew growing in the rock-storage base of greenhouses due to the moisture build-up. We had planned on insulating inside the block foundation with foam panels and covering them with a vapor barrier before adding 24 in. of gravel and a 1-in. thick slate floor. Will this approach eliminate mildew?
—*Bill & Sandy Buchanan, Pocomoke City, Md.*

Steve Andrews, a sunspace designer and passive-solar consultant in Denver, replies: There is no guarantee that you won't eventually have moisture and mildew problems in your greenhouse rockbed, either from a high water table or from the high humidity level inside the greenhouse, coupled with the relatively humid climate in Maryland. But taking the precautions you mention will help.

Put your vapor barrier (6-mil plastic) down first, then on top of that at least an inch of extruded polystyrene for insulation, and finally, 1½-in. to 3-in. dia. washed river rock to the depth required. Also include a floor drain.

You need to take steps to ensure that the greenhouse heat is distributed throughout the rockbed. These measures include installing supply and return-air plenums, a thermostatically controlled fan and a 4-in. thick concrete cap with another vapor barrier beneath it poured over the top of the gravel bed. Without these, no significant amount of heat

will get below the top 3 in. to 5 in. of slate and gravel.

A simpler, modified rockbed design uses 6-in. to 8-in. concrete block laid horizontally with the cores of the block aligned. A fan circulates air from the supply plenum through the channels formed by the cores and back into the greenhouse via a return-air plenum. Again, a concrete cap is required.

A properly functioning rockbed requires careful design. See *The Passive Solar Handbook, Vol. II* (a 1980 Department of Energy publication) for a detailed discussion of rockbed design and construction, or consult with an experienced engineer or solar designer.

If you are building a greenhouse to help heat your living area, you may want to abandon a rockbed-storage system altogether. A greenhouse rockbed will heat the greenhouse, not the house. The best place to put additional storage to heat both the greenhouse and the adjoining home is in a massive common wall. If you make two-thirds to three-quarters of this common wall out of brick, slump block, concrete or water, you will achieve the storage capacity needed.

If you are unable at this point in your project to create a mass common wall, additional greenhouse storage can still be provided—at significantly lower cost than a rockbed—by adding a variety of water containers: 30-gal. or 55-gal. drums, stacked 5-gal. honey tins, fiberglass watertubes, plastic-lined 10-gal. milk containers, etc. While metal drums take up space and aren't very attractive, they do provide the cheapest storage and also give you a place to locate raised planting beds.

Sweating ducts

The air-conditioning ducts in the crawl space under my house are sweating. The condensation appears on the outside of the fiberglass insulation that wraps the ducts. What can I do about this?
—*George Pearl, Warner Robins, Ga.*

John Porterfield, a research architect at the University of Illinois and a professional energy auditor, replies: Your sheet-metal ducts filled with cold air are inadvertently performing the same task as the evaporator coil in your air conditioner— condensing water vapor from the humid summer air. The result, unfortunately, is that your ducts are trying to cool the ambient air in your crawl space, which is sucking in air from the great outdoors through foundation vents, rather than delivering this less humid air to the living space above. The appearance of moisture on the outside of the duct insulation means that the full thickness of the insulation as well as the surface of the duct is wet. The solution is to use a vapor barrier to keep most outside air from contacting the air-conditioning ducts. There are two ways to do this. One is to seal the entire crawl space, and the second is to fit just the ducts with a moisture barrier.

To prevent much of this moisture from entering the crawl space, first close and seal all vents from the outside. Then lay polyethylene sheeting, at least 6 mil, on the ground. Lap and seal all joints, and seal the edges to the foundation walls. This in effect includes the crawl space in the area to be conditioned. You were doing that when the crawl space was vented to the outside, but without hot air coming in, the crawl-space temperature should be low enough to save you some money on your energy bills. You can also trim your wintertime fuel usage by leaving the crawl space sealed, as long as you check occasionally for water leaking into the area around the foundation, and monitor the level of humidity to make sure it isn't getting too high.

If you choose just to shield the ducts from the moisture in the crawl space, both foil and polyethylene can be used as vapor barriers. However, foil is difficult to seal at joints, and it can develop pinhole leaks when it is folded and fitted too much. I like to use a second layer of insulation with a polyethylene vapor barrier attached to it over the existing layer of insulation. Wrap this along the length of the ducts, sealing the joints with 2-in. polyethylene tape. Remove the hangers that are suspending the ducts from the joists as you go, and replace them with strips of 6-in. wide sheet metal bent into a U-shape, to minimize flattening the insulation.

Where ducting connects with another run in a coupling, or ends in an outlet or register, remove about 2 in. of insulation from the polyethylene to create tabs that can be stapled together, folded down, and taped. Use a foam sealant where ducts penetrate the subfloor.

Damp and chilly below grade

A very common home style in my part of the country is the bi-level, or "raised ranch." From the front entry, the main living area is a flight of stairs up; a flight down are the garage, family room, spare bedroom and laundry. The lower level sits directly on a poured concrete slab.

In the winter, the downstairs rooms are chilly, particularly near the floor. In the summer, the air in those rooms becomes objectionably moist, and a dehumidifier is needed. I understand that the musty air and dampness are due to the fact that the concrete slab floor is colder than the ambient air temperature, resulting in condensation in summer and chilly room air in winter. The floors are fully carpeted, and the exterior ground level is only about 3 ft. to 4 ft. above the floor.

How can the downstairs rooms be kept warm and dry? Should we insulate the floor and the concrete-block portion of the lower walls? What about a vapor barrier? What products are recommended for insulating, and how should they be installed? The room ceilings are standard height.

—*Paul W. Sigmund,*
Morris Plains, N. J.

Charles Lane, a consulting engineer, replies: The cold concrete floor slab is indeed a major source of discomfort in the lower level of your house. The uninsulated below-grade part of the lower-level walls also keep the area chilly. Like the concrete floor slab, the below-grade walls will be cooler than the better insulated above-grade wall sections.

Several steps can be taken to make the lower level more comfortable. First, I recommend that you seal the inside of the foundation wall with a urethane or epoxy concrete sealer. This will help keep out mois-ture vapor from the ground. Second, insulate the below-grade wall sections. This can be done either with furring strips and rigid insulation board or with 2x4 studs and fiberglass batts.

Be sure to install a polyethylene vapor barrier on the inside of either assembly, and finish with plasterboard. Most building codes require rigid insulation board to be covered with drywall for fire safety. Fiberglass insulation should also be covered to prevent glass fibers from becoming airborne. You could also use extruded polystyrene board on the outside of the wall, but that would require considerable excavation.

Unfortunately, there is little that you can do to insulate the concrete floor slab unless you're willing to put in a floor system. This could be done like the walls, with sleepers, rigid foam between them, a vapor barrier and plywood. At the very least, the next time you replace the carpet, paint the concrete floor with a concrete sealer. This will help prevent moisture vapor from the soil from passing through the slab. Also place a foam carpet pad underneath the new carpet for added warmth and walking comfort. Adding ceiling-mounted radiant-heat panels to the lower level may also provide greater warmth and comfort.

Finally, eliminate any sources of excess moisture to the lower level by correcting water leakage from the ground, venting the clothes dryer, removing firewood stored inside, and installing outside exhaust fans in the bathroom.

Jim Gambone, of Portsmouth, N. H., also replies: As I was reading Charles Lane's solution to Paul

Sigmund's problem of damp and chilly below-grade living areas, I noticed something that could become a problem. To insulate the concrete floor, Lane recommended that a vapor barrier be put beneath the plywood and over sleepers and foam insulation. My concern is that this will allow moisture to pass from the slab into the sleeper/insulation cavity, which will then be trapped by the vapor barrier. Over time, this could result in damage to the sleepers.

I would first seal the floor slab with an epoxy sealer, then glue and power-nail sleepers to the slab. Insulation can then be added between the sleepers, and plywood can go over the top. This is the safest way to avoid moisture build-up in the floor cavity.

Waterproofing for block

I'm building a passive-solar home using surface-bonded concrete block, which will be set into a hillside. What inexpensive waterproofing system will be compatible with the surface bonding and also with the extruded-polystyrene insulation?
—*Don Lauer, Woodbridge, Va.*

Paul Hanke, author of "Surface-Bonded Block" (Fine Homebuilding #12, pp. 34-37), replies: I suggest using either Volclay panels (American Colloid Co., 5100 Suffield Court, Skokie, Ill. 60077), which is a bentonite material, or a narrow-width rubberized sheet material laid in mastic such as Bituthene (W. R. Grace, 62 Whittemore Ave., Cambridge, Mass. 02140) or Vaporseal (Noble Co., 614 Monroe St., Grand

Haven, Mich. 49417). I recommend narrow rolls (3 ft. wide or less) for do-it-yourself application, since they are relatively easy to handle. The panels or sheet material should be applied according to the manufacturer's instructions.

If you plan to contract the job, the choice of rubberized sheet material is wider, including roll manufacturers such as Carlisle Tire & Rubber (Box 99, Carlisle, Pa. 17013), Noble Co., and Gates Engineering (100 South West St., Wilmington, Del. 19801). Before choosing any of the above products, you should read *Underground Waterproofing* by Brent Anderson ($9.50 from WEBCO Publishers, 110 S. Greeley, Stillwater, Minn. 55082), which is the best general reference on the subject.

Finally, an interesting product that you might use is not a waterproofing material at all, but a form of insulation. Owens-Corning (Fiberglass Tower, Toledo, Ohio 43659) is now marketing Warm-N-Dri, a rigid fiberglass insulation board with oriented strands that allows water to drain rapidly downward when installed vertically. I saw a demonstration where a totally saturated piece of this stuff was removed from a bucket of water and held horizontally. Not a drop of the water dripped out. However, when it was turned vertically the water drained immediately. A similar product, Baseclad (Fibreglas Canada Inc., 3080 Yonge St., Toronto, Ont. M4N 3N1), has been used as foundation insulation in Canada in recent years (it's not available in the U. S.). Field experience there indicates that it keeps basements dry, insulates them, and it is never wetted more deeply than $\frac{1}{4}$ in. when in contact with soil.

Horizontal rigid insulation

Rigid insulation was applied below ground to the outside of the concrete foundation of my neighbor's house. During the winter the ground froze, heaved against the foundation and seriously cracked it. Extensive repairs were required. I have heard that the rigid insulation should have been laid out perpendicular to the foundation wall for several feet to incorporate the adjacent ground in the insulated area. Is this a good idea? Would it eliminate frost heaves?
—*John Lawless, Montreal, Que.*

Peter Mann, who teaches passive-solar house design at Mohawk College in Hamilton, Ont., replies: The techniques of laying rigid insulation horizontally just below the surface of the soil is normally used in retrofit situations where full-depth excavation is impractical. In new construction in cold climates, however, full-height vertical rigid insulation is standard since the soil is already excavated. The horizontal approach might well solve the frost-heave problem caused by full-height vertical insulation, provided that the soil against the foundation is not abnormally wet.

In dry soil (top drawing at right), heat from the basement is essentially trapped under the horizontal insulation. This effectively raises the frost-line depth and helps minimize frost heaves. The situation is quite different in wet soils (bottom drawing at right), where heat is rapidly conducted away from the wall in a horizontal direction, which makes horizontally placed insulation ineffective.

Should wet soil prove to be the problem (check in the fall before the

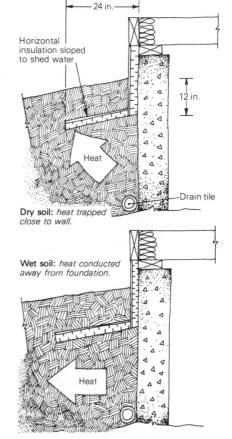

Horizontal insulation sloped to shed water

24 in.

12 in.

Heat

Drain tile

Dry soil: *heat trapped close to wall.*

Wet soil: *heat conducted away from foundation.*

Heat

ground freezes), then the ultimate answer lies in how well your surface drainage and below-grade drain tile are working.

If your soil proves to be wet and you find yourself excavating, then investigate a new product called Baseclad. It is produced by Fibreglas, Canada, Inc., and is made purposely for below-grade, exterior vertical-insulation applications. Baseclad has two unique properties that should prove helpful. The first is its semi-compressibility, which allows it to give under frost-heave pressure. The second is that it acts as a vertical drainage layer, conducting surplus water through the insulation down to the drain tile. This material has been used extensively in Scandinavia with excellent results.

Alternatives to foam?

Is extruded polystyrene really the only product I can use in insulating a slab?
—Steve Scheller, Falls Church, Va.

Bill Lotz, an engineer who specializes in insulation and moisture problems, replies: Soil, insects, water and corrosive compounds all take their toll on subsurface insulation. The foil facing used on many sheathings will corrode away in days in some soils. Fiberglass fills with water and becomes useless. I have even seen carpenter ants eat urethane insulation.

As far as I know, the only insulations that resist subsurface deterioration are extruded polystyrene and Foamglas. Foamglas is usually eliminated because of expense. Expanded polystyrene (EPS) is acceptable, but not as durable as its extruded cousin. That leaves extruded polystyrene as the primary subsurface insulation. Do remember with any foam insulation, however, that it will need to be protected from the sun so that it doesn't degrade.

Foam insulation for a slab

I'm planning to build a passive-solar house, and I'd like to do as much of the work as possible. Can you tell me the standard way to insulate my slab and foundation for a cold climate?
—Dennis Shapson, Shutesbury, Mass.

Alex Wade, an architect and author of several books on energy-efficient design, replies: The best material for the job is extruded polystyrene board. The most commonly found brand is Styrofoam blueboard (Dow Chemical, 2020 Dow Center, Midland, Mich. 48640), and many builders use the term blueboard generically. The foundation section shown below shows where the insulation goes and how it's protected. The horizontal band of insulation just below the topsoil has proven very effective in severe climates. I wouldn't use it in areas with less than 4,000 degree days.

The biggest problem is the band of insulation that remains exposed between the bottom of the finished siding and grade. This area will need to be covered to protect it from leaks, abrasion and sunlight, which degrades polystyrene. To make flash-

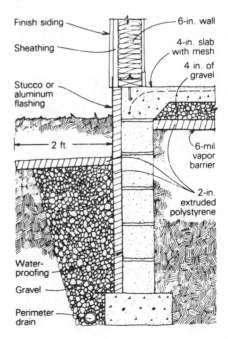

Finish siding

Sheathing

Stucco or aluminum flashing

6-in. wall

4-in. slab with mesh

4 in. of gravel

2 ft.

6-mil vapor barrier

2-in. extruded polystyrene

Water-proofing

Gravel

Perimeter drain

ing this area easier, install your foundation insulation flush with the sheathing on the outside of the stud wall. This will require offsetting the frame from the foundation, but makes it easier to produce an attractive weathertight joint.

If the grade around the building is fairly close to the floor height and reasonably level, I flash the insulation with 24-in. wide, dark brown, baked-enamel aluminum coil stock. If the sheathed wall and the insulated foundation are in the same plane, this flashing can be nailed to the bottom of the sheathing, and the finish siding will cover the exposed nails.

For a top-notch job, I use one of the new synthetic cement-stucco coatings. I like a product called Pleko Therm System (Kern-Tac Inc., 4421 Orchard St., Tacoma, Wash. 98466). It comes in 5-gal. buckets and is mixed 50-50 with portland cement and troweled onto fiberglass mesh. The resulting finish is tough and flexible.

Basement insulation

I am insulating the basement of my 150-year old stone house. First I sealed the fieldstone with a waterproof masonry paint. Then I built 2x4 stud walls inside, and will use foil-faced fiberglass batts. On which side of the wall should I put the polyethylene vapor barrier, or should I forget it entirely?
—*Gary M. Coppola, Lockport, N. Y.*

Dan Desmond, a specialist in restoration and energy conservation, replies: This is the kind of question that can warrant at least six defensible, and contrary, answers. My own inclination is to use the foil-faced insulation and forget the poly vapor barrier. Theoretically, you want to prevent moisture condensation on the inside of the cool stone wall. However, even without poly, vapor transmission from the inside to the outside of the wall is not likely because the vapor content and vapor pressure of the moist soil outside are substantially higher than those of airborne moisture, and the mortar itself is generally saturated below grade. Even above grade, not enough water is likely to be transmitted to saturate the mortar, which could then freeze and crack.

I think you should be more concerned with the seepage of water in its liquid form from the outside of the wall into your basement. With a house this old, the mortar between the stone is probably transmitting water like a sieve. In moist or saturated soils, this worked to some benefit because the passage of water through the wall kept the adjacent soil from becoming saturated, and thus prevented frost damage. Masonry paint or no, some water may still pass through from the outside of the wall, and you would risk rotting your framing by sealing this moisture behind the vapor barrier. In fact you may want to notch the bottom of your stud plates to hold sections of reamed ⅜-in. copper tubing to serve as drains or weep holes.

Chapter 2:

Carpentry

Regional building methods

I have been a California carpenter for 18 years, but am preparing for a permanent move to Connecticut. During a trip to the East Coast, I noticed that most framed houses were sheathed with a solid layer of 38-in. plywood before siding, while in earthquake-prone California, 1x6 diagonal bracing is acceptable. I'm wondering what other regional differences in construction methods I'll encounter.

—*Michael Bartlett, Vista, Calif.*

Connecticut builder Jim Picton replies: My western carpentry experience was in Alaska. Most of the carpenters there are transplanted Californians, however, and although the weather is reminiscent of New England, many of the building styles and techniques are distinctly western.

Like California, Alaska is prone to earthquakes, and this is probably the greatest source of differences between East Coast and West Coast building practices. Many of the building codes followed in the West are not used, or not strictly enforced, in the East. I've met builders with decades of experience who didn't know that nails used on a joist hanger should be of hardened steel to resist shear stresses, and that roofing nails in this application are a poor substitute.

Many builders in the East don't consider it necessary to double up the trimmers under headers that span more than 6 ft. Fire blocking is used, but structural blocking between both horizontal and vertical load-bearing members is sometimes sparse or non-existent. I've also seen mudsills put down in the East without bolts—just tacked down with concrete nails and anchored by the weight of the building.

Putting steel in footings is a conscious decision in the East; you do it to span a soft or wet area—or to "overbuild" if that is your intention. In the constantly shifting ground of Alaska, you put in two #5 bars continuous, period.

If you apply what you already know about earthquake protection in the West to your efforts in the East, the quality of your work will be much appreciated by those who recognize it. After all, the ground moves here too, just more slowly. Wind, floods, fires, frost and the occasional earth tremor are all good reasons to apply standard Western-style framing precautions.

Putting a plywood skin on buildings in lieu of let-in bracing is common in the Northeast and in Alaska as well. It's probably not much of a structural advantage, since the redundancy of solid sheathing is offset by the fact that there are joints every 4 ft. and 8 ft. Solid sheathing does provide one more layer of protection against cold wind; but I've worked on projects in Connecticut that used diagonal bracing and a non-structural sheathing such as Homasote or extruded polystyrene as a weather barrier under siding. As for the 3-in-1 alternative, I've managed to dodge T-111 siding since moving back East, but it's never far away.

The Northeast is proud of its record on insulation, and carpenters must stay alert to fill with fiberglass any voids in the framing that will be inaccessible after sheathing is installed. Sometimes vapor-barrier strips are also tacked onto the inside face of the exterior walls before interior walls are connected. With new double-wall and furring-over-vapor-barrier techniques being tried, a lot more attention to detail is required in framing. This slows the job down, but it's very important to get these details right.

Stringers for an arched bridge

I would like to build an arched bridge by edge-gluing 2x8 redwood together and cutting the arches with a bandsaw, as shown in the drawing. Do you think this

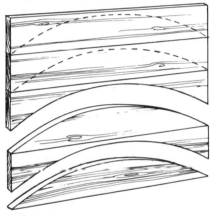

design will hold up to seasonal changes, and can you suggest the proper exterior glue?
—*Bruce Anderbery, Axtell, Neb.*

Architectural woodworker John Leeke replies: I see two problems with your method for making bridge stringers. First, I wouldn't depend on such a narrow glue joint in an exterior application. If any part of the joint failed, your entire bridge would be liable to collapse. I would redesign the stringer with a much larger glue area to increase its strength.

Second, your curved stringer has grain running straight from one edge of the stringer to the other. Ideally, and for maximum strength, the long grain should run parallel to the curved edges of the stringer.

The stringer design shown below solves both of these problems. Here, relatively thin wood (¾ in. to 1 in. thick) is laminated on its wide face into a blank with staggered joints so the long grain follows the overall curve.

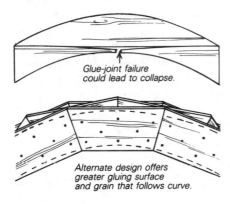

Glue-joint failure could lead to collapse.

Alternate design offers greater gluing surface and grain that follows curve.

To make the stringer, lay out the span, curve, width and angles on paper—full size if possible. Select flat boards, and cut the angled ends. The accuracy of the angles is important, but much of the strength of the construction comes from the glue joint and from the grain of the wood aligning with the curve.

This stringer will be outdoors, so it has to hold up to severe weathering and provide support for many years. Safety is a major consideration, so don't skimp when it comes to choosing glue. A Type 3, resorcinol-formaldehyde type exterior glue like Weldwood Waterproof Glue, or Epoxy Adhesive (West System, Gougeon Brothers, Inc., P. O. Box X-908, Bay City, Mich. 48707) is best for applications like this.

If you're using resorcinol glue, spread it on all mating surfaces of the joint, then tack the piece in place with small nails. Build up the entire stringer, then clamp every 6 in. in each direction. Clamping is very important with resorcinol, so be sure you have plenty of clamps on hand.

With epoxy adhesive you can get by with fewer clamps by screwing the parts together. Drill shank holes every 4 in. in all the parts, then begin gluing and screwing. Use a variable-speed drill or screw gun with galvanized drywall screws. The screws provide an extra measure of security in the finished stringer. When the glue has set, use a bandsaw to cut the curved shape.

Camber up?

While working on an apartment job, my partner and I were given the job of setting posts and laminated 4x12 beams for balconies. We were nearly finished when the foreman wanted to know why we had installed the beams upside-down, with the edges stamped "TOP" by the manufacturer facing downward. We were taught to install crowned lumber with the crown edge up. Were we right to disregard the stamp on the beam, or is there something special about the camber of a laminated beam we should know?
—*Doug Burke, Mormon Lake, Ariz.*

Russell Moody, a project leader for Engineered Wood Structures at the Forest Products Lab in Madison, Wis., replies: The "TOP" stamp of glued laminated beams must not be ignored if the beams are to work as designed. Here's why.

Glued laminated (glulam) timber is manufactured according to American National Standards Institute specification ANSI A190.1 (Structural Glued Laminated Timber) and stamped by an inspection agency to so indicate. Under this standard, many species and grade combinations are possible, and the most economical beams are commonly manufactured from a mixture of grades. The poorest grade is usually placed near the middle of the glulam. The remaining layers aren't symmetrical as to grade, though. The bottom laminations (which will be in tension) are higher grade than the top laminations (which will be in compression). Because the design of these beams depends on their proper orientation in the field, the ANSI standard requires that the compression lamination be stamped "TOP." If beams are installed "upside-down," they're likely to be weaker—in bending stress, the reduction in strength could be as much as 50%.

Camber—a slight bow from one end to the other—is often manufactured into custom-made glulam beams to offset expected deflections. Normally it's provided in the way you assume, with the curve, or crown, facing up. However, there are sometimes special situations (such as with cantilevers) where the camber may be reversed. The installer won't always know how or why the glulam was designed. So your first priority should have been to install the glulam as the stamp indicated. If you're certain that a mistake was made in applying that stamp, you should consult the manufacturer for more details on its cambering practices.

Readers interested in glued laminated timber can obtain additional information by contacting the American Institute of Timber Construction at 333 West Hampden Ave., Suite 712, Englewood, Colo. 80110.

Testing levels

I own several professional-quality levels, some with fixed vials, and a couple of the less expensive ones with adjustable vials. I would like to know the proper way to test and recalibrate them, without relying upon another level to do it. Do you have any suggestions?
—Elizabeth O'Brien, Exeter, N. H.

Consulting Editor Tom Law replies: The easiest way to test a level is to place it against a surface that is known to be plumb or level. If such a surface isn't available, you can establish a plumb edge with a plumb bob. When the level is against the plumb edge, the bubbles in all the vials should agree no matter which end is up. With an adjustable level, you can loosen the screws on either side of the window and adjust each vial, through patient trial and error, until all the bubbles are right.

Another way to test for plumb is to place the tool flat against a wall (so that it reads plumb) and draw a line along its edge. Flip it over, with the other face against the wall and the opposite edge against the line. If the bubble doesn't read plumb, adjust the vials until both edges read plumb along the same line.

To test for level, you could use a framing square to make a perpendicular line from the plumb line you've just established. Again, every bubble should agree regardless of how the tool is placed.

Testing for level can also be done by placing the tool on a horizontal surface that's not level itself. Shim up one side of the level until the bubble reads level. Turn the level over, then turn it end for end; it should read level in every position if the tool is properly adjusted.

With non-adjustable levels, broken vials can be removed and replaced if new ones are available from the manufacturer. You'll have to remove the protective windows and the glazing compound that holds them in place. It would be best to clamp the tool in position on a true level surface when doing this. Then replace the vial, put the window back in and seal it with glazing compound.

If every effort fails to bring each vial into agreement, check the edges of the level to see if they're parallel and straight; they must be absolutely true. If they are not, perhaps a machinist could correct then for you if the tool is worth the expense. Otherwise a new level is in order, but be sure to check it for accuracy before you leave the store.

Bill Crick, of Independence, Mo., also replies: The following method is a simple but very accurate way to check the accuracy of a level.

You will need two flat-head wood screws about ¾ in. long, and a rigid place where you can drive them in both horizontal and vertical positions (you can use a mudsill, a rim joist, a corner post, a door frame or even concrete by using plastic anchors). Nails are not acceptable because adjustments needed later cannot be made easily. You will soon be surprised by how little turning of the screw it takes to change the reading of a level.

To check the level vial, drive the screws into a horizontal surface and leave the heads protruding about ¼ in. The screws should be placed at a distance about 2 in. less than the length of the level. When the level is placed on the screw heads, it should touch nothing else. Center your view on the vial by using only one eye and look at one bubble from as near a vertical downward position as possible. Adjust either screw until the bubble is centered. Keeping the same edge of the level up, swap ends of the level and look at the same bubble. If there is an error, the level is off by half the distance it shows when "reversed." Check the other level vial in the same manner. Remember that each bubble must be checked against itself, not against the other bubble.

To check the plumb vial, drive the screws into a vertical surface. Placed against the screw heads, the level should touch nothing else. Sight the bubble in the manner described above, and adjust one of the screws until the level reads plumb. Keeping the same end up, turn the level to read the same bubble from the opposite side. Again, any error is half of that shown by the bubble. Check the other plumb vial in the same manner.

I don't recommend that a novice replace vials. Instead, the level should be returned to the manufacturer or a competent repair shop (sorry, I repair only levels I manufacture).

It is difficult to check out a level before you buy it by holding it against another level—the one you are checking it with may be inaccurate, too. A level is a measuring tool, so any reputable level manufacturer will repair or replace a new level that does not read accurately when purchased.

Looking for a hook

I have seen framers whose worm-drive saws are equipped with a large metal hook so that they can hang them on joists or rafters between cuts. Do you know where I can find such a hook?
—*Rick Hawks, Weott, Calif.*

The editors of Fine Homebuilding *reply:* We know of two manufacturers of these devices. In both cases, the hooks are made to replace the top handles of particular worm-drive saws.

Concept Builders Supply (P.O. Box 456, Wauna, Wash. 98395) makes an insulated steel version for either the Black & Decker or the Skil wormdrive. Marketed as the Sawklip, it is designed to fit over surfaced 2x lumber, and sells for $19.95 postpaid.

The Spoiler Sky Hook is made by Pairis Enterprises (P.O. Box 436, Walnut, Calif. 91789). It is made for the same two worm-drive saws. It is aluminum and carries a lifetime guarantee. The suggested retail price is $12.95.

Pulling in floor plates

We sheathe exterior walls before we stand them up. Sometimes the sheathing or the warp of the floor plate makes it hard to pull the wall in to the chalkline. I've heard of devices that carpenters used to make for this purpose, but I've never seen one. Do you know of any solutions to the problem?
—*Len Prelesnik, Holland, Mich.*

California builder Don Dunkley replies: The best solution is to avoid the problem in the first place with a trick used by concrete contractors

who set up foundations for prefab walls that have exterior siding already installed. In order to avoid problems of walls not lining up with the exterior layout line on the slab, the contractor sets his foundation about ¼ in. to ⅜ in. shy of actual size. This gives enough play to move the walls to the line. You could do the same with your foundation, whether wood-frame or slab (A in the drawing below.

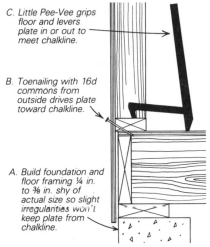

C. Little Pee-Vee grips floor and levers plate in or out to meet chalkline.

B. Toenailing with 16d commons from outside drives plate toward chalkline.

A. Build foundation and floor framing ¼ in. to ⅜ in. shy of actual size so slight irregularities won't keep plate from chalkline.

If you come on the job after the foundation has been poured, you will have to deal with the problem in another way. Often the easiest solution is to toenail through the sheathing and floor plate into the subfloor with 16d commons (B in the drawing above). You'll have to measure up from the bottom of the sheathing to know where to nail.

The device that you mention is available commercially. Proctor Products Co., Inc. (210 8th St. South, Box 697, Kirkland, Wash. 98033) makes one called Little Pee-Vee (C in the drawing above). It retails for about $14. I've never used one, but it looks like it would do the job.

Sawhorse for a table saw

What kind of sawhorses should I use under a site-built table saw? I am looking for a sawhorse that is very stable when in use, but folds or disassembles for carrying in my van. —*Mike Ramey, Seattle, Wash.*

Sam Clark replies: I use 1x6 stock to make all the parts, cutting the legs to an 18° taper before joining them to the crossmembers with 1¼-in. drywall screws (drawing below). It's a good idea to drill pilot holes for the screws. This makes it faster and easier to screw the joint closed. I also counterbore them about ¼ in. to ensure maximum penetration. Hinges can be either strap or butt style, but choose stout ones that will stand up to heavy use.

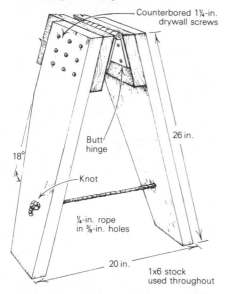

Counterbored 1¼-in. drywall screws

Butt hinge

26 in.

18°

Knot

¼-in. rope in ⅜-in. holes

20 in.

1x6 stock used throughout

Rope is actually superior to chain for holding the legs; it is more than strong enough and allows the horse to be folded flat for storage and transport. For maximum stability, there shouldn't be any slack in the rope when the horse is being used. I've found this design to be strong, rugged and reliable, although I wouldn't use these sawhorses for staging. You could beef them up by using 5/4 stock rather that 1x6s, but then they'd be heavier and less convenient to lug around.

What wood is it really?

What am I really getting when I buy lumber stamped "Hem-Fir?" —*Roo Sten, Montrose, Colo.*

The editors of **Fine Homebuilding** *reply:* Lumber-grade stamps typically give the initials of the certifying organization, the number of the originating mill or firm name, the grade, the moisture content and the species. Hem-Fir is a species stamp that refers to a large group of western softwoods. This group includes western hemlock and many of the true firs.

Two excellent brochures that explain grade stamps and have accurate color photographs of the grades within each species are Western Wood Species Book, Vol. 1, "Dimension Lumber," and Vol. 2, "Selects-Finish/Commons-Boards." These are produced by the Western Wood Products Association (Yeon Bldg., Portland, Ore. 97204), a trade and certifying organization, and can be purchased for $1 and $2 respectively. Vol. 2 states:

"Hemlock is a strong wood, free of pitch and easy to work. It is classified as a white wood, its color ranging from a pleasing off-white to a faint reddish-brown heartwood. When green, it has a relatively high moisture content but dries well by air seasoning or kiln-drying.

"The true firs included in the grouping include pacific silver fir, white fir, grand fir, California red fir, and noble fir. The characteristics of the individual species differ somewhat, but after manufacture into lumber, the wood fibers are indistinguishable from one another. Together they provide one of the nation's most versatile softwoods."

Tom Currans, of Dundee, Ore., also replies: May I add the following comments to your answer about hem-fir from one who lives in the midst of D-fir (Douglas fir)- country where hem-fir is a poor second cousin.

You gave the book answer, and the WWPA (Western Wood Products Association) has a good selection of helpful general-information publications. But let me give you the working man's comments. Here in Oregon where D-fir is readily available, a builder feels dumped on if the lumberyard sends out a load of hem fir unless the price is considerably reduced to make it worthwhile to fuss with it. It warps something fierce if left exposed in sunlight for any length of time. It splits much worse than D-fir, and splinters more than I care to say. In other words, if you are accustomed to D-fir and think hem-fir is just about the same thing, you are in for a real eye-opener.

Our local lumberyard manager once sent a load of hem-fir studs out to a building site. It was about three weeks before the builder got around to using them. By then some of the studs would have made excellent support ribs for a parabolic solar collector. The manager told me that he would never allow another load of hem-fir in the yard.

If hem-fir is all you can get, make sure it is straight when you get it, don't leave it sitting around in the sun, and get it nailed down as quickly as possible. Never use it for decking material, where the splintering would be very disconcerting. This applies if it is hemlock that is being sold under the hem-fir stamp. I haven't had experience with the other firs lumped into this category.

Woods for sauna construction

I plan to buy a heater and build a sauna room, and I'd like to know which woods are suitable. Several people suggest clear grade-A cedar. Is there anything less expensive that will work as well?
—Mark Goldfield, Brooklyn, N. Y.

Frederic Hanisch of Quakertown, Pa., replies: Wood that comes into body contact—particularly benches and walls, and the floor to a lesser degree—should have low thermal conductivity. As thermal conductivity is pretty much directly proportional to density, choose a light wood over a heavy wood. I used Philippine mahogany for the interior walls of my sauna because it was the cheapest T&G material I could find. It has worked well. I used catalpa for the benches because I had some available. In general, softwoods are lighter than hardwoods, and most of the lighter pine, cedar, spruce, redwood and fir species are suitable for a sauna, provided they are knot-free. Knots and exposed nail or screw heads become painfully hot (they don't actually get any hotter than the sauna's ambient temperature, but they feel hotter because they conduct heat so well).

Don't use finish on interior wood in the sauna. The wood for the sauna must breathe to moderate the moisture content of the air. Log saunas need a breaking-in period before they perform correctly—the wood needs to dry out before it can absorb the excess moisture produced by sweating. If you want to get an idea of what a particular wood will be like a short time after the sauna is in use—take a piece, wet it and oven-dry it several times.

It is also nice to use woods that don't splinter readily. Unless the planer blades are extremely sharp, machine-planed lumber will become rough to the touch. Be prepared to do some additional smoothing on benches. I hand-planed the catalpa bench slats, and there is a remarkable difference between the planed areas and a few places that I missed.

I used yellow pine for the ceiling and wasn't concerned with knots as it wasn't to be touched. The yellow pine, however, has exuded resin from knots and pitch pockets, and in fine beads over the entire surface—this is okay as long as it doesn't drip. Steer clear of resinous woods.

In my sauna, I used soft maple for interior trim, and it has worked well. Poplar should be fine also.

Building with ash

I want to build a house in the spring with lumber I mill myself this winter. I have heard that ash is drier than other species, but I'm wondering if it is suitable for house construction.
—James Lucas, Goshen, N. Y.

Paul Fuge, a sawyer and architectural woodworker in Shelton,

Conn., replies: Ash is a wonderful choice for building a home. It has plenty of strength to be used for beams, and is very handsome as finished work. It doesn't have oak's nasty habit of rusting nails, and tends to be easier to work. It is not as rot-resistant as white oak, so keep it out of the basement and away from the foundation. Use trees 14 in. in diameter and larger for your sawlogs. Small trees produce lumber that bows and crooks. For timbers 4 in. and larger, box the hearts as

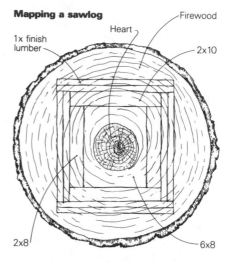

Mapping a sawlog

1x finish lumber

Heart

Firewood

2x10

2x8

6x8

shown in the drawing, and save the best 1-in. lumber for finish work.

Any wood is as dry as you make it. Ash does have one of the lower initial moisture contents among common eastern hardwoods, but a lot of time and care still have to be taken in the drying process.

Deck on grade

I plan to add a 15-ft. by 15-ft. deck to my house and would like to keep it close to the ground so that it will

be even with an existing concrete slab. I plan to use pressure-treated 2x4 decking attached to pressure-treated 1x4 sleepers laid flat on a bed of sand. I'd like to screw the decking from underneath so that no fasteners will show.

The deck will occupy the highest point in the yard, with the area around it sloping gradually away (about 1 in. every 10 ft.). I plan to level and pack the sand, then build the deck as one piece and lay it in place (with a little help from my friends). Does this sound feasible?
—*Dan McCubbin, Bedford, Tex.*

Paul Pieper, a union carpenter in Abbington, Pa., replies: Your 15-ft. by 15-ft. deck sounds feasible, but if you make it much larger, you should excavate for joists. Even with the size you have planned, I recommend using crushed stone instead of sand. Stone is easier to grade and will drain water away quicker and dry much faster than sand. Even treated lumber will mildew and smell if it's allowed to remain wet when resting on wet sand. Remember that the sand won't get any sun under the deck.

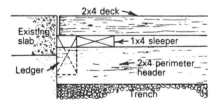

You'll need a ledger at the existing slab to hold the deck in place and at the proper elevation (drawing above). You'll also need 2x4 perimeter headers to keep the stone from escaping, and I would add a 2x4 center support as well. Some excavation should be done underneath these 2x4s to provide for adequate French drains around the perimeter. The drains should be about 12 in. wide, 2 in. to 4 in. deep, filled with stone and pitched about ¼ in. per ft. The perimeter headers and center support should be fastened to the ledger and should rest on the drain stone.

Most of the water will run off the deck, so provisions must be made to lead it away. The trench along the end 2x4 header (opposite the slab) should be deeper and wider than the rest. I recommend using 6 in. of stone below the header, projecting 1 ft. beyond the deck (drawing below).

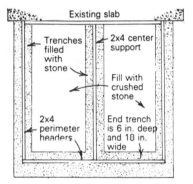

These trenches keep run-off water away from the wood while the water perks into the ground. If you find that your ground perks slowly, just dig deeper and add more stone. Once the digging is done, fasten the ledger to the slab with stainless-steel or galvanized anchors. Then, fill the trenches with stone and grade them to a pitch of ⅛ in. per ft. of run. Fasten the perimeter headers and center support to the ledger and fill the area between them with more crushed stone. The stone can be screeded and lightly tamped with a long 2x4, much as you would do when leveling concrete.

Build your deck right beside its final location so it needs only to be flipped over, end for end. Use the largest gauge 2-in. stainless-steel screws you can find (the larger the number, the larger the head). This will help hold the thinner 1x4 sleepers against the deck 2x4s, helping to keep the 2x4s from cupping. The 2x4 is thicker and stronger than the 1x4 and will twist unless you use good-quality lumber.

Keep in mind that you are working upside down when you select the proper side of the 2x4 to place up. Orient the growth rings with the convex side up. If the board cups, you want the water to run off. On the end that adjoins the slab, let the 2x4s overhang the 1x4 by the thickness of the ledger. All you have to do now is flip the deck over and nail it to your ledger. I suggest nailing each 2x4 to the ledger, keeping each one ⅛ in. from the slab. I also recommend nailing every 2 ft. along the supports.

Deck flashing

How do I flash both a standard add-on deck and a cantilevered deck (one where the floor joists of the house also support the deck)? Does a deck need flashing if it's built with pressure-treated lumber? —*J. Christie Lash, Atlanta, Ga.*

Dan Rockhill, a builder and professor of architecture at the University of Kansas in Lawrence, replies: Pressure-treated 2x lumber costs about twice as much as untreated deck joists in my part of the country, but I use it in almost all exterior applications. Still, flashing deck joists is a good idea, especially

with a cantilevered design that requires tearing up the house to replace the joists when they rot. However, flashing cantilevered joists is tricky. Cantilevered deck joists also create the problem of "stepping up" to the deck. Because decking boards are thicker in most cases than interior floor sheathing, this condition invites stumbling out onto your deck. The height of the joists can be cut down outside the house, but this weakens them considerably. The only solution that I've found to this problem so far was on a house that we built last summer. The interior slab that we poured on top of the wood floor brought the floor higher than the cantilevered joists out on the deck.

Still, if it's possible to achieve the effect you want with an add-on deck, you'll invite fewer problems. Add-on decks can easily be flashed at the juncture with the house by wrapping the ledger board with wide coil stock. This flashing should continue up under the siding 4 in. to 6 in.,

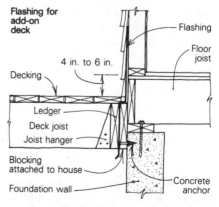

Flashing for add-on deck

Flashing

Floor joist

4 in. to 6 in.

Decking

Ledger

Deck joist

Joist hanger

Blocking attached to house

Foundation wall

Concrete anchor

as shown in the drawing above, or in the case of a door, wrap back under the sill.

However, if cantilevered deck joists remain your choice, the draw-

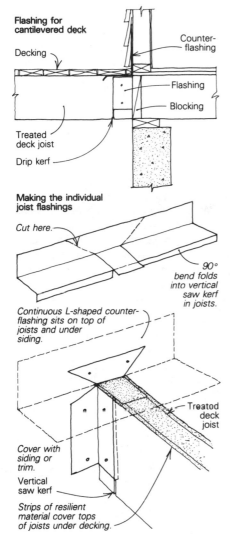

Flashing for cantilevered deck

Counter-flashing

Decking

Flashing

Blocking

Treated deck joist

Drip kerf

Making the individual joist flashings

Cut here.

90° bend folds into vertical saw kerf in joists.

Continuous L-shaped counter-flashing sits on top of joists and under siding.

Treated deck joist

Cover with siding or trim.

Vertical saw kerf

Strips of resilient material cover tops of joists under decking.

be bent over the joist and nailed to the building. The drawing shows one that's quite simple. Follow this with an L-shape flashing between the building and decking on the top of the joists.

The top of the joists is where the most deterioration will occur. Moisture gets trapped between the decking and joists and causes rot in a very short time. The trick is to cover the joist tops with some impervious material that won't trap water when it's punctured with a decking nail. Standard metal flashing just won't work. I would suggest that you try resilient materials like those used in masonry flashing systems: 90-lb. felt strips, heavy-gauge vinyl, asphalt-coated copper or other synthetic products that are used in commercial building.

Finally, don't forget to cut a drip kerf in the underside of each joist. The kerf will keep water from flowing back against the building when it rains.

Swimming-pool deck

I want to build a low wood deck on an existing concrete patio that surrounds an oval swimming pool. What's the best way to proceed?
—Leonard Fuscaldo, Miami, Fla.

Dan Rockhill, a builder and professor of architecture at the University of Kansas in Lawrence, replies: Although pressure-treated lumber is often less expensive, I like redwood for a pool deck and the sleepers it will sit on. If knots are acceptable, use construction heart grade, usually referred to in lumberyards as con heart. It is less expensive than clear all-heart redwood.

ing above shows how they can be effectively flashed. Cantilevered decks have two areas that are vulnerable to water damage. One is where the joists break through the wall at its outside edge, and the other is the tops of the joists themselves.

At the outside surface of the wall plane, you need to install flashing to protect this joint from water penetration. Any number of shapes can

However, in some parts of the country, clear redwood can be found green, and costs considerably less per board foot than kiln-dry redwood. These grades are free from sapwood, which is usually a creamy white in color and doesn't contain the natural chemicals that the heartwood does which resist rot and termites.

Use 2x4 redwood sleepers on 24-in. centers. Run them perpendicular to the pool and set them right on the patio. The concrete will be pitched away from the pool, and it's important not to obstruct the path that the water naturally takes with these sleepers. You can rip the sleepers to compensate for the slope of the patio, or shim under them until the deck is level. Cover the ends of the sleepers where they terminate at the edge of the pool with a ⅜-in. thick redwood band. This material is sold in 4-in. and 6-in. heights as an edging for landscaping, and is usually referred to as bender board.

Nail 2x4 or 2x6 decking to the sleepers, making sure to keep the bark side up with the pieces that are flat grained. Space the decking boards ⅛ in. apart if they are dry; less if they're wet. Nail with hot-dipped galvanized nails or aluminum nails to minimize streaking. Be careful if you are thinking of treating your decking with a wood preservative that contains toxic chemicals since water splashed on the decking can run back into the pool.

Steel studs for a fire wall

My living-room fireplace is on an inside wall that is shared with my downstairs bedroom. The house was built in 1921, and the walls are lath and plaster. I burn my fires hot, and at the end of an evening, the bedroom side of the wall is very warm to the touch. The paint-covered wallpaper is somewhat discolored on that wall, and although I'm not certain that this has anything to do with the heat, it worries me.

My plan is to replace all the wood studs in the wall with metal ones and then to hang drywall. What can you tell me about metal studs? Should I put insulation or maybe asbestos between the brick and the new wall? I also plan to run enough wire for several new circuits for the upstairs. Can Romex be attached to metal studs?
—*Paul McGuire, Seattle, Wash.*

Contractor Steve Mead from Lakewood, Colo., replies: Metal studs are ideal for situations where combustibility is a problem. Drywall and metal-stud assemblies comprise the majority of today's fire-rated wall systems.

After removing the existing plaster, inspect the brickwork thoroughly for cracks, loose mortar and settling. If there is a lot of damage, it may be wise to call in a qualified mason to do the work. Otherwise, repoint the bricks and fill cracks as necessary.

Use 2½-in. or 3½-in. wide metal studs, and leave a space between the new wall and the existing masonry. This space will act as an insulating air cushion and will prevent direct heat transfer from the brickwork to the studs. Screw the studs into the tracks (these are analogous to top and bottom plates in conventional wood framing) with pan-head screws. Be sure to face all of the stud channels in the same direction. When you apply the drywall, be sure to locate seams on the open side (flange side) of the studs. This prevents the studs from buckling, and will prevent finishing problems later on.

No insulation should be necessary, but if you are concerned, apply two layers of ⅝-in. firestop gypboard instead of one.

Romex cable can be attached by using standard metal cable clips, available at electrical-supply houses. Attach utility boxes in the same fashion. If you are in a pinch, simply screw a piece of wood to the studs, then nail or staple the electrical work in place. Before applying the drywall, inspect all the wiring to be certain that it hasn't been skinned by any sharp edges on the studs.

For further information on metal studs and related assemblies, consult the brochure "Steel-Framed Drywall Systems" (SA-923), which is available at no cost from U. S. Gypsum Co. (101 S. Wacker Drive, Chicago, Ill. 60606).

Cupola framing

I am interested in building a cupola for my house, but haven't been able to find a plan for one. Can you give me some information to get me started?
—*R. G. Magnan, Miller Place, N. Y.*

Consulting editor Bob Syvanen replies: There are two basic kinds of cupolas—the add-on ones that are attached to the finished roof with screws, and the ones that are framed as part of the roof structure. This latter kind of cupola is built just like a dormer, and the cheeks, or side walls, are step flashed into the roof-shingle courses. The section and plan drawings below will give you a rough idea of how to frame one of these.

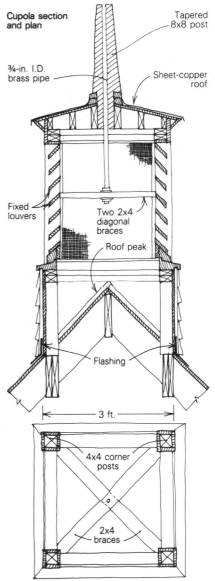

Cupola section and plan

Tapered 8x8 post

Sheet-copper roof

¾-in. I.D. brass pipe

Fixed louvers

Two 2x4 diagonal braces

Roof peak

Flashing

3 ft.

4x4 corner posts

2x4 braces

Adding a shed dormer

The roof pitch on my 1½-story frame house is 12-in-12. I want to put a nearly full-length shed dormer on the back of the house. Can the existing roof somehow be jacked up in place as a unit, and a new supporting structure built underneath?   —Jay Enloe, Portland, Ore.

Sam Clark, a carpenter in Cambridge, Mass., who writes design and construction books, replies: Although you can jack up one side of an existing roof to create a dormer,

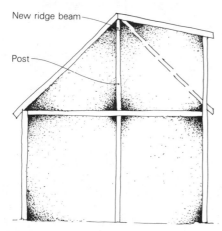

New ridge beam

Post

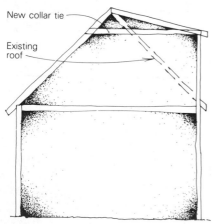

New collar tie

Existing roof

doing so could take longer, be more dangerous, and require a broader range of skills for a partial dormer than the more conventional approach of building one in place. You would also be letting your technique dictate your design—a common pitfall. Why go to the trouble of a virtuoso performance when a routine method works well?

The drawings below left illustrate two common solutions for supporting a new dormer. In the upper one, a ridge beam replaces the collar ties of the original roof, making two shed roofs in effect. This beam would have to be sized along with posts to support this load right on down to the ground. The second drawing shows an extended collar tie that would lower the ceiling, but keep the roof rigid and not require a ridge beam.

In either case, check your plans with a professional designer or builder to guard against underbuilding or overbuilding. The latter is often the case with novice builders, since a roof, once it's sheathed, is usually stronger than the timber sizes would suggest.

Figuring pitch

I recently built a bay whose roof framing was independent of the rafters over the house. I got the pitch of rafters A and B (drawing below) through trial-and-error. The tops of all of the rafters had to end up in the same plane for the

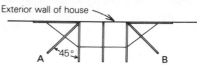

Exterior wall of house

A   45°   B

sheathing and fascia, yet it seems rafters A and B have to drop faster (a steeper pitch) in order for them to bear on the top plates. I've got another 6-in-12 octagonal roof coming up, and this time I'd like to know how to do the figuring on it.
—*John Shoneman,*
Hillsborough, N. C.

Jud Peake, a contractor and carpenter in California, replies: The way that you framed your bay will work, but in its classical form, this bay is really just three sides of a full octagon (as shown in the drawing below), and the key rafters are hips.

Octagonal-bay layout

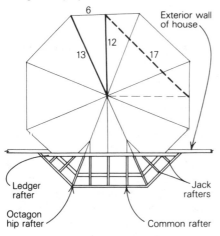

When projected on paper, they meet at the center of the octagon. I have shown the relationships of the runs of the octagon at the top of the drawing. The common rafters are figured and cut just as you would any common rafter; in your case that means using 6 and 12 on your framing square. Where a common or jack rafter comes off one of the angled walls of the bay, its top plumb cut will have to be made with a 45° bevel. Octagon hips, on the other

hand, can be found by using your rise figure, 6, with 13 on the square. The hip top cut, where it meets the ledger, will be beveled at 22½°.

The ledger that supports the common rafters that rest on the front wall of the bay should be level. But the ledgers for the angled walls should be sloped—these are often called ledger rafters. You can figure them by using 6 and 17 on the square, just as you would a standard hip.

One last piece of advice—beware of architects who give too many dimensions in situations like this. What their plans describe may not be a true octagon. If this happens, you're on your own.

Calculating the rise

How do you use a calculator to figure the height of a rake wall that is 13 ft. long and rises at a 4-in-12 slope?   —*G. Schelvan,*
Huntington Beach, Calif.

Jud Peake, a contractor and carpenter in California, replies: This is a simple proportion problem. What you are doing is trying to create a triangle that has a 4-unit rise and a 12-unit run where you know that the actual run is 13 ft., and you don't know the rise.

Mathematically, the problem is written: 4/12 = actual rise/13 ft. The units of measure of the 4 and 12 are not indicated because they aren't important—they express the proportion, the ratio of rise to run. Notice also that the rise figures are kept on the top of the equation and the run figures are lined up on the bottom. To solve the math you can cross-multiply and divide, the way we learned in school, or you can do exactly as you suggest with a calculator. The keystrokes are: $4 \div 12 = .3333 \times 13$ ft. $= 4.333$ ft. Because the actual run was entered in feet, the answer is also in feet. That's great until you try to lay out your rake wall in decimal feet with your tape measure.

There are several ways to deal with the problem of decimal feet. 1) Store the whole feet (in this case, 4) in your own memory and multiply the .333 feet by 12 to get 12ths of a foot, or inches. 2) Deal only in inches from the beginning. Here it would be: $4 \div 12 = .3333 \times 156$ in. $= 52$ in. If in some other example you wind up with decimal inches, you can work it out in a manner similar to the first method above. 3) When the actual run can easily be punched in in decimal feet, here simply 13 ft., just multiply the actual run in feet times the unit rise, and neglect to divide by 12. The answer will then be in inches: 13 ft. $\times$ 4 = 52 in.

Forming a curved roof

I plan to build a house with a bowed roof, and I am considering various options for the rafters. Two labor-intensive options I've thought of are building curved box-beam trusses, and making curved laminated rafters of 1x2s sheathed on both sides with plywood so I won't have to glue separate laminations. However, since the house will be less than 24 ft. wide, I could build curved gable walls and run straight rafters parallel to the ridge and bend sheathing over them. Would curved blocking be needed between the rafters, or would bending sheathing over their contact points be sufficient to form a true curved roof? —Tom Sullivan, Vineyard Haven, Mass.

Jud Peake, a contractor and carpenter in California, replies: Making curved laminated beams might not be too difficult if you jigged them on the floor before framing the walls. You could glue the laminations with panel adhesive and nails rather than clamp them while the glue sets. I think this would be easier and much better-looking than sheathing the sides of the laminations with plywood. You could also opt for fewer, heavier curved beams rather than closely spaced curved rafters.

I have built a vaulted-roof/ceiling along the lines of your second idea. It turned out to be relatively easy and gave me the results I needed. The 2x10 joists ran parallel to the vault and spanned almost 20 ft. Because the vault was a simple radius (about 5 ft.), the joist blocking that ran from the top of one exterior wall up to the ridge and down the other side formed an arch and really did reduce deflection in the joists over that long span. However, if your roof is more bowed than it is vaulted, I'd be concerned that the arch of the blocks might push out on the side walls.

I didn't bandsaw the blocks to conform to the curve. Instead, I used 2x8s in the 2x10 space. The interior was plastered over expanded metal lath. The exterior was sheathed with two layers of $\frac{3}{8}$-in. plywood bent with the grain. Roll roofing, hidden by parapet walls, made it watertight. You might not like the looks of roll roofing, but remember that a curved roof has almost no slope right at the ridge, and roofing shingles of any variety will tend to leak.

Tools for tricky angles

I am building a traditional 1½-story cape with a 12-in-12 roof pitch. It will have two gable dormers with roof pitches of 24-in-12. The compound angles involved in the cheek cuts of the valleys and jacks for the gables appear to be beyond the capacity of table saw, radial arm saw and skillsaw. How do I cut them?
—John Archard, Mt. Vernon, Maine

Don Dunkley, a carpenter and framing contractor in Cool, Calif., replies: Side cuts for 24-in-12 jacks used to be made with a handsaw, but that takes some patience. If you're good with a chainsaw and you've got one on site, you can make these cuts quickly and cleanly in one pass. If not, you'll need a hand-held circular saw that cuts at least 4 in. deep. I use a 16-in. Makita circular saw, which is also handy for beams and header cutting. Saws like this can be rented for the day, or even for half a day.

To make the cut with a big circular saw, begin by scribing the side cut in the direction you need it, on the top of the rafter stock. Hold the framing square at 13⅜ and 6 on the edge of the board, and draw your line along the 13⅜ side of the square (top drawing, above right). Next scribe the plumb-cut line, 24 and 12, down along the face of the rafter from the long point of the side cut. Do the same on the other face from the short point. These are all the layout marks that you'll need.

Two sawcuts, shown at bottom below, are required to get the correct side cut using this method. The first cut establishes the plumb-cut angle on one side of the rafter, and removes enough stock to allow the shoe of the saw room to make the second cut. This second cut uses the

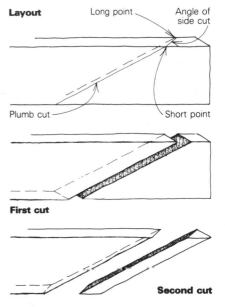

Layout

Long point

Angle of side cut

Plumb cut

Short point

First cut

Second cut

line of the first cut as a guide and gives the rafter the necessary bevel.

To make the first cut, follow along the plumb line on the face of the rafter that connects with the long point of the side-cut line on the top edge. Keep the saw shoe set at 0°, which leaves the blade perpendicular to the shoe. Any circular saw will be able to make the first cut.

For the second cut, use the big saw set at 0°. Secure the rafter or have someone hold it up on edge. Then screw up your courage, and line up your saw so that the blade will follow the line of the first sawcut on the long point face of the rafter, and the plumb-cut pencil line on the short point face simultaneously, as shown. You will have to keep the saw up at an angle, freehand, on one edge of the shoe to make the cut. At first, it may seem impossible to eyeball the sawblade on both sides of the cut, but with a little practice you can get quite good at this maneuver.

Sizing a gable overhang

We are in the design stage of our new passive-solar home. The gable end of the house, which will face south, is shown in the elevation below. The style of the house calls

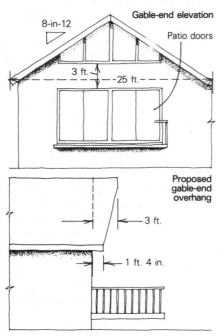

Gable-end elevation

8-in-12

Patio doors

3 ft.

25 ft.

Proposed gable-end overhang

3 ft.

1 ft. 4 in.

for a gable overhang that angles back toward the house from the ridge, rather than being a uniform width. Since the literature we've read deals in straight eave overhangs, we're only guessing that we'll need a 3-ft. overhang at the

top, which will be reduced to 1 ft. 4 in. by the time it reaches the bottom. Is this correct for our 41° N. latitude and 73° 08' longitude, and if not, how can we calculate the correct overhang?
—Mike & Sue Barra, Rocky Point, N. Y.

Jeff Ellis, a solar designer and builder in Boulder, Colo., replies:
You are correct in thinking that simple shading diagrams will not work with your house design, but the approach will be the same. Still, be aware that fixed overhangs are a compromise at best on optimum winter vs. summer performance.

The simplest way to size an overhang is to draw a section of the south wall—in your case both at the gable peak and at the outside edge of your windows. You can approximate winter sun angles with 26° from the horizontal, and summer sun at 70° for your latitude (I use Edward Mazria's *The Passive Solar Energy Book* as a basic reference). You may be surprised to find that with your present plan, very little winter sun will penetrate the trapezoidal upper windows, while the patio doors below will remain entirely unshaded during the summer, spring and fall. This is the reverse of what you want. With your climate, I would go with smaller overhangs, to get better spring and fall performance. You can always add thermal curtains or blinds later, but it's not so easy to cut off the overhangs.

There are a couple of design options you might consider. The first is to lower the trapezoidal windows. As a rule of thumb, the length of the overhang should be twice the distance from the top of the glass to the underside of the roof. In your design, if you reduced the 3-ft. space between the windows and the patio doors to 1 ft. and kept the windows the same size, you could then increase the width of your overhang to 4 ft., tapering to 3 ft. or 2 ft., and achieve a respectable compromise.

The other option is to treat the windows and patio doors as separate systems. The gable overhang could be calculated exclusively for the upper windows, while another overhang (perhaps a boardwalk to aid in cleaning windows) would serve the lower patio doors as shown in the drawing below. This

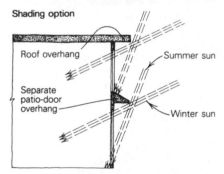

Shading option

Roof overhang

Summer sun

Separate patio-door overhang

Winter sun

system would be particularly nice if the upper windows belong to a separate floor of the house.

A good way to test these adjustments is to construct a model at ⅛-in. or ¼-in. scale with window cutouts, and actually see the effect of sun angle and overhangs, using the sun or a floodlight as a source of light.

Framing with 2x6s

I am the draftsman for a project governed by the new strict California residential energy standards. Since we are using 2x6 stud walls

to house R-19 insulation, the typical 2x4 detailing at windows and doors no longer works. Could you identify some of the critical problems and give me some simple solutions? —*Richard Gage, Glendale, Calif.*

Eric Rekdahl, an architect and builder in Berkeley, Calif., replies: Framing exterior walls with 2x6s rather than with 2x4s doesn't really alter the basic approach. The various members of a stud wall—studs, cripples, plates, sills, blocking and headers—should all increase from 2x4 to 2x6.

Doing it this way doesn't change any of the standard connections. The impact on labor costs is minimal, affected only by having to frame walls in shorter sections because of the added weight, and because of the added time required to run a skillsaw through that extra 2 in. There is, however, an increase of roughly 50% in material costs that applies not only to the framing but to some finish costs as well. Exterior door and window jambs, sills and thresholds will also need to be stretched that additional 2 in.

One way that you can save money in 2x6 framing is by using studs on 24-in. centers rather than 16 in. o. c. Although this theoretically reduces the number of studs by one-third, it doesn't translate to a one-third reduction in material. The other members in any wall—sills, plates, fire stops, header cripples and drywall backing—all remain the same. When considering the economy of going to 2-ft. centers, pay close attention to the thickness of the exterior and interior skins applied over the studs. I find ½-in. drywall over studs at

24 in. o. c. to be very flimsy, so I generally use ⅝-in. drywall. The same is true for ½-in. plywood sheathing. I use at least 58-in. and preferably ¾-in. thickness when spanning 2 ft. from stud to stud.

I've begun using a built-up box-beam header with 2x6s (drawing below). It's installed like the typical

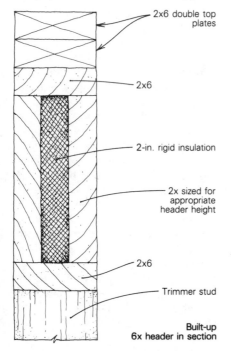

2x6 double top plates

2x6

2-in. rigid insulation

2x sized for appropriate header height

2x6

Trimmer stud

Built-up 6x header in section

solid 4x stock we used to use, and yet its parts can all be cut in one pass with a skillsaw. It gives an overall R-value of about 14, depending on what kind of rigid insulation board you use, compared to about R-7 for a solid 6x header.

Wide mudsills

In my area of northern California, on most older houses the mudsill is wider than the cripple-wall studs. Typically, the sill is a 2x6 or 2x8, and the studs are 2x4s. How then does one connect the plywood shear-wall sheathing to the sill? Your suggestions would be appreciated, since this problem affects my own home.
—*Daniel T. Wagner, Lafayette, Calif.*

David Helfant replies: The description of the mudsill and cripple-stud situation you give is one that we commonly confront in our subfloor reinforcing work. When the sill is wider than the studs, it is necessary to create a shear surface, i.e., a totally flush surface. This can be done by installing 2x4 blocks between the studs at the base of the mudsill and nailing the blocks to both the studs and the mudsill (drawing, below).

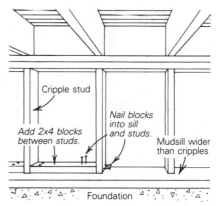

Cripple stud

Add 2x4 blocks between studs.

Nail blocks into sill and studs.

Mudsill wider than cripples

Foundation

Then drill a hole through the block and the mudsill and use a hammer drill to bore a hole in the concrete. Use a larger anchor bolt so that its embedment in the concrete satisfies the engineering specifications of the anchor. This approach gives you a blocked and bolted mudsill and a flush nailing surface for the plywood shear wall that includes the plate, the stud and the blocks.

Another way is to rip the mudsill to create a new edge that's flush with the edge of the studs. In this case you shear off the side of the mudsill.

Assessing rafter strength

I am enclosing a back porch to increase the size of an existing room. I have some doubts about the strength of the porch roof. It has 2x4 rafters on centers from 19 in. to 24 in. They are covered with 1x6 tongue-and-groove sheathing and shingles. The roofing is new, and I don't want to pull it up and start fresh. How do I strengthen my present roof?
—Ron Honthaner,
Studio City, Calif.

Sam Clark, a carpenter and author in Cambridge, Mass., replies: Small structures, even if they are significantly underbuilt, rarely fail unless they are damaged by rot or violent weather. Your problem is one that is best solved by applying rules of thumb and practical experience.

First you need to determine whether or not you really have a problem. Check the toenailing or joist hangers of the members that support the roof to see if they are loose or missing where they are fastened to the house. On the other end of the span, look for a sag in the beam or plate that supports these joists. If they are supported by a wall, make sure that it's sound. Also sight the rafters along their length. If you can see a sag of ¾ in. or more, then the rafters are too small for the span.

If you do need to re-engineer your porch, there are several manuals

you can consult. *Wood-frame House Construction* by L.O. Anderson (USDA Agricultural Handbook #73) is an excellent guide to simple, straightforward building. It is available free from The Forest Products Laboratory (Current Information Section, P.O. Box 5130, Madison, Wis. 53705). Rafter size and spacing can be found in reference books such as *Architectural Standards,* many building textbooks, and your local building code.

When I need to consult span tables, I use a chart that the Western Wood Products Association calls a span computer. This useful tool is actually a pocket-sized cardboard slide rule for comuting joist, beam and rafter sizes for woods of different strengths. It costs $2 including postage (WWPA, 1500 Yeon Building, Portland, Ore. 97204), and is the easiest way I've found for sizing the beams that are needed in typical wood-frame construction.

If your porch rafters prove to be undersize, the correctly sized lumber, probably 2x6s, can simply be scabbed onto the existing 2x4s with a pair of 10d common nails every foot. As long as the 2x4s themselves are well supported at both ends, the added pieces need not be fastened directly to the walls.

Designing trusses

I want to use home-built trusses on the house I'm building for myself. The truss I designed is 36 ft. long with a total rise of over 12 ft. The gussets will be ½-in. plywood on both sides. There are 13 pairs of them for each truss. These trusses will allow me a more open

floor plan of 36 ft. by 54 ft., with a room above the lower chord of the trusses that has a usable 12 ft. by 54 ft. Is this design structurally feasible?   —*Jack Reynolds,
Mission Hills, Calif.*

Consulting editor Bob Syvanan replies: Trusses save time and money if they are simple and light. A 24-ft. truss made of 2x4s or 2x6s can easily be handled by three people. Your 36-ft. 2x6 and 2x10 truss is extremely heavy, and uses more lumber than conventional framing. Also your room above the trusses using the 2x10 lower chord as a floor joist will span nearly 14 ft. This is all right at 16 in. o.c., but trusses to be economical have to be 24 in. o.c. This would put your 14-ft. floor joists at 24 in. o.c., not good enough for the building code.

Because of the serious nature of calculating roof loads using truss systems, you should consult a structural engineer with your complete plans if you are unsure about the structural feasibility of the design. You can either buy a few minutes for advice, or pay for the full calculations that result in an engineering stamp on your plans. Your local building inspector is a good person to consult about structural engineers in your area. You can also get good advice from companies that make trusses.

Beam size questioned

Last year I finished building a house for myself and family. It's a split-entry bilevel, 28 ft. wide by 48 ft. long. The architect called for a W8x28 wide-flange beam to span the 24-ft. rec room on the first floor. The beam is supported at each end by a 3½-in. concrete-filled Lally column. Now that the project is finished, an engineer informs me that a W8x28 is too light for the application.

If my friend is correct and the beam is too light for the load, is there any chance of failure by the beam or the columns that support it and the house? The floor supported by the beam is 2x10s spaced 16 in. o. c. with ¾-in. T&G plywood glued and nailed on top. The ceiling below is ½-in. drywall glued and nailed. The joists are toenailed to a 2x8 laid flat on the beam. There is no flooring laid in the attic at that end of the house.   —*H. J. Barfield,
Morganville, N. J.*

Thomas Rewerts, a licensed structural engineer and professional engineer with the consulting firm of Wiss, Janney, Elstner Associates, Inc. in Chicago, Ill., replies: I agree with your friend that a W8x28 is not deep enough for this application. A W12x26 or larger member should have been used.

The W8x28 that was installed will support only 18 lb. per sq. ft. of live load. In this application, the beam should support 40 psf live load plus 15 psf partition load, a total of 55 psf.

The existing beam doesn't meet standard building codes for this application. But it isn't likely that the beam will fail. It will be highly stressed, however, and if fully loaded, it will deflect up to 2 in.

The best solution to your problem would be to add a column, with an appropriate foundation, to support the beam at midspan.

Beam split

The roof I built last year is supported by several 10x14 larch beams that span 26 ft. One of these beams has checked almost entirely through, effectively rendering it two separate beams. A consulting engineer states that there is still plenty of "reserve," but I wonder if there is some way to reunite the pieces.
—*Stephen A. Smith, Concord, Mass.*

Bruce Hoadley, a professor of wood technology and author of Understanding Wood *(The Taunton Press, 63 S. Main St., Box 355, Newtown, Conn. 06470), replies:* It's difficult and risky to answer a question involving the failure of the beams without inspecting them. I have never known beams to check through entirely. But in the case of a boxed heart beam, it is common for a large single check to develop, opening the beam along one face to relieve the shrinkage stresses.

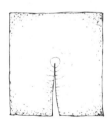

In a beam stressed in bending, if the separation is vertical, such as the one pictured on the left above, it is probably of little consequence. In fact, any minor strength loss due to checking or shrinkage would probably be compensated for by the added strength the beam had gained in drying.

If the check is horizontal, however, as at right above, it could lead to horizontal shear failure, separating the remainder of the beam into two planks. These would bend independently, making the beam weaker. But as long as the halves hold together, it will remain strong, functioning as an I-beam.

There is no natural way to reunite the halves of a beam or reclose the checks. If the checking worsens, consult again with a structural engineer for safety and peace of mind.

Cutting trusses

I want to install a pull-down staircase in my upstairs hallway so the attic can be used for storage. Unfortunately, the staircase needs to be installed perpendicular to the attic trusses. The rough opening I need is 22½ in. by 54 in., which would require cutting two of the trusses (they are 24 in. o.c.). All truss members are 2x4 lumber. How would I cut and frame out the rough opening without compromising the structural integrity of the trusses or cracking any of the ceiling plaster below?
—*Mike Brooks, Lutherville, Md.*

Consulting editor Tom Law replies: There has been a gigantic boom in house building in Maryland recently, and local building officials have tried hard to keep up with the times. In doing so, they have adopted some very stringent code requirements. Roof trusses are one of the few engineered structural components in a house, and when they are in place, they're expected to perform just as they do on paper; loads, stresses and connections all should work according to design. Disturbing any segment or connection in a truss destroys this calculated concert. For that reason, the cutting of any truss in the field is not permitted by code.

Alteration to the truss must take place in the manufacturing plant and carry an approved stamp. The easiest solution would be to find a place where you can install the stairs parallel to the truss chords. Cutting through the plaster can be done with a reciprocal saw on slow speed with a hardened blade made for tile cutting.

Replacing floor joists

In many old structures the floor has a sag that you want to correct without damaging the original floor. How do you remove the sagging joists without disturbing the T&G floor above, and how do you retie the floor for subsequent sanding and finishing?

—*Thomas A. Larkin,*
Lucasville, Ohio

Michael Zelver replies: There are several ways to deal with the removal of joists. In the case of a sagging floor, I would leave the original joists in place and nail new ones (sisters) to the original to take out the sag. If you do this, be sure to kerf the original joist to help it bend. Or you can attach a 2x2 cleat on both sides of the old joist, nailing or screwing up through the cleats into the original subfloor (don't use a fastener that's too long). Then you pull out the joist and replace it. If you have a big sag, use two joists and a flat 2x6 to make an inverted box beam and nail up through the 2x6 into the floor. Another solution is to put in a conventional joist and face-nail through the floor. Then you fill the nail holes and sand, or you can use screws and plugs.

Building a girt in place

My wife and I built the home we live in. One of the worst jobs was placing the 40-ft. girder that spans our full cellar. We used 2x8s and nailed them together four wide. We assembled the beam on one of the foundation walls. But putting it in final position was a terrible job. We needed all sorts of heavy temporary supports and trestles to get that monster across the span. There must be a better way.

—*Fred Jabour, Old Tappan, N. J.*

Consulting editor Bob Syvanen replies: When it comes to anything that is heavy or unwieldy, try to construct it in place. Since building a

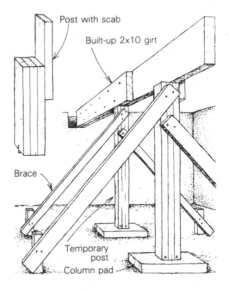

girt like this requires some support along its length, use temporary posts set on column pads, and brace them back to stakes or sills. When you are placing these temporary posts, keep them out of the way of the permanent support columns. The pads under the posts can be concrete or a header offcut that will spread the load of the beam on the ground. To keep the girt in place, make sure you scab a 2x on the outside of the post that can be nailed to the girt as well.

Jacking up a house

I need to elevate a two-bedroom frame house approximately 14 in. so I can pour a footing and foundation wall to replace the old metal underpinning. I was fortunate to find some 5x7 33-ft. long fir girders to replace the inadequate ones that held this old place up for so many years. I have the new girders positioned from 4 ft. to 4 ft. 8 in. apart under 2x6 floor joists. I want to raise this house myself using a single hydraulic jack. The girders are sitting on 12-in. wide by 8-in. thick 16-in. long concrete blocks. Can I jack up one point at a time and insert a 2x10 spacer until I reach the height of another building block? There are about 50 jacking points. I plan to lower the house about 6 in. of the 14 in. back onto the new foundation wall and girder supports.

—Joe Foust, Grandview, Tex.

Restoration specialist Dan Desmond replies: Realizing that most home-owner repairs of this kind are born of necessity and the materials at hand, I will give some advice of a general nature regarding your proposal. People attempting structural work of this nature should consider that every house has unique prob-

lems, and they should not forge ahead without the benefit of some expert on-site advice.

If the joists are undersized, the strain of concentrated force in lifting may cause them to break. If at all possible, face-nail properly sized "sister" joists to the originals before you attempt to lift the house. Remove any rotted wood completely so it won't contaminate the replacements. The new joists should also enable you to lift the house with fewer girders in place.

Don't use concrete blocks as a jack stand. Without the benefit of mortar and a proper footing to distribute the load, they could shatter. If you have enough 5x7 timbers to spare, cut them up into 3-ft. or 4-ft. lengths to use as cribbing.

Lift points must be placed uniformly under the bearing walls, not just uniformly under the floor. Lift the bearing walls, and the floors will come along without any special effort. You should use gangs of jacks, and not just one, so that you can lift each girder as a unit.

Lifting 1½ in. is a bit much; I'd suggest no more than ½ in. at one time, and even then, keep a close eye on plaster, windows and doors for signs of racking. Use ½-in. steel plates as shims, and always keep one under the ram of the jack so it won't punch a hole in the girder.

Don't work alone. You need eyes and ears other than your own to let you know what's happening. Dress for the job—this means a hard hat, gloves and steel-toed shoes.

Chapter 3:

Roofing

Lightning protection

I'm building a house on the crest of a hill, and the chimney extends 5 ft. above the house. The ground is Normanskill shale with quartzite. It was necessary to drill to 300 ft. to obtain water, although moisture was observed at around 2 ft. because of poor percolation. Many of the houses in the area have no lightning protection. It has been suggested that lightning rods attract lightning and should be avoided. I haven't been able to locate anyone knowledgeable about this subject. What can you tell me about lightning protection? If rods are recommended, I'd like information on the size and location of rods and ground rods and copper conductor wire.

—G. Salensky,
Whitehouse Station, N. J.

Marvin Frydenlund, managing director of the Lightning Protection Institute, replies: It is the purpose of lightning rods, technically called air terminals, to attract lightning, taking any current onto themselves and directing it, through large-diameter metal conductors, to a buried grounding system where the lightning will dissipate harmlessly.

A properly installed and maintained lightning protection system of air terminals on the roof and other points, copper or aluminum conducting cables, buried copper grounding system, and surge suppressors or arrestors will intercept and lead harmlessly into the ground any lightning current that might otherwise start a fire, cause structural damage, or damage electrical systems and components.

Shale and quartzite don't provide much resistance to the passage of electrical or lightning current, so the heavy charge of a lightning stroke, normally negative, is likely to damage wiring and appliances. Moreover, if the lightning flash is a "hot bolt," it will contain at least one long-duration flow of current, which will transfer enough heat to cause a fire unless proper grounding is provided.

In a case like yours, there are a number of ways that grounding can be enhanced. Laying lightning conductor cable atop the rock strata in long trenches is the most common solution. For best results, the entrenched cable should make a closed loop around the building.

We ran information about your house through a "Lightning Risk Assessment Guide" prepared by the Lightning Protection Code Committee of the National Fire Protection Association. Because the house is on a hill it is a conspicuous target during a thunderstorm. But as the owner of a single-family residence, you do not face the liability exposure that owners of public buildings do. Your lightning risk is between "light to moderate" and "moderate." If the structure were a larger, publicly occupied building, such as a nursing home, the risk would be "moderate to severe."

For a copy of "Lightning Protection for Home, Family and Property," you can send $1.00 and a stamped, self-addressed No. 10 (business-size) envelope to: Lightning Protection Institute, P. O. Box 1039, Woodstock, Il. 60098; (815) 337-0277.

Problematic roof design

I plan to build a 16-ft. by 18-ft. addition to my house. The roofline I have designed presents some seri-

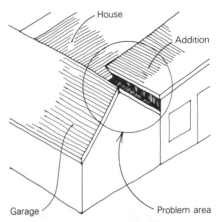

ous problems where different roofs intersect. The extended roof of the addition, shown above, will create a long valley with one side of the gable roof of the house. All the runoff from these roofs (as well as the water from one side of the existing garage roof) will drain into one small area. I can end the long roof in a vertical wall short of the garage roof to create a wide valley, but how can I flash it?
—*Bill Fosbury, Poughkeepsie, N. Y.*

Consulting editor Bob Syvanen replies: In this situation, I would build an end wall for your new roof that stops it short of the garage, as you have suggested. But this is as bad a roof condition as you will find— three slopes all draining against a vertical wall. If you simply cannot figure a way to change your design, you will have to have a gutter made that will fit this narrow area. It should be supported a few inches above the V created where the sidewall of the addition meets the sloping roof of the garage. A cant strip that is beveled from bottom to top as well as tapered along its length would do nicely.

Copper is the only material to use for this gutter, and it should be one piece if possible. The gutter will slope in two directions—toward the exterior of the house, and away from the sidewall. Because of the possibility of snow building up in the gutter and then slowly melting, the leg of

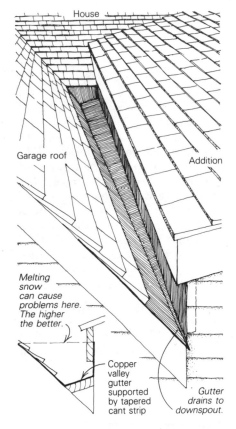

House

Garage roof

Addition

Melting snow can cause problems here. The higher the better.

Copper valley gutter supported by tapered cant strip

Gutter drains to downspout.

the roof side of the gutter should extend up the slope a minimum of 2½ shingle courses. However, because the gutter is sloped across the horizontal courses of shingles on the garage, this leg of the gutter will have to cut in behind several courses to get the needed 2½-course protection at any given point. The wall leg

should be the same height as the one on the roof side.

David Cumins Mitchell, of Washington, D. C., also replies: I'd like to comment on the answer Bill Fosbury got when he asked how to flash his roof. Although Bob Syvanen did call this the worst possible roof condition, fine home building really begins with design. If someone designs in a problem, why not just tell him to go back to the drawing board? Syvanen should have taken into account the debris that will collect in such a nasty interstice and the resulting ice dams and related backup, not to mention the discoloration and mildew that will streak down the siding below.

Flashing a hip-roof addition

I want to install a pitched roof on my flat-roofed garage, which shares a wall with the house. What kind of roof will look best? Also, how can I best flash and gutter the new roof where it meets the house?
—*Ron Austin, Park Ridge, Ill.*

Consulting editor Bob Syvanen replies: In your sketch, there appears to be a hip roof on the house. Therefore, a hip roof (see drawing on the facing page) should go on the adjoining garage. I tried out other roof designs, but nothing else looked quite right. Unfortunately, this creates the worst roof-flashing condition there is, so use the best material, copper, and install it with care. Don't forget to stick the building paper and shingles to the new roof with a tar-base cement.

As with all flashing, consider the course that rain will take as it hits

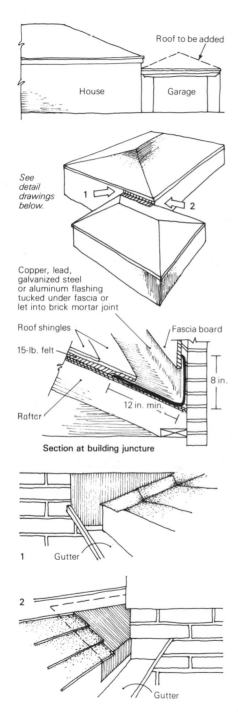

Roof to be added

House

Garage

See detail drawings below.

1

2

Copper, lead, galvanized steel or aluminum flashing tucked under fascia or let into brick mortar joint

Roof shingles

Fascia board

15-lb. felt

8 in.

12 in. min.

Rafter

Section at building juncture

1   Gutter

2

Gutter

the roof. Follow that drop of water until it reaches the ground. This will tell you how to install the flashing properly. Also pay close attention to the wind—it drives water off its natural course.

Skylight in a metal roof

I installed a 30-in. by 30-in. Plexiglas skylight in my standing-seam metal roof. The mistake I made was probably classic. I didn't build a curb around the rough opening. I installed the skylight at roof level so the flange at the base of the bubble is covered by the sheet metal. I've sealed the 2-in. overlap several times with different kinds of caulking. But the two materials expand and contract at different rates, and the sealed joints never last very long. Is there a super-adhesive sealant that has enough flexibility to hold the two seams together? I need some advice.
—*John Cole, Freedom, Maine*

Matt Holmstrom, a remodeling contractor who specializes in sheet-metal roofing in Bedford, Va., replies: Your problem is indeed classic. Incorrectly flashed skylights and curbs seem to be commonplace. I wouldn't attempt to install a curbless skylight in a metal roof. The whole point of a standing-seam roof is to have a long-lasting metal "skin" between your house and the weather, uninterrupted by fasteners and not relying on short-term sealants or caulks to keep water out. There are no super sealants that will work here. Building a curb is the only way to go.

Flashing a curb in a standing-seam metal roof is just like flashing a chimney. Turn the roof metal itself up the side of the curb (built from 2x stock) 1½ in. to 2 in. as the base flashing, as shown in the drawing below. Don't fasten the flashing to the

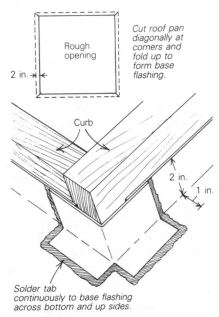

Rough opening

2 in.

Cut roof pan diagonally at corners and fold up to form base flashing.

Curb

2 in.

1 in.

Solder tab continuously to base flashing across bottom and up sides.

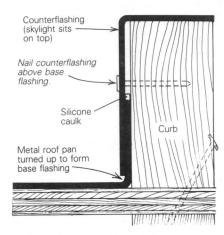

Counterflashing (skylight sits on top)

Nail counterflashing above base flashing.

Silicone caulk

Curb

Metal roof pan turned up to form base flashing

curb at all. As extra insurance apply a bead of silicone caulk. Then counterflash the curb with identical metal, coming down over the base almost to the roof, as shown in the drawing above right. Fasten this flashing into the curb *only,* above the height of the base flashing. This way the roof and skylight curb can expand and contract independently of each other. This is probably not as critical as it is with masonry, but it does help.

The only tricky part is at the corners of the curb, where folded tabs of metal (3 in. by 6 in.) must be soldered in place to make the base flashing continuous. Sorry, but its the only permanent solution. No sealant will last very long. For terne,

galvanized steel or copper use 50-50 solder and a 175-watt or higher iron (one made for sheet-metal and stained glass work, not some tool for radio work). The type of flux you use depends on the metal.

The glory of this method is that the roof and the skylight are independent of each other. If any problems develop with the glazing on top of the curb, they can be dealt with without disturbing the roof: at the worst the counterflashing might have to be replaced while reglazing or remounting the skylight.

In your case, you can simply bend up your 2-in. overlap of metal on all four sides (if you don't have metal-working tongs, sheet-metal vise grips will probably do), remove the flanged skylight and drop in a curb made from 2x4 or 2x6 stock to the inside dimensions of this opening in the metal. No alteration of your rough opening should be necessary. Toenail this curb from the inside to the roof deck and proceed with this flashing method. Finish with either a prefab skylight that will fit over this curb, like the one you have, or use a site-built skylight.

Flashing a terne roof

Please tell me how to flash a standing-seam galvanized steel (terne) roof around chimneys, skylights and vent pipes.
—*Thomas N. Towle, Chichester, N .H.*

Alex Wade, an architect in Mt. Marion, N. Y., replies: Terne roofs are flashed much like other roofs, except that terne metal is used for the flashing material as well. The only trick is

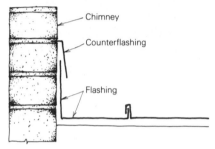

Flashing locked into flat seam

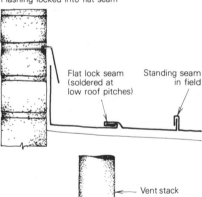

Flat lock seam (soldered at low roof pitches) Standing seam in field

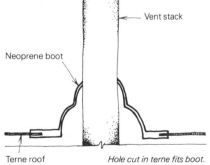

Neoprene boot

Vent stack

Terne roof   *Hole cut in terne fits boot.*

the method of joining the terne flashing to the surface of the terne roof. If the joint between flashing and roof surface is parallel to a nearby standing seam, the flashing can be bent right into the seam as an integral part of the roof. If the joint runs laterally across the roof or at a distance from a vertical seam, a flat lock seam (drawing, below left) is used. This seam, soldered after it has been hammered flat, should be used wherever a roof surface meets a vertical plane, as at a dormer, a chimney or a skylight curb.

Where the roof is punctured, as at a plumbing vent stack or an electric service mast, use a standard commercial neoprene boot-type flashing. Neoprene boots usually come attached to a square of flimsy aluminum flashing, which you can use as a pattern to cut a neat hole in the roof. Then insert the boot into the hole and slide the pipe through. Try to position the pipe so that it misses the standing seams.

Curbless skylight on metal roof

Could you describe the modifications necessary for installing a curbless skylight where a corrugated metal roof will be used?
—*Bill Stephenson, Denver, Colo.*

Rob Thallon, an architect-builder, replies: Fitting the curbless skylight into a metal roof presents a few difficulties when the panels are corrugated. The flashing details will basically be the same, except that the step flashing on the side of the skylight should be replaced by a single piece, and the depth of the flashing may have to be increased slightly to accommodate the roofing. Using a narrow piece of corrugated roofing for this side flashing will allow the horizontal leg to fit tightly under the panel of roofing near it by matching up the corrugations, as shown below. Add a bead of caulk

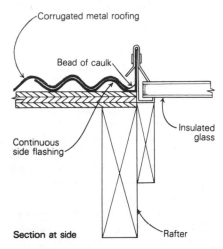

Corrugated metal roofing

Bead of caulk

Insulated glass

Continuous side flashing

Section at side

Rafter

ing where the cut edge of the roofing dies to prevent water seeping between it and the horizontal leg of the side flashing.

This side flashing isn't something you'll be able to make up on site. Since the horizontal leg requires corrugations but the vertical leg doesn't, you'll have to get your local sheet-metal shop to solder two compatible pieces together. The problem then is to coordinate the alignment of the corrugations laterally between the roofing in the field and the side flashing, neither of which can be adjusted during the process of roofing. The sheet-metal fabricator I use shakes his head at the kind of precision and coordination between the site and shop that is required here.

Air infiltration could also be a problem at the top and bottom of the skylight. Seal these areas with foam, which will act as a gasket.

Weatherproofing a skylight

I'm interested in using a curbless skylight, but I live in a cold climate where condensation would form on the exposed flashing (or even on the glass itself) on the interior. Could the same skylight be built with a thermal break?
—*Dale M. Johnson, Deerfield, Ill.*

Rob Thallon replies: Since I live in Oregon, where the temperature rarely drops to 0°F, this hasn't been a problem in the skylights I've built. But your observation is a good one. A combination of cold weather and humid inside air would almost surely produce some condensation on the flashing at the sides of the skylight where the flashing is continuous from the exterior to the interior of the building. A thermal break could be accomplished by adding two pieces of non-conductive rigid plastic at the location shown in the drawing below. This would isolate

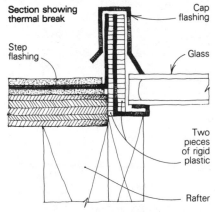

Section showing thermal break

Cap flashing

Step flashing

Glass

Two pieces of rigid plastic

Rafter

the exterior from the interior flashing with the exception of the three through-rivets on each side of the skylight that hold the cap flashing, step shingles and vertical leg of the interior side flashing together.

The installation would be complicated only by having to figure out how to seal the notch at the top of the side flashing.

A simpler and possibly easier solution would be to insulate all of the flashing from the inside—in effect preventing the warm moisture-laden interior air from getting to the cold flashing. In our climate, the interior wood trim provides this thermal break. The addition of a layer of rigid insulation in extremely cold climates would provide more protection. In either case, the wood trim at the bottom should be held down from the underside of the glass at least ¼ in., so that moisture that condenses on the glass itself has a chance to reach the channel in the bottom flashing that was designed to collect it and drain it away.

Flashing for brick veneer

In north Texas, the most popular exterior material is brick veneer. Many homes have areas on exterior walls that are interrupted by a roof. What is the best way to support and flash brick veneer in these areas?
—*John Brooks, Allen, Tex.*

A. *Rhett Whitlock, a research engineer at the Brick Institute of America, replies:* The best way to support brick masonry in residential construction is on concrete footings. In cases where the veneer is interrupted, its weight has to be carried by an engineered system of steel beams and columns that have a direct connection with the foundation.

As shown in the drawing above right, two flashing techniques must be used where a roof section meets

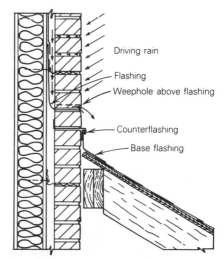

Driving rain

Flashing

Weephole above flashing

Counterflashing

Base flashing

brick veneer: one to keep water from entering the building where the roof and the wall intersect, and the other to drain moisture that has penetrated the brick veneer back to the exterior of the wall.

Information on brick veneer, flashing and other aspects of brick masonry construction can be obtained through the BIA Publications Dept. (11490 Commerce Park Dr., Reston, Va. 22091).

Metal roof on stress skins

I am building a timber-frame house with a large garage (30 ft. by 60 ft.) and plan to install a prepainted galvanized standing-seam roof. Should I build an air space between the metal and the stress-skin panels? Also, would it be advisable to sheathe the rafters in the garage and then add an air space instead of just attaching the metal roof to purlins? I'm worried that condensation will form under the roofing and soak the attic insulation.
—*Michael Sheehan, Annville, Pa.*

Matt Holmstrom, a remodeling contractor who specializes in metal roofing, replies: I advise using an air space between your stress-skin panels and the metal roofing. Although many metal-roofing manufacturers and fabricators specify solid sheathing under their products, I'm convinced this will severely shorten the lifespan of any steel roof. Galvanized steel is no exception. Its initial rust resistance may help for awhile, but constant exposure to moisture, even backside condensation, will break the resistance down. It would be best to run vertical nailers (1x stock should do fine) on 16-in. centers over the stress skin with your purlins on top of these. Vent the air spaces into the cornice. The point is to get air to the backside of your roofing to remove condensation. I wouldn't bother with solid sheathing on your garage roof. The air flow that results from roofing directly over purlins should minimize condensation.

From roof to deck

I recently bought a house with an attached garage that has a flat tar roof. The top of the garage could be converted to an excellent balcony or deck with an appropriate surface, but the tar on the roof is brittle, blistered and crumbling. I live in a part of the country where roof temperatures often change as much as 75°F in a single day. What type of roofing would stand up to the climate and also serve as a deck surface?
—F.B. Green, Boone, N. C.

Ed Carlson, a roofing contractor in Rockford, Ill., replies: Your best

bet is to have a coal tar pitch roof applied over the deteriorated tar roof, with a dense layer of roofer's pea gravel set into the new tar compound. This roof covering is applied hot by a roofing contractor, and is designed for flat roofs.

For the balcony, build a slatted deck (duck boards) with 2x4 sleepers and your choice of decking material. This will be easier on the feet and also protect the new roof. Build the deck in sections, so you lift them up to remove leaves and trash from the roof.

Before you go ahead with the renovation, though, check the roof framing in your garage. Supporting the new roof shouldn't be any problem, but make sure that the existing frame is strong enough to hold people safely.

Quarry tile on a roof terrace

I am now in the planning stages of a large town house. I'd like to incorporate some roof terraces in the design. Instead of wood decking, though, I would like to use quarry tile. Is this compatible with wood-frame construction? If so, could you suggest possible detailing? *—Robert Kelly, Lexington, Ky.*

Michael Byrne, a tile setter in Walnut Creek, Calif., replies: Quarry tiles make an excellent outdoor paving surface. Their ability to resist the elements, however, depends on the system of waterproofing that begins with the joists and ends with the grout.

Adjust the joists at the terraced areas to allow for a slope of ¼ in. to 1 ft. toward the edges of the roof, and use ¾-in. CDX plywood for the subfloor. Instead of installing in-floor drains, which clog and cause leaks, use gutters on the perimeter of the roof. A waterproof membrane such as Laticrete 301/335 (Laticrete International Inc., 1 Laticrete Park, Bethany, Conn., 06525) or Vaporseal (The Noble Co., Box 332, Grand Haven, Mich. 49417) will give longer service life than hot-mopping with tar. Whatever material you decide to use, lap it 6 in. up the walls and columns and down 6 in. over the edges.

A 1-in. to 2-in. bed of mortar reinforced with 2-in. galvanized mesh

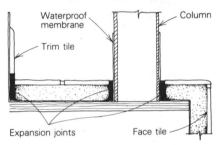

Waterproof membrane · Trim tile · Column · Expansion joints · Face tile

will cushion the membrane against the forces of the finished floor. The addition of latex mortar additives to the setting bed and to the grout will offer extra protection against the freeze/thaw cycle. Provide for expansion joints as shown in the drawing above, at all abutments and every 12 ft. to 16 ft. in the field. These joints should extend down through the mortar base, but stop short of the membrane. Fill them with silicone caulk, or use extruded polystyrene strips with ½ in. of silicone on top if you want to save money.

Brick patio on a flat roof

The hilly site where I will soon build a home lends itself to a garage with a flat roof doubling as a patio. For the floor of the patio, I prefer brick set on sand, but am apprehensive about the choice of a supporting system with respect to moisture and freeze/thaw cycling. A membrane over precast concrete panels or galvanized steel decking has been suggested. Is there a dependable system you can recommend?
—I. J. Fuchs, Hoboken, N. J.

Architect Harwood Loomis, director for Technical Services with the New Haven, Conn., firm of Hoffman Architects, replies: The idea of a garage roof as a patio is, of course, a familiar concept. The problem has always been finding a covering that will withstand traffic while remaining watertight. While you don't say what type of construction is involved, I would say that this appears to be an ideal application for a loose-laid, ballasted EPDM (ethylene propylene diene monomer) rubber-membrane roof. This type of system is attached only around the perimeter. The field of the roof is free to move laterally, and is held in place by the weight of the ballast. If the garage is not unusually large, the rubber can be applied in a single sheet that will cover the entire area with no seams. It is available in rolls up to 40 ft. wide by 100 ft. long.

The minimum weight for ballast is 10 psf, and more is recommended if high winds are likely. We routinely specify 15 psf, or even more for certain projects. Brick weighs roughly 120 lb. per cu. ft., so a single layer of brick would yield about 25 psf, which should be plenty unless your home will be subject to ocean gales. The weight of the ballast must be supported by the structure, in addition to the weight required by code for live load. For an outside patio, this is probably 100 psf, so the garage-roof structure is going to have to be fairly substantial, whatever roof system is selected.

If the walls can be load-bearing masonry, concrete plank would seem an ideal roof system, as the rubber membrane can be laid directly on it, with just a layer of heavy felt (supplied by most of the rubber-roof manufacturers) to act as a cushion and slip sheet. I would put another layer of the same felt on top, between the rubber and the brick, to prevent sharp edges from punching into the membrane. Sand isn't a very good idea—it would work its way under the bricks and abrade the roof membrane. The bricks should be as hard as possible, and should have the bottom side finished fairly smooth. Concrete bricks would be better for this application than fired clay because they can be cast much smoother.

For more information on single-ply roofing, contact the Single Ply Roofing Institute (104 Wilmot Rd., Suite 201, Deerfield, Ill. 60015-5195).

Counterflashing a chimney

I recently completed a modest ranch-style home with a stone-veneer fireplace and chimney. The roofers and masons were supposed to work together on flashing around the chimney. They say they did, but when it rains, water pours in. Both subcontractors are now out of business. My objective is to correct this problem.

I strongly suspect that no counterflashing was used. I'm thinking of using a masonry saw to cut a 2½-in. deep groove for copper counterflashing at the base of the chimney. A cut of this depth would penetrate through the 1-in. stone veneer and make a 1½-in. cut in the brick behind. Is this the best way to correct the problem? And if so, what kind of saw and blade would be best for the job?

—*Lanny W. Robinson,*
Winterville, Ga.

Contributing editor Scott McBride replies: Counterflashing is the exposed part of a chimney's flashing system. The other part, the base flashing, is covered by the counterflashing and the roof shingles, except on the downhill side where the base flashing is exposed. So if you don't see counterflashing, you haven't got it. Adding it will probably stop the leak, assuming, of course, that the chimney does have base flashing.

From the slight thickness you give for the stone veneer (1 in.), I imagine it must be fairly uniform material, and that it would thus present a fairly flat surface. In that case a circular saw fitted with a masonry blade would be appropriate to make the kerf you desire. Be sure to wear safety goggles when you do this. Setting up some surface as a fence will give you a nice, straight cut. If the chimney surface is very irregular, however, the saw will tip from side to side as its shoe rides the contours of the stone. This could make the abrasive wheel bind in the cut, causing premature wear or, even worse, shattering the wheel.

In the case of an irregular surface, you would be better off freehanding the cut with a portable grinder or cutoff saw without a shoe. Snap a line first and take light successive cuts. As the cut gets deeper, be sensitive to any rubbing of the disc against the side of the kerf: this indicates that you are tipping the machine, risking the same bad results mentioned earlier. Cutoff saws, in both gas and electric models, are available at tool-rental yards.

Basically, there are two types of masonry-cutting blades: abrasive discs and diamond blades. Discs are much less expensive, but they wear down quickly. If you buy a disc, make sure it's labeled "masonry" rather than "metal." Metal-cutting discs use a different type of abrasive. Also, be certain that the rpm rating of your saw or grinder doesn't exceed the rpm rating printed on the disc.

Diamond blades are steel discs with a lip of industrial diamonds bonded to the rim. Some require a constant spray of water to cool them, and some can used without water. Porter-Cable has recently come out with a dry-cutting diamond blade for their "Saw Boss" circular saw. Unfortunately, it costs about as much as the machine. As with abrasive discs, it's best to take repeated light cuts with diamond blades.

Once you've cut the kerf, use lead plugs to wedge the prebent flashing in place. Take a small strip of lead sheet about 1 in. wide, roll it up until its diameter is about equal to the width of the kerf and cut it off. Make a handful of these little plugs and drive them into the kerf above the flashing. You might be able to get some scraps of lead sheet from a plumber, or you could forge the plugs from bullet slugs or from lead masonry anchors. Once the flashing

is secured, fill the kerf with silicone caulk to complete the job.

If you still have leakage after the counterflashing is installed, there are two possibilities. First, the base flashing may have been improperly installed. Checking this will mean removing shingles. The second possibility is that water is migrating through the masonry. Painting the chimney with a silicone masonry sealer may stop this, but the only foolproof solution is a through-pan flashing.

Log-house chimney

My wife and I are about to build a stone chimney for our log house. We need to know what accommodation to make for the logs' settling, and how to flash the chimney. —*Stephen Rosen, Duluth, Minn.*

Charles McRaven, log builder, restorationist and author, replies: Since all logs settle, your chimney should ideally be built after seasoning and shrinking are complete. Wait at least a year, more if possible. In any case, the chimney should not be attached to the house, but built independently up alongside the gable end. This way the expansion and contraction of the logs won't affect the chimney. Use an elastic caulking at the joint between the stonework and the house.

Flashing should be laid into the horizontal joints between the stones. Aluminum, copper and galvanized sheet iron are the common metals used. They should be fastened with nails of the same metals to avoid galvanic corrosion. The traditional method is to use two 90° bends on each of these step shingles, as shown in the drawing below. This flashing may be nailed down over the roofing material or under it, as is

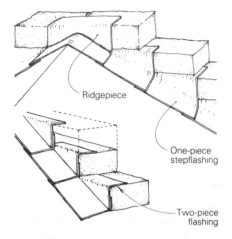

Ridgepiece

One-piece
stepflashing

Two-piece
flashing

usually done with wooden shingles. If the chimney is located at the peak of the gable, a piece of flashing should be fabricated to fit the ridge.

A two-piece step flashing will allow much more movement. Each piece of flashing is set into the stonework to overlap a corresponding one nailed to the roof. This lets the two pieces slide with the settling of the house.

Gable-dormer retrofit

I want to add a gable dormer to my house. The roofing is composition shingle and has been on for about three years. What is the best way to cut back the existing roofing? How do you pull or cut the nails so that you can get the metal flashing in without tearing the shingles to pieces? Should the valley flashing go on top of the 15-lb. felt or under it?

—*Alex F. Ramsay, Somerset, Calif.*

Carpenter Scott McBride replies: After framing in the common rafters of your gable dormer, use a straight-edge to project the dormer roof planes onto the main roof. The lines of intersection will be the centerlines of your two valleys. Snap chalklines parallel to and about 3 in. away from these centerlines. This is where you will cut the existing shingles. If the shingles are not too brittle, you can use a utility knife equipped with a hook blade to cut them. The hook blade is pulled through the roofing material like a linoleum knife, and

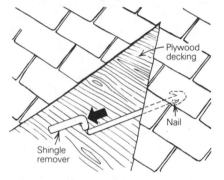

Plywood
decking

Nail

Shingle
remover

will work better than an ordinary straight blade, which will dull immediately on the gravel surface of the shingles. You can also cut the roofing with an old carbide blade that is mounted in a circular saw, or use a sawblade made just for this purpose. Use goggles here.

To slip the valley flashing under the existing roof shingles, you must remove some hidden roofing nails. Again, a lot depends on the state of the shingles. If they are still pliable, you may be able to peel them up enough to catch the nail heads with a cat's paw or flat prybar. If the existing shingles aren't pliable, you'll need a shingle remover (drawing, above) to remove them. This tool has a long flat blade with V-notches at the end. To use it, slip the blade up under the shingles and poke around until you hit a nail. Slide the end of the blade up past the nail and then pull down, hooking the nail in one of the notches. Now beat down on the offset handle of the tool with a hammer until the nail is yanked free. It takes a bit of practice to master this technique, and even then the task can be frustrating. Shingle removers can be found at roofer's supply houses or at some hardware stores. One mail-order vendor that carries them is U. S. General Hardware (100 Commercial St., Plainview, N. Y. 11803).

When flashing the valley, the flashing material should be slipped under the 15-lb. felt as well as under the shingles. That way any water that gets through the shingles will drain off the felt and onto the valley flashing.

Sawing white-oak shingles

I have access to an antique machine that saws 16-in. shingles out of squared timber. I plan to cut shingles for my new home's roof using white oak, which is available in my area. Does it matter which way the growth rings run on the sawn shingle? I also need to know if the shingles should be nailed up green or seasoned?
—Christopher Z. Nestor,
Onalaska, Wis.

Dave Geisler, a wood-products research specialist, responds: White oak is dense and hard. It can be difficult to work, but if it's available at a low enough price, it's a good choice for shingles.

Shingles should be cut radially to the growth of the rings, producing quartersawn pieces. Quartersawn shingles shrink and swell less, exhibit less twisting and cupping and suffer less surface and edge checking. Use the heartwood of the timber. Heartwood resists decay because of the presence of natural tannins, oils and phenolics, which discourage fungal growth. Dip them in a water-repellent preservative for even greater decay resistance.

Shingles should be seasoned outdoors under cover with good air circulation before installation. This will keep dimensional changes after installation to a minimum, and will result in a more attractive job.

One other suggestion: If you drill pilot holes in the oak, you'll save yourself a lot of wasted shingles.

Roll roofing

The 100-year-old rowhouse I'm renovating has a roof that slopes 5 ft. in the 55 ft. from the front to the back of the house. It has had hot-tar roof coatings in the past, but it has developed some leaks. I've talked with several neighbors who swear by their cold-laid roofs of heavy mineral-covered felt, saying that they have lasted 10 to 15 years so far without problems. Can you tell me a little more about this kind of roof covering?
—Taylor Baxter, Baltimore, Md.

Consulting editor Bob Syvanen replies: For moderate-priced roofing on a low-pitch roof, I like to use 140-lb., 19-in. selvage double coverage. My own house on Cape Cod has such a roof and it still looks good after 14 years. The 19-in. selvage

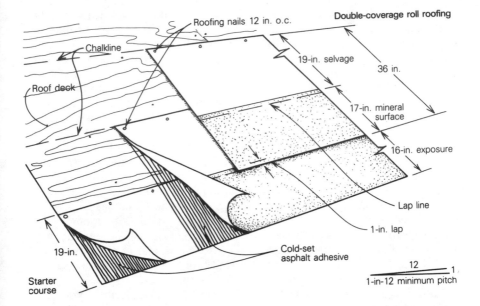

Roofing nails 12 in. o.c.
Double-coverage roll roofing
Chalkline
19-in. selvage
36 in.
Roof deck
17-in. mineral surface
16-in. exposure
Lap line
1-in. lap
19-in.
Cold-set asphalt adhesive
Starter course

$$\frac{12}{}\,1$$

1-in-12 minimum pitch

rolls come 36 in. wide and 36 ft. long. It takes two rolls to cover a square (100 sq. ft.). The lower 17 in. (which is overlapped 1 in. by the course above to give a total exposure of 16 in.) is mineral surfaced; the remaining 19 in., called the selvage, is smooth (see the drawing above for details).

The roof is started with a 19-in. wide strip of selvage, nailed at the top at 12 in. o. c. The first 36-in. strip is rolled over the starter strip and nailed at the top at 12 in. o. c. The second strip is then rolled out over the selvage, lapping 1 in. onto the mineral surface and nailed at the top at 12 in. o. c. Some roll roofing has a 1-in. overlap line on the mineral surface for a guide. If there is no line, I snap parallel lines on the roof deck at 16 in. o. c. to align the top of each row.

Short lengths of this roofing (12 ft. to 18 ft. long) are easier to work with and lie flatter than long lengths. Us-

ing shorter lengths, however, means making a side lap or two in each course. These should be overlapped at least 6 in.

Try to pick a sunny day to do this kind of roofing so that the asphalt-impregnated felt is pliable. Even if it is cold, there is often enough sun to make the roofing lie flat if you leave it out in the sun for an hour or so before proceeding.

Flexibility is important because each course, including the starter strip, must be rolled back on itself and a coat of cold-set asphalt adhesive brushed or squeegeed underneath. This will cover the 19-in. selvage surface, stopping just short of the 1-in. lap line. I pour gobs of adhesive from the can along the entire course and then smooth it with a long-handled squeegee. However, if the adhesive is laid on too thick, it is apt to squeeze out at the seams.

When you work with asphalt, take care where you step. A gob of asphalt on the soles of a shoe will leave its mark wherever you walk. If there is asphalt on the mineral surface, I carefully lift the bulk of it and then cover what is left with a piece of paper. That way I can at least keep it from following me all over the roof. Granules from a piece of roofing scraped onto such a blemish can sometimes mask it quite well.

It's possible to keep most of the cold asphalt off the surface of the roofing, but you're guaranteed to be wearing some when you're finished. Cleanup is easier than it might appear—throw away the tools and clean your body with lard, butter or vegetable shortening. You can salvage squeegees, but forget brushes. Lathering with lard dilutes the asphalt as you rub, and a rag or paper towel cleans it all off.

Looking for cypress shingles

My Monticello, Ga., home, built in about 1820, has a bottom layer of wooden shingles labeled OCKLHA PRIMES, WILSON CYPRESS CO. I'd like to replace these shingles with ones of the same kind. Can you tell me where to get them?
— *G. Speights Bollard, Atlanta, Ga.*

Tom Law replies: Cypress is being produced in greater quantities recently with the development of machinery that can traverse swamp lands. I'm now using a lot of cypress boards, but I don't know if any sawmills are cutting shingles. You could try writing to the trade association: Southern Cypress Manufacturers Association, 805 Sterick Building, Memphis, Tenn. 38103.

The shingles on a house I recently worked on were in excellent condition where they were not exposed to direct sunlight. The shingles on the porch walls were brown from aging and some staining along the way. I brought them back to a new look by sandblasting with low air pressure. Shingles like these could also be salvaged from an old building.

Fire safety and wood roofs

My wife and I are building a log home. We would like to use cedar shakes on the roof, but we are concerned about the danger of fire. What can we do about this?
—*Steve Rosen, Duluth, Minn.*

Dave Geisler, a wood-products researcher, replies: Anything that reduces the the risk of fire on the roof is worth doing. Installing a good chimney screen, or spark arrestor, will help. Flue maintenance to prevent chimney fires is important with any kind of roof covering.

Although wood roofs have been restricted by some communities in the past, the treated shakes and shingles now available meet many fire-code and insurance requirements nationwide. Treating shakes and shingles with fire-retardant chemicals helps to minimize two major hazards. First, it prevents your roof from igniting when burning airborne debris from other sources lands on it. Just as important, your roofing won't become firebrands that are scattered by the wind to start fires on other roofs.

The fire retardants used are organic resins dissolved in water. Pressure treating and then prolonged high-heat kiln drying polymerize the resins and leave them attached to the cells of the roof. This process requires extensive handling and equipment, which can double the price of the roofing. The process results in a Class C rating by the Underwriter's Laboratory. Use of a solid roof deck and foil underlayment or treated asphalt felt can raise this rating to Class B. The U.S. companies that treat shakes and shingles are: J. H. Baxter Co., Box 10797, Eugene, Ore. 97440; Hoover Universal, Knox Shopping Center, Thompson, Ga. 30824; Koppers Co., Inc., 750 Koppers Building, Pittsburgh, Pa. 15219; and Wesco Cedar, Inc., Box 2566, Eugene, Ore. 97402.

Sheathing under shakes

Many builders in my area use a solid-plywood roof deck as an underlayment for cedar shakes. However, in my remodeling experience I have torn apart old roofs to find shakes nailed to 1x6 purlins. If I use plywood, will my shake roof be likely to rot because of poor air circulation? —*Glenn Raleigh, Woodland Park, Colo.*

The editors of Fine Homebuilding *reply:* According to Frank Welch of the Red Cedar Shingle and Handsplit Shake Bureau (Suite 275, 515 116th Ave. N.E., Belleview, Wash. 98004), the choice of solid or open sheathing depends on the demands of local codes, but is otherwise optional. He states that there is no difference in the longevity of a cedar roof using either kind of roof deck. The same applies to red cedar shingles. However, in the case of shakes the Bureau recommends solid sheathing in areas with wind-driven snow.

Installing a shake roof

I am presently looking at a roofing job involving cedar handsplit shakes on a 12/12 pitch. The manufacturer and helpful local builders have recommended, since shake roofs are "so difficult to weatherproof," that each course of shakes be preceded by a course of 90-lb. roofing, which gets hidden by the shakes. Thus the cedar part of the roof is strictly visual. Besides adding significantly to the cost of the job, this approach just doesn't appeal to me. For what this roof will cost, I certainly don't want to have to do it more than once, but it would be much more satisfying to know that the cedar shakes are really doing what they appear to be doing. Is the double-roof approach really necessary, or is it merely a catch-all technique to correct for sloppy shingling? —*Jeb Smith, Ithaca, N. Y.*

Consulting editor Bob Syvanen replies: There is a difference between shakes and shingles, and the application of each is different as well. The flatsawn tapered shingles commonly used are installed with or without roofing felt underneath. An 18-in. shingle should have a maximum exposure of 5½ in. to ensure three layers of shingles at each butt (triple coverage).

Most shakes are split and resawn to create a taper on the back side. The split top surface of the shake is irregular, with the result that there are a lot of air spaces between courses. Shakes won't lay down as flat as shingles will. Because of this extra bulk, the exposure is usually increased to 10 in. for 24-in. shakes and 7½ in. for 18-in. shakes. To get triple coverage at the butts, an 18-in. strip of 30-lb. roofing felt should be applied over the top portion of the shakes and onto the sheathing, as shown in the drawing below. The

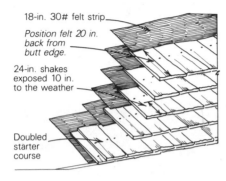

18-in. 30# felt strip

Position felt 20 in. back from butt edge.

24-in. shakes exposed 10 in. to the weather

Doubled starter course

bottom edge of the felt is positioned above the butt equal to twice the weather exposure of the courses. A 24-in. shake with a 10-in. exposure will have the bottom edge of the felt 20 in. above the butts, covering the top 4 in. of the shakes and extending 14 in. onto the sheathing.

The 18-in. felt strip can be eliminated when certain kinds of shakes are applied with exposures that are less than one-third the shake length (triple coverage).

Roofing with cedar shingles

Here in Maine, our shingles are northern white cedar, and the best grade available is #2. I want a roof for my house that will last. Will these work? —*Richard W. Aishton, Farmington, Maine*

Consulting editor Bob Syvanen, who builds on Cape Cod, replies: In my experience, red cedar lasts much longer on a roof than white cedar, although the difference in price between the two is forcing a lot of people in the Northeast to use the local white cedar. I have been watching the aging process of a shed roof near my home that has red cedar on one half and white cedar on the other. The roofing was done about 1973, and although I'm told that neither section leaks, the superior wearing quality of the red cedar is already obvious. There is much more splitting, warping and general deterioration on the white-cedar part of the roof.

You'll have to judge for yourself whether #2 shingles will meet your needs. Generally they make a good weathertight roof, although there will be more waste, and shaving the shingles with a hatchet will be more difficult when you're laying the roof. Even accounting for the differences in grade, I have had to return many shingle shipments because of poor quality—too many hard shingles, very narrow shingles, thin butts, shorts and splits. Watch for knots, too. These just aren't acceptable on the roof of a house.

Chapter 4:

Siding and Exterior Trim

Applying gold leaf

A year ago I bought a 27-in. eagle weathervane made of copper. At the time the gold market was erratic and the manufacturer refused to cover the weathervane with gold leaf. I tried to get the weathervane plated, but the $1,200 quote for the job was unacceptably high. It looks like I'm better off doing the job myself. Can you furnish information for applying gold leaf to a copper weathervane? Please include some sources of supply if possible.
— *Paul Sundback, Hartstown, Pa.*

Ted Ewen, a specialist in traditional construction and restoration techniques, replies: In terms of expense and personal satisfaction, you are definitely better off doing the job yourself. Gold leafing isn't difficult to do provided you have a good place

to work, patience and the necessary materials. The tools and supplies you'll need are listed below; they should be available at either an art-supply store or a paint store.

No. 0 steel wool
Fine (120 grit) and extra-fine (220 grit) sandpaper
1 soft-bristle brush (1½ in.)
1 rabbit-hair brush for leafing
1 gilder's tip (about 3¾ in. long)
Good-quality, exterior-grade oil-base primer
Slow-drying oil size for leafing
One or more books of 23K XX-quality gold leaf (one book should cover about 1½ sq. ft.)
1 package clean cotton

Rub the entire surface of the vane with steel wool, using light to moderate pressure to remove any loose scales, tarnish or paint. Brush the copper clean with a soft brush. Using a soft scrubbing brush, wash the vane off with hot water. Do not use any soap or detergent. Allow the surface to dry for 24 hours in a heated room. Throughout the leafing process you should try to maintain a warm temperature (70°F) in the work area, with consistently low humidity (50% or less).

Cover a large table with clean kraft paper and position the weathervane on this surface so it stands vertically. Remove any dust and then apply an even coat of exterior-grade alkyd (oil-base) white primer. I suggest Moorwhite Primer, made by Benjamin Moore Co. Allow the paint to dry for at least four days. Then sand the surface lightly with fine sandpaper, wipe the weathervane clean with a tack cloth and apply a second coat of the primer, letting it dry as before. Next use extra-fine sandpaper to smooth the painted surface and to give it the required tooth to hold the size.

With a soft-bristle brush, apply a thorough, even coat of slow-drying oil size; either the clear or the yellow kind will do. When all surfaces to be gold leafed are completely covered, allow the size to dry for 12 to 18 hours, or until it is just barely tacky to touch. The surface should hold its tack for 10 to 12 hours, giving you ample time to complete the leafing.

Open the books of gold leaf on a level surface to avoid spilling the leaves. Stroke your gilder's tip across your hair to pick up static electricity, place it along the outer edge of the first sheet of leaf, and carefully pick up the leaf and place it against the surface of the vane. It will cling fast. You will probably find it easier to start leafing from the back of the vane and work forward,

completing one side at a time. Overlap each sheet of leaf at least ⅛ in.

As the job progresses, don't be discouraged by the spots you will miss or by the leaves that may adhere in clumps. Let them remain until you have worked your way to the front of the weathervane. Then with your rabbit-hair brush, lightly brush down all the leafed areas. Avoid brushing in areas where there is no leaf. Catch the resulting gold "debris" on a piece of clean white paper; this can be used for brushing into crevices and indentations.

Continue this procedure until you have leafed the entire surface. To cover small spots, cut leaf sheets to approximate size (use sharp scissors lubricated with silicone spray) before applying them; this can save quite a bit of leaf.

Give the leafed surface a final light brushing with your rabbit-hair brush. Then with a piece of clean cotton, gently rub down the entire surface. This burnishing will bond the leaf to the vane and make the surface gleam beautifully. Do not apply varnish or any other protective coating over the leaf. It will last for many, many years just as it stands.

Health hints for painters

As a painter, I am exposed daily to oil and latex paints, surface preps, varnishes and stains. What ingredients in these products have been shown to be harmful, and what precautions can be taken?
—*Eric S. Butterfield,*
Wethersfield, Conn.

John Leeke, an architectural woodworker from Sanford, Maine, replies: You can get an idea of the hazards of finishing products by considering a couple of examples. Benzene, used in finish coatings and some paint strippers, has been linked to leukemia and cancer (chemicals in its vapors attack the bone marrow). It can also cause nausea, dizziness and loss of coordination. Cadmium, a yellow pigment, can effect the respiratory tract, prostate and kidneys.

Follow directions and heed all precautions on labels, especially when using wood preservatives that contain pesticides. Assume that most finishing products can be hazardous when exposure is daily over long periods. A notable exception is latex paint, which does not contain large proportions of hydrocarbon solvents, and for that reason is good to use on interior areas that cannot be easily ventilated.

Airborne particulates from spraying and sanding can be kept out of your lungs with a good-quality respirator, but adequate ventilation is the best defense against solvent vapors. For protection from remaining vapors, be sure your respirator cartridges are rated for organic vapors. Some materials can be absorbed through the skin and affect other parts of the body. Wear unlined protective gloves when pouring, mixing and cleaning brushes. Eye protection is a good idea when splashing or splattering is likely, and is a requirement when you're spraying. Be sure to clean your hands thoroughly before eating or smoking.

Once you acquire the habit of being cautious, you will not notice the slight inconvenience it causes. Think of any expense involved as an investment with the most important return of all: your good health.

An excellent respirator, Comfo II 460-968, is available from Mine Safety Corp., 1100 Globe Ave., Mountainside, N.J. 07092. It costs $12.90 ppd. The filter you need is Type H 464-035; a box of ten costs $32.20.

Long-lasting finish

The toughest problem so far in my home-building project is what to use for a low-maintenance, clear preservative on my redwood siding. Nothing here seems to last more than 18 months.
—Chris White, Koloa, Kauai, Hawaii

William Feist, a paint technologist with the Forest Products Laboratory in Madison, Wis., replies: An effective natural-wood finish has three components: a mildewcide to protect the wood surface against fungal decay, a water repellent to protect against weather, and an ultraviolet light stabilizer (known also as a UV protector or absorber) to minimize the degrading effects of sunlight.

There are a number of commercial natural finishes, but unfortunately, none will last more than one to three years under normal conditions. Hawaii's warm, humid climate is especially conducive to mildew growth on the wood (which will show up as a grey to black discoloration), and the large amount of sunlight will degrade both the finish and the wood itself. This relatively severe exposure reduces the life of natural finishes to a year or two at the most.

The best solution in your climate is to reapply the finish as soon as deterioration is visible. Grey blotches near the bottom edges of the siding are a telltale sign.

A toxic preservative

I've been thinking of finishing my boat with pentachlorophenol, but I read that some people use this to protect their homes, and that it's dangerous. Can you give me some information? —*R. T. Johnston, Orlando, Fla.*

Michael McCann, editor of the Art Hazards Newsletter, *New York, N. Y., replies:* Pentachlorophenol is a potent fungicide and wood preservative that can be highly hazardous when absorbed through the skin or inhaled. This can occur either with the pure pesticide or wood treated with it. In one incident, three dairy farmers were poisoned by vapors arising from chemically treated wood used to build their barns, and over 600 dairy cows died in this incident as a result of licking the wood. Pentachlorophenol may cause liver damage, birth defects and cancer. I suggest you avoid using pentachlorophenol on boats and houses.

Linseed-oil sealer

I just put roughsawn pine bevel siding on my house, and I need to seal it. I have heard of a method using linseed oil thinned with kerosene. What are the merits or faults of this sealer? Also, should I seal before or after I caulk?
—*Jim Nelson, Lake Nebagamon, Wis.*

The editors of Fine Homebuilding *reply:* The Forest Products Lab in Madison, Wis., has developed and tested a water-repellent treatment that fits your description. They warn that it is for use only above ground. It does not contain a fungicide, and

therefore may not prevent mold growth, especially in very warm climates. However, in tests done in Wisconsin, it was considered effective on exterior window sills for over 20 years, and it doesn't contain potentially harmful and toxic chemicals, as many commercial preservatives do. FPL suggested that immersion is the best application technique, closely followed by brushing the solution on. Caulk or paint after applying the sealer.

For each gallon of solution, use 1½ cups of boiled linseed oil, 1 oz. of paraffin wax and 3 qt. of solvent (turpentine, mineral spirits or paint thinner.) Mix the linseed oil with the solvent, then cut the wax into thin shavings and add it to the mixture. Set the container in the sun where it will reach a temperature of 75°F or more. As the solution warms, the wax will dissolve. Do not melt the wax over an open flame, or it may ignite. Apply the sealer after the wax has dissolved, and let it dry for several days before painting or staining.

Fuel-oil sealer

I've recently sided my house with cedar siding, which I intend to leave a natural color by using clear sealer. I have a fuel tank with about 200 gal. of fuel oil in it. Is there any way I can mix the fuel oil together with something else and use it as a sealer?
—*Curtis G. Junket, Alliance, Neb.*

Kevin Ireton, associate editor of Fine Homebuilding, *replies:* According to a handbook prepared by the Forest Products Laboratory (FPL, One Gifford Pinchot Drive, Madison, Wis. 53705), the answer is yes. No. 1 grade fuel oil may be mixed with boiled linseed oil, preservatives (such as fungicide or mildewcide), paraffin wax and tinting colors to produce a natural finish. The exact formula will vary according to the appearance and durability desired, and depending on where in the country it's being used. Be forewarned, however, that fuel oil does have a disagreeable odor that may persist for at least several weeks after application.

Because you want a clear finish, you can leave out the tinting colors, but doing so will decrease the durability of the finish. Use an effective mildewcide in the formula, and be prepared to recoat the siding about every two years.

For more information, you can send for a copy of "Finishing Wood Exteriors: Selection, Application and Maintenance" (stock no. 001-000-04450-8). It costs $3.25 and can be ordered from the Superintendent of Documents, U. S. Government Printing Office, Washington, D. C. 20402.

Fading stains

Please help me solve the fading problem I have with the stain that was applied to cedar siding early in 1985 on my new home. The product was a mixture of Martin Senour semi-transparent natural cedar stain (1 part) and clear wood finish, or CWF (2 parts). The stain was applied with a hand-pressure sprayer and has already lost almost all its color on the southeast wall. The west wall has also faded a good deal. The contractor doesn't know what to do to slow or stop this rapid fading. He thought the stain would not show signs of fading for at least a year and a half and would not need restaining for three years.
—Paul Skoglund, Tallahassee, Fla.

William Feist, a wood finish technologist with the Forest Products Lab in Madison, Wis., replies: The first application of unpigmented (clear) finish on smooth cedar siding will generally last only one to two years in a climate like Florida's. An undiluted semi-transparent oil-base stain will usually last two to three years. Better durability will result when the finishes are applied to roughsawn or weathered cedar, since more finish can be applied to the wood surface. The first indication of finish failure is a bleaching, fading or greying, especially on the south and west sides of the house.

You diluted one part of a semi-transparent stain with two parts of an unpigmented finish. This means you have less pigment on the wood surface and, as a result, you find relatively rapid fading on the south and west sides of your house. The more pigment in a finish, the longer it will last (paints last longer than stains, and stains longer than clear finishes). This means you need to get more pigment in your finish or live with the fact that you will be refinishing every year or two.

If you wish to correct the fading problem, you'll need to apply the stain in an undiluted form. Brushing is usually a much better method of applying stain than spraying because you can work the stain into the wood. Apply as much stain as possible without causing runs. Be sure the semi-transparent stain you use has a good mildewcide in a concentration recommended for use in Florida. Mildew growing on the surface of siding (whether finished with a clear or pigmented finish) is the primary cause of greying in your area. Colors are usually available that will approximate a natural cedar color. Remember, the more pigment in a stain finish, the longer it will last before needing refinishing (this is true only when high-quality pigments of the right type are used in the formulation of the stain).

Diagnosing stains

I built my home in 1979 and used 6-in. beveled cedar siding, installed with a 4-in. reveal. I used galvanized nails and put two coats of Cuprinol Wood Preservative on it immediately. Since that time, I have not treated the cedar at all.

Small black dots, which I thought to be mold resulting from the wooded setting, began to appear on the siding after about five years. I washed some of the siding with a bleach solution, but was not satisfied with the results, and stopped.

I was told by a contractor that the black dots were related to tannic acid in the wood. He said that bleach wouldn't do much good, but that washing with an alcohol solution would remove them and restore the original appearance of the cedar.

Is this assessment accurate? Is the siding in any real danger if nothing is done? Also, I have considered simply staining over the siding, but am not sure if doing so without removing the black spots is advisable.

—*Jim Imhoff, Milford, Mich.*

Pete Kent of the Western Wood Products Association in Portland, Ore., replies: Without repeated applications of a moisture sealant, cedar siding will naturally weather either to a tan or a soft grey. During the first stage of this process, however, the wood will darken as water-soluble extractives are drawn to the surface. This darkening effect is more pronounced in areas of high moisture, where the wood may even turn black for a time.

In addition to extractives, other factors may cause discoloration like the smattering of black dots you describe. The most common causes are soot and grime, iron contamination and mildew.

You can identify a particular cause through visual clues and by doing simple tests using separate solutions. These clues and tests are from William Dost's "Procedure for Classification of Stains which Develop on Wood in Service," courtesy of the Wood Building Research Center, (University of California, 1301 S. 46th St., Richmond, Calif. 94804).

For example, extractives that leach from the wood are light tan to nearly black and often have reddish hues, whereas soot, dirt and ash produce a black-grey or earth color. Iron from filings or dust will show up as discreet grey to black flecks, often surrounded by a lighter grey zone. Mildew also turns up grey to black and usually is spread unevenly across the siding.

To test the stains, wash small sample areas of the siding with three different solutions: oxalic acid, chlorine bleach, and liquid detergent and warm water. Do not mix the solutions together. Oxalic acid is available in crystal form from most pharmacies. Mix 4 oz. of the crystals with 1 gal. of warm water. Wear rubber gloves and avoid inhaling the fumes. Rinse the areas with clear water and let the siding dry completely before judging the results. If the discoloration is caused by soot, grime or ash, neither oxalic acid nor chlorine bleach will have an effect, but liquid detergent mixed with water will remove part or all of the black color.

For extractive-caused staining, oxalic acid will give the best results, with liquid detergent a close second. Only repeated washings with chlorine bleach will remove the blackened stains.

If iron contamination is the problem, oxalic acid will usually completely remove the black color. The detergent wash will reduce the stain, but will rarely remove it entirely. However, if the iron has leached from contaminated finishes, such as aged water-repellent penta solutions, chlorine bleach usually intensifies the black color of the stains.

The detergent wash will usually eliminate mildew stains and will leave the wood a tan color. Oxalic acid will lighten some of the blackness, but chlorine bleach will have little to no effect.

When you have determined the cause, wash the rest of the siding with the appropriate solution and rinse thoroughly with clear water. Reapplication of a water-repellent preservative would be wise. If mildew is the cause, use a preservative that contains a fungicide.

Discoloration usually occurs only on the surface of the wood and will have no effect on the wood's strength if not removed. But it looks bad and could get worse, depending on the cause. Remove the black spots if you decide to stain the siding because they could intensify or reappear if you don't.

For more information, write to the Western Wood Products Association (Yeon Bldg., 522 S.W. Fifth Ave., Portland, Ore. 97204-2122) for a free copy of their publication "Exposed Cedar: Color variations in exposed cedar; causes, cures and controls."

Staining rough siding

I have a 14-year-old house with rough cedar siding that has had only one paint job in its life. There are also some areas under the eaves that have never been painted. The paint that is left is peeling badly. What has caused this problem, and what can I do about it?
—Donald Shaw, Montague, Calif.

John Leeke, an architectural woodworker in Sanford, Maine, who specializes in restoration, replies: Even the best three-coat paint job will need at least partial recoating in five to seven years. Your paint may have begun to fail earlier than that because it was applied on rough siding. Paint is a film, and works best when it is applied on a flat, smooth surface. The paint on the high points of a rough surface are thinner, and will weather away before the rest of the film. Then, these small spots with no paint allow moisture to get behind the rest of the paint, causing peeling. A more suitable product to use on rough-textured wood is exterior stain.

One solution to your peeling-paint problem is to stain the siding as the paint wears off. This method requires patience since it will take several years before your house will look uniform again. But the alternative is trying to scrape all the paint off the rough surface, which is both difficult and costly. Instead, use a stiff bristle brush to remove peeling paint that will come off easily. Then give the entire house one coat of an oil-base, transparent or semi-transparent exterior stain that is close to the color of the peeling paint. The house will look at least 50% better, but don't get carried away with a lot of hard work trying for 100% yet. In a couple of years, more paint will have peeled. Brush it off, and give the house another coat of stain. It will look even better, and you might be able to skip the full coat, and just touch up the less noticeable parts of the house. If it still looks good under the eaves, skip that too. Soon you will be on a schedule of recoating with stain every seven to ten years.

Latex vs. oil-base primers

I build houses for a living, and a question that continually arises is whether to use latex or oil-base paints as primer coats on new wood exteriors. Many painters insist on using oil-base primers and following with a latex base for the finish coats. I think that latex acrylics are as good as if not better than oil-base paints and perhaps adhere better to a latex primer than to oil. Is there any reliable, published information that can settle this expensive, recurring argument? —*Douglas A. Carroll, Santa Ynez, Calif.*

William Feist, a paint technologist at the Forest Products Lab in Madison, Wis., replies: Commercial paint producers have developed

acrylic latex paints with superior adhesion as compared to the latex paints of a few years ago, and most companies sell both acrylic latex primers and top coat paints. Their current popularity over oil-base (or alkyd) primers seems to be merited, according to a recent study done by the American Plywood Association (PO Box 11700, Tacoma, Wash. 98411). The study concluded that a good-quality acrylic latex primer followed by an acrylic latex top coat was the very best paint system of dozens evaluated on new unpainted plywood. Acrylic latex primers were found particularly suitable for use over woods that stain, like redwood and cedar.

The Forest Products Lab has a number of studies underway that are designed to evaluate the performance of stain-blocking acrylic latex primer paints. We have not published any of this data as yet, but the excellent performance of these primer paints over bare-wood and wood-related products (plywood, hardboard, waferboard) is already apparent. These studies are all on new wood.

Factual information on the performance of acrylic latex primer and topcoat paints is available from most paint manufacturers and their raw-material supply companies. You might begin by getting in touch with the E. I. Du Pont de Nemours Co. (Wilmington, Del. 19898), the Rohm and Haas Co. (Philadelphia, Pa. 19105) and the National Paint and Coatings Association (1500 Rhode Island Ave. N.W., Washington, D.C. 20005).

Oil-base primers are still useful in applications where some control over water-vapor movement is necessary. They also have better adhesion over old, heavily chalked or dirty paints, although surface preparation is an important factor in the success of any paint application, latex or oil-base.

Exterior woodwork

A porch reconstruction that I will be doing this spring entails building twelve newels. I am worried about material shrinkage. After one summer with an unobstructed southern exposure, the resulting gaps at the joints would be unacceptable. Can you recommend materials, adhesives (is resorcinol the only candidate?) and designs to help minimize the problem?
—Jim Picardi, Arlington, Mass.

Architectural woodworker John Leeke, from Sanford, Maine, replies: You can control the shrinkage of exterior woodwork and the resulting gaps by paying special attention to three major areas:

Construction details: For the base and cap of the newels, I would use a splined miter joint, as shown in detail A in the drawing at right. The miter eliminates having the end grain of the wood exposed to the weather, but does not provide a good gluing surface. The side grain of the spline gives the glue something to grab onto and locks the joint.

I cut the molding directly on rails and stiles of exterior panel work rather than apply a separate molding to hold the panel in place (detail B). This makes fewer joints to open up and holds the panel better. Drill weep holes from the groove of bottom rails to the interior to let water drain that may collect there.

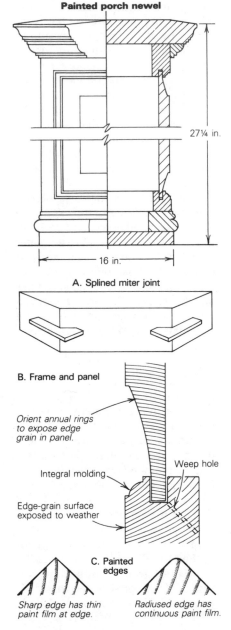

Painted porch newel

27¼ in.

16 in.

A. Splined miter joint

B. Frame and panel

Orient annual rings to expose edge grain in panel.

Weep hole

Integral molding

Edge-grain surface exposed to weather

C. Painted edges

Sharp edge has thin paint film at edge.

Radiused edge has continuous paint film.

The panels should be completely free-floating in the framework. You should be careful that you don't inadvertently glue the panels in place by assembling the frames before the paint has had enough time to dry.

Radius the edges and corners of the newels so paint will form a continuous film around the edge (detail C). If edges are perfectly square, the paint film will be thinner at the edge. The thin film at the edge will weather away quickly and allow water to enter.

Materials selection: Eastern white pine is my choice for exterior woodwork here in New England. It has the right combination of workability, availability and reasonable cost. To ensure added decay resistance, I select all heartwood. Mahogany is more decay resistant than pine but more expensive too. Recently its cost has been comparable to redwood or western fir.

You should select wood with vertical or edge grain. It will expand and shrink less with changes in moisture content. An edge-grain surface also holds paint better than a flat-grain surface. Edge-grain pine is more stable than edge-grain mahogany.

Resorcinol adhesive is very weather resistant. But it may be too brittle to use if weather conditions lead you to expect a lot of wood movement. Epoxy adhesives like The West System (Gougeon Brothers Inc., P.O. Box X-908, Bay City, Mich. 48707) can be mixed to retain a certain flexibility and move with the wood.

Moisture control: Controlling moisture in the newel will keep wood movement to a minimum. Use wood with a moisture content that is similar to existing wood on the house. Vent the pedestals at the bottom and top so air movement can remove moisture from the interior.

Paint is the first line of defense against weather and moisture. For complex exterior woodwork I always back prime all surfaces of each piece before final assembly, and follow with a top coat right after installation. A second top coat is a good idea, but can wait for painters.

Even after all this attention to detail, the wood may move enough to crack paint at joints, especially around the panels. Some touchup later on may be necessary.

Installing wood gutters

I plan to install cedar gutters using wrought-iron gutter supports. What spacing would you suggest I use for the supports, and how should I install them?
—*A. L. Cummings,*
Owings Mills, Md.

Consulting editor Bob Syvanen replies: The spacing will depend in part on the size of the gutter. A standard 4x5 wood gutter with wrought-

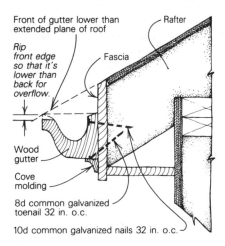

Front of gutter lower than extended plane of roof

Rafter

Rip front edge so that it's lower than back for overflow.

Fascia

Wood gutter

Cove molding

8d common galvanized toenail 32 in. o.c.

10d common galvanized nails 32 in. o.c.

iron supports at 48 in. o. c. should do the trick.

I fasten my gutters hard against the fascia, using 10d common galvanized nails through the back of the gutter into every other rafter tail. You should use a nail in between if the gutter isn't completely tight to the fascia. I also toenail 8d common galvanized nails at the bottom, taking care not to split the corner of the gutter. I set all the nails, and then I cover the bottom joint between gutter and fascia with a small cove or scotia molding.

Some builders space the gutter away from the fascia with ¼-in. by 1¼-in. blocks. I have found that the space behind the blocked-out gutters fills with dirt, which traps moisture, and is followed by rot. I have been nailing my gutters hard against the fascia for 30 years with no problems.

I also rip about ¼ in. off the top front edge of the gutter before installing it to make sure that if the gutter fills up, the overflow will drain over the front of the gutter and not behind it. This is particularly important in a cold climate, where ice can form and act like a prybar between the gutter and the fascia.

Ideally, the gutter should be set low enough to allow ice (or a piece of wood if you're testing) to slide off the roof past the gutter. Along the length of the gutter, I try to set a slope of ¹⁄₁₆ in. per ft. for good drainage to the downspouts, but it isn't always possible. On a roof as long as 40 ft., the gutter should slope from the middle to each end. This creates two 20-ft. runs, each of which will require 1¼ in. of slope. If the fascia is narrow, there won't be enough room to drop the gutter that much, and you'll just have to do the best you can. You can also cheat a bit by raising the middle some. But as long as there is a slope, with no low spots, the gutter will work.

Clapboard sunburst

I am currently building an addition to a Victorian house. The original structure features a gable-end bracket with a beautiful sunburst of clapboards. I would like to duplicate this ornamentation within a panel I've provided on the new addition. Can you tell me how?   —*Robert M. Gould, Buffalo, N. Y.*

Stephen Sewall, an architectural woodworker in Portland, Maine, replies: The Victorian gable-end sunburst is an architectural feature most often found in late Victorian (Queen Anne) wood-frame construction. The basic design consists of a half-circle or half-ellipse, in which a smaller half-circle or half-ellipse (representing a sun) sits. Clapboard rays radiate from the smaller curve to the larger one.

The motif of the Victorian sunburst may have been borrowed from earlier styles. Some 14th and 15th-century Elizabethan furniture incorporated a carved sunburst feature. Although the Victorian sunburst looks somewhat similar, it did not evolve from the Federal-period fan.

I recently made the half-elliptical sunburst shown below with leftover

Elliptical sunburst

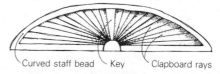

Curved staff bead   Key   Clapboard rays

clapboard. It was a little over 8 ft. long and about 2 ft. high.

I began by cutting a piece of ¾-in. fir plywood to the overall size and shape of the unit. Because the sunburst sat in a brick opening, it had to have a curved staff bead to seal it to the brick. Three bandsawn pieces of ¾-in. by 2-in. pine made up this curved section. I epoxied them to the perimeter of the plywood along with a lower rail. I didn't spline these pieces to each other because the plywood provided a strong and stable surface for simple epoxied butt joints. An elliptical sun was then cut from ¾-in. stock and attached to the plywood at the midpoint along the lower rail.

Clear, select-pine clapboards were used for the sun rays. I laid out marks on both the small sun and the outer curve, giving me the taper requirements for each ray. The thin edge of the clapboard was used for the narrow end of the taper, which butted the sun. I rough-cut the tapers on the table saw. Then the pieces were held between the layout lines to scribe their end cuts, which were rough-cut with a jigsaw and fitted with a block plane and utility knife.

A partial piece was used to begin the first ray, something like a starter course for clapboarding. The completed rays were nailed with 4d galvanized box nails along the lower edge, much like regular clapboards. I eased the lead edge of each piece with sandpaper before it was installed. The key, or wide central ray, was the last to be placed. It had to be fashioned from a piece of unmilled stock because there isn't any change of thickness along its width.

Scribing an arc

As part of the exterior trim on my house, I am using half-timbers cut from 1¼-in. rough cedar. On the corners I want to use curved half-timbers rather than straight diagonals. How can I best lay out the curves on boards this size?
—*Heinz P. Werner, Lutherville, Md.*

Jud Peake, a carpenter and contractor in Oakland, Calif., replies: I've seen in an old book a method of scribing the correct radius arc for any three points. Drive nails in your timber at the end of the curve. Set two 1x4 legs against the nails, and connect them at an angle so that

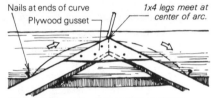

With pencil at peak, rotate pattern as shown, keeping both legs snugged against the nails.

they meet at the midpoint of the arc between the two nails. Connect them there with a plywood gusset, as shown in the drawing above. Hold a pencil at this point, and move the pattern, in first one direction and then the other, keeping both legs always in contact with a nail. The result will be an arc drawn on the timber. This method might come in handy for your situation or anytime you have to scribe an arc when the center is off the material and hard to locate.

It would probably be easier in your case, however, to spring a strip of ¼-in. or ½-in. thick stock to describe the curve. For an even curve, push in on the ends of the strip rather than pulling on the middle. Given the limitations of the width of your boards, you could get greater curvature by making an elongated S-shape.

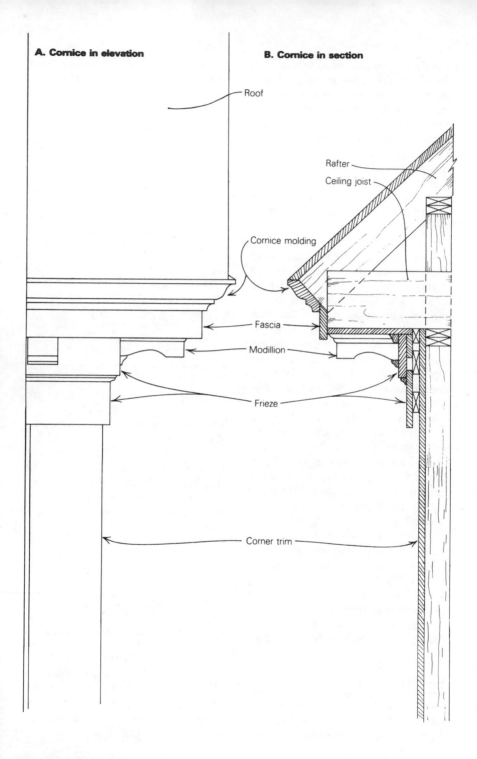

A. Cornice in elevation

B. Cornice in section

Roof

Rafter

Ceiling joist

Cornice molding

Fascia

Modillion

Frieze

Corner trim

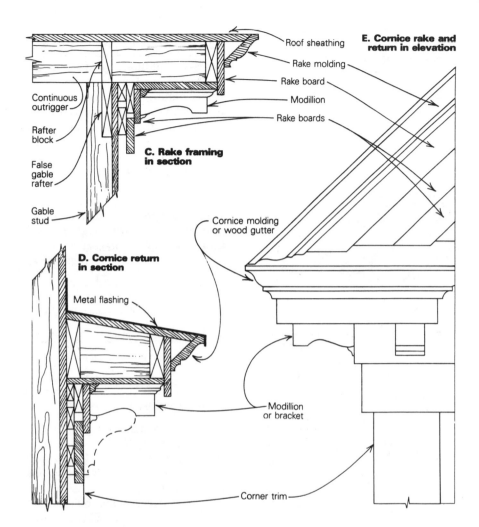

Roof sheathing

E. Cornice rake and return in elevation

Rake molding

Rake board

Continuous outrigger

Modillion

Rake boards

Rafter block

C. Rake framing in section

False gable rafter

Gable stud

Cornice molding or wood gutter

D. Cornice return in section

Metal flashing

Modillion or bracket

Corner trim

Cantilevered cornice

I am interested in learning more about cornices, and I'd like to see how decorated cantilever supports are handled for deeper gables and eaves. *—Kazuhiko Hibino, Chiba-Ken, Japan*

Bob Syvanen replies: The construction of a decorated cantilevered cornice (drawing **A**, facing page) is basically the same as for a simple cornice. The large overhang at the eaves is supported by extending the ceiling joists (**B**).

The overhang at the rake is supported by outriggers—short cantilevered members that nail to the first rafter pair inside the house, and bear on a false gable rafter that is let into the top outside edges of the gable studs (**C**).

Solid blocking runs between the outriggers. The cornice return must be extended out from the sheathing on the gable end (**D** and **E**) far enough to allow the cantilevered rake trim to die on it. To break up the large soffit surface at eaves and rake, modillions are spaced at about 12 in. o. c.

If extra support is required, brackets are used. Wooden eave gutters can be built in or applied (**F** or **G**, below).

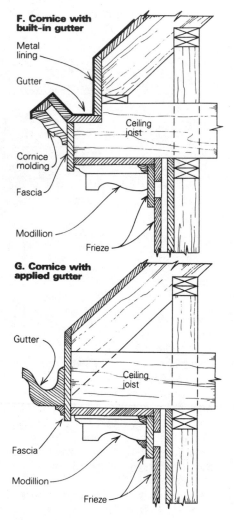

F. Cornice with built-in gutter

Metal lining

Gutter

Ceiling joist

Cornice molding

Fascia

Modillion

Frieze

G. Cornice with applied gutter

Gutter

Ceiling joist

Fascia

Modillion

Frieze

Nailing boards and battens

We are building a post-and-beam kit house, and my question concerns nailing the boards and battens. The boards are rough-cut 1x12s and the battens are 1x3s. Both are eastern white pine and appear to be seasoned. I have seen them nailed a number of ways: a) nail on one side of the batten into 1x12; b) nail between 1x12s in center of batten; or c) nail all edges with angled nails. Can you help? —*Gregory S. Kindig, Harrington, Del.*

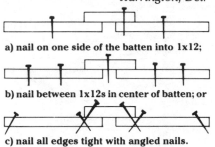

a) nail on one side of the batten into 1x12;

b) nail between 1x12s in center of batten; or

c) nail all edges tight with angled nails.

Ed Levin, a housewright in Canaan, N. H., replies: Of your methods, my first choices for nailing boards and battens would be **b**: one nail in the center of the batten passing between siding boards into framing beneath. This allows boards to shrink and expand under battens without breaking the seal. Second choice would be **a**, though wide, flatsawn pine boards are prone to cupping, a serious weakness here because the unfastened side of the board-and-batten connection is likely to open up. Method **c** comes in a poor third, because it restrains wood movement.

No method of board and batten that I have seen provides a strong defense against wind and weather. I recommend you have the boards

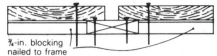

¾-in. blocking
nailed to frame

tongue-and-grooved and dispense with the battens altogether. If this is not possible, consider nailing the boards over the battens, as shown in the drawing above.

Kevin Ruedisueli, McLean, Va., also replies: There are several nailing patterns commonly suggested for board-and-batten siding, but I believe the best method is shown below.

This technique allows both boards to move as shrinkage or expansion takes place, and the double nailing pattern will also keep the batten from cupping.

Cutting beveled siding

We are renovating an old house (circa 1900) with 6-in. beveled cedar clapboard siding. We have run into a major snag: how do you cut beveled siding so there is a clean line of siding at the inside corners, especially at angles (45° or 60°), without using vertical wooden or metal strips to cover the seams? Lots of old houses around here have this detail, but without taking them apart, we are stumped about how to do it.
—*Linda Canton, Minneota, Minn.*

Consulting editor Bob Syvanen replies: I usually use a small vertical corner stick (¾ in. by ¾ in.) at inside corners when I'm installing beveled clapboards, and simply butt the clapboards to it. But I have also in-

stalled shingles without corner sticks, weaving the inside corners. Clapboards could be done the same way, with a lapped joint, alternating courses. In either case, I always start with a strip of 15-lb. felt in the corner as a precaution.

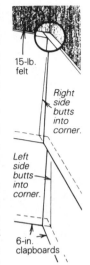

15-lb. felt

Right side butts into corner.

Left side butts into corner.

6-in. clapboards

After nailing up the starting strip, which shims the first clapboard to the correct angle, the first course, on the left side for instance, is cut to butt into the corner, as shown in the drawing. The right-side piece is cut on an angle to fit against the first piece. On the second course, the clapboard on the right side goes up first and is cut on an angle to butt into the corner. The piece on the left side is cut to fit against the piece on the right, lapping over it, and so on. The result is a tight, clean inside corner.

If the corner isn't 90°, the procedure is the same, but the cut on the end of the clapboard will be a compound angle. Set the bevel of your saw to the angle of the corner.

Chapter 5:

Concrete, Brick, Stone and Tile

Steps to a leak-free shower

I have a corner shower stall with the two sides against the tiled walls. Periodically there are severe leaks from the shower that wet the ceiling below. In the past, I've regrouted the tile on the wall that gets most of the shower spray. This remedy is usually effective, but only temporarily.
—*Steve Saweh, Syosset, N. Y.*

Michael Byrne, a tilesetter in Walnut Creek, Calif., replies: Without a visual inspection it's difficult to say whether regrouting will help. Begin by checking the obvious sources of leaks, which are also the ones most easily repaired. Check the enclosure to make sure that it is caulked properly at all seams. Sometimes water finds its way into a screw hole and out onto a stud. The shower floor, whether it is tiled or prefabricated

fiberglass, should get a careful bead of silicone where it intersects the walls and the enclosure. Also check the packing behind the faucet valve covers and shower head. These should be filled with putty to prevent the passage of water.

If all these areas are in order and the shower still leaks, you should make sure that the walls supporting the tiles are sound and that the tiles themselves are firmly attached. If they are, regrouting should take care of the problem if you do it thoroughly. Begin by purchasing a grout saw. Actually, an old hacksaw blade used to be the tool of choice, but grout saws give your fingers a break and come with replaceable blades. You can find them at masonry or tile suppliers, and often at large hardware stores. In the past, your new layer of grout failed because it was too thin. Sawing out the old grout right down to the bottom of the tile is the only sure way to waterproof the tiles. However, you do want to avoid cutting into the substrate.

For a good regrouting job, disassemble, remove and clean the parts to the enclosure and set them aside. Do the same with the plumbing fixtures. Vacuum away loose material and clean the tiles with a 10% to 20% dilution of muriatic acid or a proprietary cleaner for removing soap scum and oil (Brite 'n' Tile, Lime Kleen and Tile Kleen are common brands).

Now you can regrout. Waterproof the new grout by mixing it with a latex additive. Laticrete International (1 Laticrete Park North, Bethany, Conn. 06525) and Garland-White (Box 365, Union City, Calif. 94587) both manufacture grouts and additives that I trust. After the grout dries you can reset the enclosure and fixtures.

Recessed sink rim

How can I attach a stainless-steel kitchen sink so that the sink rim is recessed below the tiled countertop? *—Robert Sitzman, Castro Valley, Calif.*

Michael Byrne, a tilesetter in Walnut Creek, Calif., replies: Installing a stainless-steel sink under tile is no more difficult than installing any other sink. The only problem is that this type of sink may flex quite a bit when filled with hot water or when the garbage disposal is in use, so pay particular attention to the grout joint where sink meets tile.

Tiles for a wet countertop should be set on a mortar base of at least ¾ in., laid on a ¾-in. CDX plywood

base. Make your cutout in the plywood so that the screw clips provided with the sink can be clamped onto the edge of the plywood all the

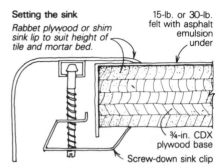

Setting the sink
Rabbet plywood or shim sink lip to suit height of tile and mortar bed.
15-lb. or 30-lb. felt with asphalt emulsion under
¾-in. CDX plywood base
Screw-down sink clip

way around the sink. Then measure the thickness of your tile, add it to the height of the mortar bed you will be using, and either rabbet out the plywood or shim up the sink with plastic tile spacers so that the quarter-round tiles you will be using around the edge of the sink are flush with the field tile at the top, and are up off the sink rim a good ⅛ in.

Before actually setting the sink, run the waterproofing membrane (15-lb. or 30-lb. builder's felt works well as long as it's glued down with asphalt emulsion) under the sink lip and over the edge of the plywood to prevent moisture from getting to the cabinet itself.

When you lay the mortar base, don't let it extend onto the lip of the sink. Holding this line with both the mortar and the field tile, and using quarter-rounds to trim out the sink edges, makes it possible to remove the sink if necessary without destroying the entire deck.

The quarter-round tiles are set entirely in the grout. After it has initially set up, cut the grout back under the quarter-round to form a ⅛-in. square recess where these trim

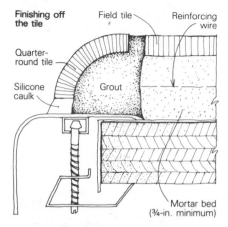

Finishing off the tile

Field tile

Reinforcing wire

Quarter-round tile

Silicone caulk

Grout

Mortar bed (¾-in. minimum)

tiles meet the sink rim. Then when the grout is completely hard and dry (about three days) fill in this void with clear silicone caulk to allow the color of the remaining grout to show through, as shown in the drawing above. The silicone allows the sink to move about while preventing water from entering.

Pigment dust for slab floor

We are planning to build a passive-solar home and want an economical and attractive finish for our concrete floor, something that will give a mottled appearance. Can you suggest a way of achieving this look (we want to avoid the costs of tile)?
—*David Sanders, Arqueta, Ill.*

Architect Max Jacobson replies: I called C. D. Sovig of Conrad Sovig Co. Inc. (35 Gilbert St., San Francisco, Calif. 94103), makers of concrete additives and coatings. He suggested that you color the slab by troweling in a dust-on topping rather than mixing in the color integrally. The product is both a concrete hardener and a coloring agent. After the slab is

leveled and the surface water has disappeared, the powder is dusted on the surface and troweled in. Variation in color will result from the uneven distribution of the powder and from troweling. Another way to get a mottled look is to use less coloring agent than normal, thereby allowing the natural color of the concrete to show through occasionally. Use two-thirds of the recommended amount. When this technique is used, the finished floor should be sealed with clear sealer.

Smoothing a rough slab

I am converting my garage to a family room. The garage-floor slab is above grade, well insulated and warm, but the concrete got rained on right after it was poured, so it is rougher than a perfectly troweled surface. I want to use a high-quality vinyl floor covering in the new room. How do I attach the underlayment to the concrete so that the floor will be smooth and permanent? —*Robert K. Searles, Wonewoc, Wis.*

Don Bollinger, a flooring specialist in Seattle, Wash., replies: Concrete makes an excellent substrate for vinyl floor coverings if the slab is smooth, level and dry. To make your slab smooth, use a power edge sander and 16-grit or coarser, open-coat paper. Sanding concrete is noisy and dusty work (use a dust mask) and wears out paper quickly. If the floor is too irregular to sand, you can pour or trowel on leveling compound. This requires damming any door openings that exist.

Because your slab is above grade and heated from below, you may choose not to seal it. In my work, I seal all concrete I lay floors on. There are many excellent sealers on the market, in a great variety of price ranges. I use an epoxy sealer called Hydro-Ban 500 (KRC Research Corp., 315 No. Washington Ave., Morrestown, N. J., 08057) and apply it with a roller. It is expensive (about $30 a gallon) and available only from the manufacturer, but can even be applied to slabs that aren't fully cured, and will prevent moisture under considerable hydrostatic pressure from reaching the living space above.

Once the slab has been smoothed, leveled and sealed, proceed with mastic and vinyl as you would on top of any underlayment.

Refinishing a concrete slab

We have completed a passive-solar home and have had problems with the living-room concrete slab, which serves as thermal mass. The slab was allowed to dry thoroughly, then stained with Olympic Exterior Wood Stain and subsequently sealed with a Varathane finish. The finish has worn badly and tends to lift from the concrete when water is spilled on the floor.

The floor will need refinishing. What stains and finishes are suitable? *—Jim Trivelpiece, Palouse, Wash.*

Malcolm Wells, architect and underground consultant, replies: If your floor finish is lifting, blistering or flaking after the concrete itself was allowed to dry thoroughly, it's almost certainly from water-vapor pressure coming from below the concrete. That problem must be solved before another finish is applied. The subsoil in time may dry out. If there's not a vapor barrier below the slab, however, the pressure may be permanent, in which case, you can either live with it, carpeting the slab with something that won't rot, or stop it by applying a vapor barrier to the concrete and pouring a new 2-in. or 3-in. slab on top of it. In any case, once your water-vapor problem is solved and a stain-sealer is applied, I recommend the use of this mixture: two parts Dutch Boy urethane wood-floor finish with one part Minwax Jacobean stain. Try a sample on a hidden area first.

Bill Zink, of San Andreas, Calif., also replies: I'd like to tell Jim Trivelpiece about a stain that I used successfully on my concrete. It gave my floor a very even, permanent color, and has not been affected by moisture coming from below the slab. This product is Lithochrome Chemical Stain, manufactured by L. M. Scofield Co. (6533 Bandini Blvd., Los Angeles, Calif. 90040). It comes in five colors and contains a dilute acid that etches the surface of the concrete. The metallic salts that produce the color penetrate the pores of the concrete and react chemically with it.

Warner Babcock, of Fairfield, Conn., also replies: Jim Trivelpiece described the common problem of moisture migrating up through an existing concrete slab, causing blistering and delaminating of the floor finish. One effective remedy for this problem, not mentioned by Malcolm Wells in his answer, is the use of a cementitious membrane to seal the slab. As the president of U.S. Waterproof, Inc., I can recommend our

Waterproof Cement Membrane System. It is a one-coat, rigid, self-curing surfacing that can be applied directly to the positive side (nearest the moisture source) or negative side (top) of the slab by spraying or troweling. This membrane can be used even if an existing slab or wall is damp; and it will prevent even high hydrostatic pressure from ruining sensitive finishes such as stain and paint. This waterproof cement can also be troweled into concrete as a dry-shake powder at the time the slab is poured. For brochures, technical bulletins and the nearest distributor, write U.S. Waterproofing, Inc., 425 Stillson Rd., Fairfield, Conn. 06430.

Cleaning granite

The house we're building will have a large fireplace built with granite taken from several stone walls on our property. We need to clean the silver gray moss and the lichen off the stones. I can't seem to pin down the best method. Do you have any suggestions?
—*Edward W. Lawler,*
Portland, Maine

John Benson, a stone carver in Newport, R. I., replies: Many preparations for cleaning stone are used in the monument industry. One such product is Stone Clean (available from Granite City Tool Company, 11 Blackwell St., Barre, Vt. 05641). Like most stone cleaners, it is a fairly strong acid, and its use would indeed be labor-intensive and potentially hazardous. A biologist and lichen expert tells me that copper or copper salts would most likely kill the moss and lichen, but here too some risk and considerable labor would be involved. An old remedy for removing moss on roofs is to lay pieces of copper on the peak and let the run-off from it kill the growth.

The chemical that most threatens moss and lichen is sulfur dioxide, but application would be troublesome and the dead growth might still cling. On the whole, sandblasting would probably be best.

Curiously enough, I once heard of a builder who had laid up a fireplace with stone such as yours and periodically sprayed it with water to keep the lichen alive.

Coatings for concrete floors

I recently completed a residential project in which we used a decorative concrete slab as the first-floor finish material. We poured a 5-in. thick slab with control joints at approximately 3½ ft. o. c. The concrete pour was very successful, and we allowed two months of curing time before we applied the finish. We then applied two coats of Olympic dark stain to the concrete, allowed the stain to dry, and then applied two coats of gloss polyurethane to seal the floor.

The floor finish was beautiful, but maintenance is becoming a problem. When a scratch occurs it goes down to the concrete, exposing the white finish. We're looking for a stronger plastic coating that can be applied over the polyurethane and provide a high-gloss finish. Do you know of a product that would be compatible with the existing finish and provide a more durable surface? —*J. Yonushewski,*
Colorado Springs, Colo.

Dan Rockhill, an architect in Lawrence, Kans., replies: There are many kinds of concrete coatings available to the industry, and they can be categorized in three groups: urethanes, epoxies and polychloroprenes or neoprenes. Your choice of urethane was a good one, but was the one you used formulated for industrial use?

Urethanes made for industry are formulated to resist heavy traffic in contaminated industrial environments. In a residential project such as yours you shouldn't have problems with deep scratches. I suspect the problem lies with compatibility between the stain and urethane.

Most urethanes are compatible with each other, but I would try a test strip in an out-of-the-way spot just to be sure. A product representative will probably give you a sample to test. If you find the two finishes are not compatible, you'll have to start over. Also, consider that some urethanes are two-part, so improper mixing and application could render a good product less effective.

If you start over, you should strip down to the concrete with a chemical stripper, wash it with trisodium phosphate, etch it with muriatic acid and put a finish on it that has the color "built in." You might consider an epoxy, which has higher tensile and compressive strength than urethane. However, epoxy comes in only two colors: clear and grey. Built-in colors for urethane are costly and perhaps beyond your budget.

If color is what you're after, consider a top-quality concrete paint, which comes in a high-gloss finish and a wide range of colors. After years of experimenting with various approaches, I prefer using paint. It's the least expensive, and quite suitable for residential applications.

The coatings industry compares products in this line with an abrasion-resistance test. One fairly common product, often used for warehouse floors, is Sonneborn's Sonothane (Sonneborn Building Products, 57-46 Flushing Ave., Maspeth, N. Y. 11378).

Eliminating efflorescence

The central stone chimney on my new house looked great until the first rain, when a white powder appeared on much of the masonry and even spilled down onto the roofing. I've been told that this is efflorescence from the portland-cement mortar. How do I clean it off and keep it from reappearing?
—Jim Long, Monroe, N. C.

The editors of Fine Homebuilding *reply:* Efflorescence is a crystalline deposit that can develop on the surface of almost any kind of masonry given the right conditions. The basic concern here is appearance, since efflorescence is basically harmless. It is the result of soluble salts—typically sulfates of sodium, potassium, magnesium, calcium and iron; carbonates of sodium, potassium and calcium; or sodium bicarbonate or silicate—that are carried to the surface by moisture. Although efflorescence is most noticeable when a structure is new, changing weather conditions like rain, humidity and wind can draw these salts to the surface even if they occur only in tiny amounts in the masonry.

The Portland Cement Association suggests several ways of preventing the problem; all of them are based on eliminating either the salts or the moisture that brings them out. The biggest source of salts is contaminated mixing water and unwashed sand, but even something as seemingly inconsequential as a mortar box or shovel that has been used with de-icing chemicals or beach sand can cause a problem. The suggestions for eliminating moisture from the masonry are the standard admonitions: use high-quality concrete or mortar (properly cured), self-draining mortar joints, adequate flashings and wide overhangs.

To remove the efflorescence from your chimney, Glen Simon of the PCA recommends using a dilute (5% to 10%) solution of muriatic acid. Be sure to wear protective clothing, rubber gloves and eye protection when handling the acid. Work on only a small area at a time, and dampen it well with water before applying the acid. A stiff bristle brush should be used for scrubbing the surface of the masonry. Once the efflorescence is removed, the area should be thoroughly rinsed and allowed to dry. It can then be sealed by spraying all surfaces with a clear silicone acrylic or silicone alkyd solution, or an acrylic emulsion.

There are also proprietary products designed to remove efflorescence and keep it under control; one of these is Sure Klean Efflorescence Control System (ProSoCo, Inc., 1040 Parallel Parkway, Kansas City, Kans. 66104). This system uses a water-soluble cleaner followed by a penetrating preventive treatment.

Peter K. Newman, of Orange, N. J., also replies: In answering Jim Long's question about how to clean efflorescence from his brick chimney, you state that the "basic concern here is appearance, since efflorescence is basically harmless." Our company has been involved in restoring and preserving masonry for 75 years. Our experience with this problem leads to exactly the opposite conclusion.

Efflorescence can be harmful because it leads to deterioration of mortar joints and masonry units through expansion of the efflorescence itself when it is located beneath the surface. This results in spalling masonry and deteriorating mortar, often thought to be caused by a freeze/thaw cycle.

Should any readers desire to research the subject of efflorescence further, I recommend *The Weathering and Performance of Building Materials*, edited by John W. Simpson and Peter J. Horrobin (Medical and Technical Publishing Co., Ltd., Chiltern House, Oxford Road Aylesbury, Bucks, United Kingdom).

Heat-absorbant colors

What are the best colors to use in a passive-solar system for absorbing heat effectively? Obviously, black is tough to beat, but black surfaces everywhere can make an otherwise pleasant design awfully dreary. —*James T. Dobush, Canton, N. Y.*

Glen Tucker, a solar consultant in Danbury, Conn., replies: While flat black is the best heat absorber, sensitivity studies conducted by William O. Wray (Los Alamos Scientific Laboratory) show that certain other colors may be used without substantially decreasing the annual efficiency of a passive system.

Color largely determines the solar absorptance of a thermal-mass surface. The higher the solar absorptance, the more efficient the mass is in absorbing and storing energy. Changing the surface absorptance from 0.95 (flat black paint) to 0.80 (medium light-brown paint), for example, decreases the annual solar savings only 5% or less. A solar absorptance of 0.60 (such as uncolored concrete) reduces solar savings another 8% to 12%. Lowering the absorptance below 0.60 results in substantially greater losses in performance. (I use 0.60 as the lowest acceptable limit of solar absorptance when I design a passive system.) In passive systems with only a little thermal mass, absorptance should always be kept high to make the best possible use of what mass there is.

Here are the absorptance values of commonly used materials and colors to help you decide which would be best for your purpose:

Flat black paint: 0.95
Dark-grey paint: 0.91
Dark-brown paint: 0.88
Dark-green lacquer: 0.88
Medium-brown paint: 0.84
Medium-rust paint: 0.78
Red bricks: 0.70
Uncolored concrete: 0.65
Medium-orange paint: 0.58
Medium-yellow paint: 0.57
Medium-blue paint: 0.51
White semi-gloss paint: 0.30

Since you'll want the best payback possible on your investment, use discretion in lightening the surfaces of costly mass walls.

While the value (lightness or darkness) of the surface color has the largest effect on solar absorptance, the hue also has a significant impact.

Studies conducted by Faye C. Jones at the University of Arizona Agricultural Station indicate that for painted surfaces of equivalent lightness, the hues in the middle wavelength range, such as green and yellow, are the best absorbers. The next best hues are those in the long wavelength range, such as red. The poorest absorbers are those in the short wavelength range, a group that includes purple and blue.

Stripping paint from brick

I have recently purchased a 30-year-old red-brick home that has had the entire exterior painted white. How can I remove the paint without damaging the brick?
—Paul Ahlers, Johnstown, Pa.

Dick Kreh, a mason and author in Frederick, Md, replies: There are two methods of removing paint from bricks. The first is sandblasting. It is done by bombarding the brick face with a fine aggregate such as silica sand under air pressure. The problem with sandblasting is that it cuts away a small part of the face of the brick. This removes the crust that has developed from years of exposure to the elements. Once this protective layer is removed, moisture will begin to enter the brick, and it will cause it to deteriorate much more quickly than usual. To protect sandblasted brick, a clear silicone dressing can be sprayed or brushed on. It will need replacing in about eight years. Restoration specialists disapprove of this method of cleaning brick because of its altering effects and the need for further maintenance. If you do decide to use this method, contact an experienced sandblaster so that a minimum of damage is done to your brick.

The second method I have used with quite good results, but it requires extra time and patience. You will need a pair of rubber gloves that cover your arms completely, goggles for eye protection, caustic soda (lye), cornstarch, two plastic pails and a plastic-fiber brush. These items can all be purchased at a hardware store. Start by brushing all loose paint from the wall with a wire brush. Mix a quart of the caustic soda with a gallon of clean water in one bucket, stirring with a wooden paddle. Add 8 oz. of cornstarch to a gallon of water in the other bucket. Combine the contents of the two buckets slowly while stirring vigorously. Be careful with this solution—it is caustic. Wear old clothes and use your rubber gloves and goggles. If any gets on your skin, flush immediately with clean water.

Apply the mixture to a small section of wall with the plastic-fiber brush. It will adhere to the wall like gelatin and cook the paint off the brick. After one hour, remove the solution from the wall with a spray of water from a garden hose equipped with a nozzle.

A more thorough job can be done with a high-pressure water sprayer, which you can obtain from a rental company. If you use the high-pressure sprayer, run liquid soap with water through the first time, and then rinse with clear water. This will neutralize the cleaner and remove all of the paint and dirt. If all the paint doesn't come off the brick walls with this procedure, repeat it until you are satisfied.

Since this operation is very time-consuming, do a small section of wall at a time, and work your way around the house. It will not damage the brick, and it removes most paint economically. For best results, work in fairly warm weather, and be careful not to get the goop on any shrubs or plants growing near the walls where you are working.

Sand-laid bricks

My house is brick veneer, and the driveway and sidewalks are concrete crossed by redwood 2x4s every 6 ft. to 8 ft. To integrate the house, driveway and sidewalks, I have decided to pour a footer alongside the driveway and sidewalks and to have matching brick laid lengthwise (end to end) as a border.

While giving me an estimate of the cost of laying the brick, the brick contractor said that the mortar joint between the driveway and sidewalks and their brick borders may eventually crack and separate as a result of freezing and thawing.

Although I want to have a brick border, I do not want to worry about making repairs to the mortar joints every few years. It occurred to me that there might be some flexible compound, as opposed to mortar, which could be used to bond the brick to the concrete. How might I minimize the effects of the weather on this joint?   —*Michael V. Davis, Leonardtown, Md.*

Richard Kreh, a mason in Frederick, Md., replies: I know of no way to prevent mortar joints from degrading as a result of freeze/thaw cycling on flat work such as you describe. The width and size of the footing have nothing to do with the cracking. What causes it is the heaving of the ground that the footing is laid on.

My suggestion is to forget using mortar but instead lay the bricks in sand or stone dust, and sweep in the joints with the same materials. This way, there is nothing to crack. As shown in the drawing below, the edges or border bricks should be

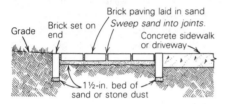

Grade
Brick set on end
Brick paving laid in sand
Sweep sand into joints.
Concrete sidewalk or driveway
1½-in. bed of sand or stone dust

laid in a different position so that they are turned down farther in the ground. This will help them to resist movement. Also, this type of mortarless brick paving is more attractive, as the bricks are laid tightly together against each other and reveal a much smaller joint between.

I have tried several different methods over the years to do what you describe, and always with the same results—the mortar joints eventually crack in time.

Jeff Bollinger, of York, Pa., also replies: I heartily agree with Richard Kreh's advice not to attempt a mortared brick edging along an existing concrete driveway and walkways, as frost heaving will surely break up the mortar joints. As a landscape designer specializing in landscape construction, I would like to share with you a technique of installing dry (non-mortared) brick paving that has performed well for me over the years.

The two greatest enemies of dry brick paving are subsidence (settling or compression of the base material into the soil) and frost heaving. The former is especially a concern in soft soils or where even occasional auto traffic could occur. Because of its very small aggregate size, the traditional sand base offers little resistance to subsidence, and also retains enough moisture to promote frost heaving.

Instead of a sand base, I suggest that a minimum 4-in. thick base of crusher run or quarry waste be installed over a properly graded soil base, as shown in the drawing below. This should then be thoroughly compacted with a vibratory plate-type compactor. A top dressing of stone dust is then applied to fill any voids and provide a smooth setting bed. If the stone dust is carefully screeded, one may quickly lay one brick after another with no need for a trowel or mallet.

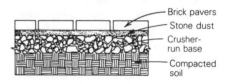

Brick pavers
Stone dust
Crusher-run base
Compacted soil

The bricks should be laid tightly together or nearly so, and the entire project can be swept with stone dust or sand to fill the joints and anchor the wobbly bricks. Where unstable soil is encountered or when a paved area is to be used for vehicular traffic, a geotextile fabric should be laid before installing the stone base to ensure the separation of the base from the soil. I have found that this technique can be used effectively for any sort of brick walkway, patio or driveway.

Fitting paving bricks

We will be installing a brick floor in our new passive-solar house according to Alex Wade's instruction in *A Design and Construction Handbook for Energy Saving Houses* (Rodale Press, Emmaus, Pa.). Although our bricks are new, their size varies enough that it's impossible to fit them tightly together. If we space them apart, then we'll have to grout between them, and this gets confusing. Wade describes applying a damp mortar mixture and tamping it in place with a narrow board, but also shows a dry mix being swept into cracks. We are also not sure whether the bricks should be dry, just damp or wet.
—*Susan Weegar and Brent Harold, Hartford, Conn.*

Alex Wade replies: The two issues of spacing and grouting are interrelated, but let's deal with size first. Paving bricks are made to a closer tolerance than regular bricks and are also designed to expose a flat face rather than an edge. If you use brick that isn't designed for floors, be sure that the dimensions are reasonably uniform. Used bricks are frequently better than new for this purpose, but don't try to butt them tightly together, even if they are only slightly uneven. Instead, space them ⅜ in. to ½ in. apart to allow room for grouting.

If you're butting your brick but there are still slight gaps to be filled, you have two choices. My favorite is to sweep sand into the cracks and seal it in place with a heavy coat of polyurethane. This works well only for cracks ¹⁄₁₆ in. and under. A second method is to sweep a damp mortar mixture—thoroughly wet, but not sticky—into the cracks with a stiff-bristled floor broom. The mortar should just barely adhere to itself (form a ball) if squeezed in the palm of your hand. This method relies on the action of the broom to compact the top of the mortar joint.

Wetting the floor is a separate issue from how much water to add to the mortar. The bricks must be thoroughly wet or they will wick the water from the mortar and it will not set properly. You can soak your bricks in a pail of water before setting them, but if you're sweeping the mortar into narrow cracks, you should spray a small area of floor with a medium spray from a hose for about a minute.

Cleaning mortar off the floor after grouting can be a headache if the brick is very porous. Paving bricks made by the Pee Dee Brick Co. (Pee Dee, S. C. 29586) have a paraffin layer to keep mortar from sticking. Another option is to coat the top surface of the brick lightly with polyurethane before grouting.

Brick care

I live in an orange-brick, one-room schoolhouse built in 1889. About seven years ago, the previous owner had the brick sandblasted, grouted and sealed. How do I know when the brick needs to be resealed? If it is something I can do myself, tell me all about it.
—*Roger Lake, Lafayette, Ind.*

Gerald Carrier, an intern architect at the Brick Institute of America in Reston, Va., replies: The first question you have to ask yourself is: "Does the wall really have to be sealed?"

Contrary to what many people think, brick walls, when built correctly, do not require any type of sealant, and in some cases, the application of a sealant may cause accelerated deterioration of the brick. If moisture isn't coming through the wall, then there's no real need to apply a sealant.

Tests at the National Bureau of Standards have shown that colorless waterproofers are ineffective on badly leaking walls. Where leakage is through fine cracks, some colorless waterproofers are effective for only about two years.

Under normal exposure, it is virtually impossible for significant amounts of water to pass directly through the bricks themselves. If moisture passes through a brick wall, it inevitably does so through cracks. Check for these cracks, or bond breaks. In some cases, especially after sandblasting, there may even be pits in the brick and mortar. Most sealants won't bridge these gaps.

Before you apply any sealant to a wall, consider other ways to reduce moisture penetration that are less likely to deteriorate the wall. If the mortar joints have softened, disintegrated or cracked open, tuck-pointing is usually necessary. Cut away defective mortar to a depth of at least 1½ times the joint thickness and then replace it with mortar (one part Type 1 portland cement, two parts Type S hydrated lime, and eight to nine parts washed building sand and potable water). Point all joints in the affected areas, since it is usually impossible to determine which joints are defective by visual inspection.

In some cases, if the cracks in the mortar arc small, it's possible that a grout coating could seal the joints. Brush the grout vigorously into the moistened joints with a stiff fiber brush, making sure that the whole joint is covered. Use a template to keep the bricks clean while applying the grout if you want to ensure a neat appearance.

For information on moisture penetration and how to prevent it, write for "Technical Notes 7," available for 75¢ from the BIA (Suite 300, 11490 Commerce Park Dr., Reston, Va. 22091).

Ultra-light concrete

I'm planning to build a multiple-dome ferro-cement house. A Pattern Language praises ultra-light concrete (using materials such as vermiculite for aggregate). I especially favor it in this design where straight ferro-cement isn't necessary structurally. Is ultra light concrete an antidote for the "heat-sink" effect that concrete has when buried in the ground? I'd like to see a graph that gives R-values as a function of the amount of lightweight aggregates used in a mix. —*Stephen Bushway, Williamstown, Mass.*

Max Jacobson, one of the authors of A Pattern Language, *replies:* The problem with an uninsulated masonry wall or roof (or floor, to a lesser degree) is not that it acts as a heat sink, but that it acts as a thermal link between the interior of the house and the virtually infinite thermal sink of the surrounding soil. While it is true that infiltration of air is eliminated, and that the outside temperature is tremendously moderated within the soil, conventional practice demands that the wall be insulated to prevent the constant, unimpeded flow of heat from the interior at 70°F to the soil at 50°F.

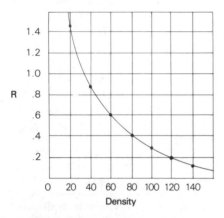

Density

It is true that the gradual replacement of dense aggregates, such as rock, with increasing amounts of lightweight aggregates, such as expanded shale, slag or vermiculite, will increase the thermal resistance of the concrete. The graph above expresses the relationship between the density of the mix (lb. per cu. ft.) and the R-value.

While the R-value curve increases dramatically with lightweight aggregates, the R-value is still very low—at best, less than 2. In contrast, the application of only 1 in. of polystyrene, which performs very well in underground applications, would increase the R-value by about 4.

Shortcut stucco

I would appreciate information on a simple method of applying stucco to the exterior of a new concrete-block wall. Can I eliminate the traditional scratch coat and brown coat and go directly to a smooth coat? If so, can I use white cement? Should I use any additives in the cement? Does the wall need any preparation? How do I waterproof the finished wall?

I also wish to achieve a plastered effect on the interior, and was wondering if ordinary drywall compound could be applied directly to the concrete block, or would the exterior mix be preferable on the inside?

—*David Vitarelli, Maui, Hawaii*

Restoration plasterer Dean Russell replies: There is a shortcut method for applying stucco over a base of concrete block. The block wall must be well constructed. Joints must be flush, as any joints which "lip out" will probably show through a thin veneer of stucco. The wall must also be straight and plumb, since you won't be able to straighten it or fill it out with the finish-type stucco mix. If the wall surface meets the above considerations you may proceed as follows:

Remove all dirt, excess hardened mortar and any other surface contaminant. If joints have been struck or finished with a jointing tool, fill in concave joint areas with a prepared mix such as Thorite (Thoro Systems Products, 7800 NW 38th St., Miami, Fla. 33166) or a mix of 4 parts fine sand, 1 part portland cement and ¼ part hydrated mason's lime. With a rubber float, make the joints flush with the wall surface.

At least 24 hours later (same day with Thorite), apply a brush coat of Thoroseal (also made by Thoro Systems Products) to prime the surface and even the suction of the masonry units and joint mortar. Allow it to cure according to the directions on the package.

Follow the guidelines for time between coats, and apply Thoroseal Plaster Mix with a hawk and trowel. Leave as few trowel marks as possible, and when the surface is ready, float finish with a wood or sponge float. This finish is extremely durable and weather resistant. When properly applied it is also impermeable.

Drywall joint compound is not the best thing to use on an uninsulated wall, as condensation may form on the inside, depending on building use, climate and how the wall's footings are waterproofed. Use the exterior mix on the inside as well. Since Thoroseal is available in white and a few colors, it may not be necessary to paint, though Thoroseal may be painted if desired.

Delaminating stucco

In October 1975 we built our house and had it stuccoed. During the late summer of 1976 the stucco began separating from the scratch coat at the grade line and up about 1½ ft. At this time we removed all the loose stucco and had the damage repaired.

Just two years later, the patched stucco and also some new spots separated from the scratch coat again. We again had the stucco removed where it had come loose, and patched.

Two years after the second patch job, the areas had to be patched again, and in the fall of 1982 we had the stucco patched for the fourth time.

The stucco is separating for the fifth time now, and we are still looking for an explanation. If the stucco is separating because of freezing and thawing moisture being drawn up from the ground, why did the stucco also fall off from the middle of the chimney 15 ft. from the ground? If the problem is being caused by moisture inside the house, why is stucco coming off the garage? If it was a bad stucco batch, why didn't it stick after the second, third or fourth application?
—G. McIntyre, Mendota Hts., Minn.

Jake Ribar, principal masonry research engineer in the department of concrete materials research at the Portland Cement Association, replies: Several things can cause a finish layer of portland-cement stucco to delaminate. A hard-trowel (smooth) finish may have beeen used on the base coat of plaster. The base coat should have a slightly rough texture that is created by floating (leveling) the surface with a wood tool It is difficult to bond a finish coat to a hard, smooth base coat. Inadequate application and curing procedures may have been used in every application attempted. Each coat should be kept moist for at least 48 hours after application.

Cracks in the base coat may have contributed to the delamination. These cracks telegraph into the finish coat. Even fine, hairline cracks will permit water infiltration and possible delamination due to freezing and thawing.

Improper installation of the substrate (under the base coat) can also lead to problems. Plywood sheathing that has been installed without gaps between each of the sheets can buckle. The gaps allow for expansion caused by increases in the humidity. Asphalt-impregnated felt should also be used to cover the sheathing before plaster is applied. This step is sometimes inadvertently omitted.

If the sheathing and the base-coat plaster are adequate, then a liquid bonding agent may be used to obtain a better bond. Such products are specified for use with concrete, concrete and plaster or plaster only, and are applied directly on the base coat. They are available from hard-materials suppliers or contractor-supply houses. The manufacturer's recommendations for application should always be followed.

If none of the above suggestions is of any help to you, talk to a professional consultant and arrange for a detailed investigation.

Removing paint from stucco

I have a 30-year old concrete-block home that is finished with plaster cement covered with a ¼-in. thick layer of smooth, white stucco cement. This chalky surface is now covered with several layers of peeling paint. I plan to have the walls sandblasted so that I can paint again. Is there anything I can do to get the paint to adhere to the chalky stucco, or do I have to re-plaster the entire house?
—*Mark De Michele, Ledgewood, N. J.*

Otto Heurer, a paint researcher and consultant in Waukegan, Ill., replies: I don't recommend sandblasting because of the danger of removing too much of that thin layer of smooth white stucco cement. Instead, rent a pressure sprayer from a rental yard or large paint dealer. It should be able to develop about 2,000 psi, and will run you about $50 a day. Removing paint from masonry

with water pressure is fast and clean, and doesn't require the experience that sandblasting does.

Once your walls are clean, use a good grade of exterior acrylic latex paint. To improve the adhesion, I would add to each gallon of paint two quarts of Flood E-B Emulsa-Bond Stir-in Bonding Primer (Flood Co., 1213 Barlow Rd., Box 397, Hudson, Ohio 44236). Though there are several brands of clear silicone waterproofing liquids that can be applied to the stucco with a small garden-type pressure sprayer, I think the Emulsa-Bond system will do the best job.

Because stucco is somewhat porous, plan on a coverage of about 300 sq. ft. to a gallon of latex paint, rather than the 400 sq. ft. that's usually claimed. Adding two quarts of Emulsa-Bond to the paint will yield 1½ gallons of paint, but its hiding power will be slightly reduced. A second coat of latex paint should be used, but don't add bonding agent to this one.

Michael Crowe, of Glenview, Ill., also replies: Otto Heurer's recommendations for painting chalky, peeling stucco are good, but I'd like to make a few additions.

When water-blasting any masonry surface, great care must be taken not to damage the surface. If a high-pressure sprayer that generates over 1,500 psi is used, make sure it has adjustable settings so that you can keep the pressure down to an effective but safe level. After you water-blast, the surfaces must be checked and hand scraped where necessary to remove all the peeling paint. Let the surface dry at least 48 hours before painting.

To restore masonry surfaces in bad painted condition, I use a two-coat system. For the first coat, I follow the directions on the Emulsa-Bond can for making the conditioning-bonding primer (3 gal. Emulsa-Bond, 1 gal. paint, ½ gal. water). This first coat gives a much better bond than just adding two quarts of Emulsa-Bond to the paint. Allowing 48 hours drying time after the first coat, I follow with a finish coat of the same paint that I used in the bonding primer, but in this case, without anything added. I use a top-quality acrylic paint for durability.

Mortar facts

Does cement mortar actually bond to bricks, concrete block and stone or is there some other force at work here? —*Manuel Perez, West Fairlee, Vt.*

Stephen Szoke, senior staff engineer for engineering and research at the Brick Institute of America, replies: At the same time it holds masonry units in place and, in a sense, apart, mortar most definitely bonds them together. Properly constructed brick masonry using Type N portland cement and lime mortar should have a tensile strength of about 19 psi.

Concrete repair

I've been using a 1-1-1 mixture of white cement, portland cement and lime to resurface badly weathered concrete patios and driveways. I dabble this in by hand with a stiff-bristled brush. Results are fair, sometimes uneven, and the procedure is tedious and time-consuming. Is there a better mix than mine and a faster way to apply it? —*Don Barnes, San Antonio, Tex.*

Steven Kosmatka, a concrete engineer in the building construction section of the Portland Cement Association (5420 Old Orchard Rd., Skokie, Ill. 60077-9973), replies: Resurfacing weathered slab-on-grade concrete with thin mixtures of cementitious materials is often a temporary repair. The 1-1-1 mixture you mention may be improved by the addition of about 3 parts of fine sand to reduce shrinkage and crack development. The mixture should then be troweled onto a clean surface. Unfortunately, this and other repair procedures take time.

More successful alternatives for repairing weathered concrete are full-depth slab replacement or resurfacing with a ¾-in. minimum thickness bonded concrete overlay.

For bonded resurfacing, the old concrete surface must be clean and have a rough texture. It should also be sound and relatively free of cracks. Old concrete surfaces ideally should be cleaned by hydrochloric acid etching, scarification, water-blasting or sandblasting. If the surface is acid etched, all the acid should be rinsed away before the repair application.

Next, a ¹⁄₁₆-in. to ⅛-in. thick bonding grout consisting of 1 part portland cement, 1 part fine sand and enough water to make a creamy consistency should be brushed onto the dry slab just ahead of placing the concrete overlay mixture. The grout must not be allowed to dry before the concrete is placed.

The concrete overlay mixture should consist of about 1 part portland cement, 2½ parts sand, 2½ parts ⅜-in. maximum-size coarse aggregate and ⅔ part water by volume. The mixture may be made more workable through the use of a superplasticizing admixture. Don't add more water at this point because you'll increase the potential for shrinkage cracks and reduce the strength of the mix.

After the concrete overlay is placed, consolidated and finished, let the surface cure for at least three days. The best curing is with wet burlap. Polyethylene sheeting may be used to cover the burlap to retain the moisture in the burlap.

Additional information on concrete overlays is given in the PCA publication IS144T, "Resurfacing Concrete Floors."

Finishing concrete stairs

I would like some help with concrete stair finishing—when to pull forms, how to fill voids, etc. Also, I have noticed two types of finishes in my area—smooth finishes on old work, and brushed finishes on most new work. I would prefer a smooth finish and would like to know the proper procedures involved.

If I must go with the brushed finish, what materials would you recommend to make the paste, and what are the proper tools to apply it with? I've done a considerable amount of flat finishing, and if I can get some solid facts, I can do a good job on these new stairs.
—Larry Steinbach, Chicago, Ill.

Kevin Ireton, assistant editor of Fine Homebuilding, replies: This

answer comes from the recent edition of the "Cement Mason's Guide" (PA112), a very useful 24-page illustrated booklet available for $5.95 from the Portland Cement Association (5420 Old Orchard Rd., Skokie, Ill. 60077-4321).

"Before placing concrete for steps, forms should be wetted with water or coated with a form-release agent such as form oil. Forms to be removed the same day may be wetted; those to stay in place several days should be oiled.

"Placing starts with the bottom step and continues upward, filling against side and riser forms as work progresses. The concrete should be carefully spaded or vibrated, especially along the inside edge of forms, to ensure that the face is free of voids and honeycomb. Each tread should be floated off as it is filled. Care should be taken while spading or vibrating so that pressures do not push out the tread that has previously been floated. The top step or landing is filled last, then struck off with a straightedge and darbied. The forms should be tapped lightly to release air bubbles that could cause bugholes.

"After all of the steps have been filled and floated, it may be necessary to wait for a time before proceeding to the next operation.

"When the concrete has partially hardened and bleed water has disappeared, finishing starts at the top and continues down the steps....

"Each tread is hand-floated and then edged along the riser form, usually with a ¼-in. to a ½-in. (6mm to 12mm) radius tool. Use a level to check that each step has its proper fall—¼ in. (6mm) is normal—for drainage.

"This is followed by the first troweling. Hold the trowel relatively flat against the surface, and trowel the step.

"After all the step treads have been troweled the first time, there is normally a waiting period until the steps set sufficiently to hold their shape when riser boards are removed. At the proper time, each riser board should be carefully removed. The riser is floated in a circular motion, using a cork or rubber float and a little mortar (mud) to apply a smooth finish. An inside step tool is used to smooth the cove where the riser meets the tread below. The radius of this tool is usually the same as that of the outside step tool used to smooth the top edge of the riser. Matching inside and outside step tools are available for this purpose.

"If sufficient mortar cannot be worked out of the concrete for proper finishing, a little mortar (mud) consisting of 1 part cement to about 1½ parts fine sand by volume should be applied. After troweling, a damp brush should be drawn lightly back and forth across the riser and tread to obtain a fine-textured, nonslip surface. These operations are repeated for the next lower riser, etc. Fast and careful work is essential since too much time on any one step may cause the others to set too firmly for proper finishing....

"Nonslip finishes for better safety on steps can be obtained in a number of ways. Brushing, swirl-floating and swirl-troweling produce satisfactory rough textures, but these finishes may wear smooth under heavy foot traffic. A more permanent nonslip tread can be obtained by using a dry-shake of abrasive grits, such as silicon carbide or aluminum oxide. The most permanent nonslip steps are built with special abrasive strips and nosings that are embedded in the surface of the treads. A lightweight, hand-held power groover can be used to cut evenly spaced safety grooves in hardened concrete."

I still found myself wondering how soon after pouring the concrete I could safely pull the forms. I asked the Portland Cement Association if they could be more specific about when to strip forms and found there are too many variables in the mix of the concrete and in weather conditions to give an exact length of time. The forms can be stripped the same day that they're poured, but how soon will vary with each pour (two hours is about the minimum amount of time). You should strip the forms after the concrete has taken its initial set—when you can't easily leave a thumbprint in it. The concrete has to be stiff enough to hold its shape, but green enough that you can still slice off high spots and work up mortar to cover blemishes.

Doggy door through masonry

My wife and I have recently purchased a 15-year-old, stone-veneer home in Maryland. As far as I can determine, the stone is laid up over concrete block. How do I go about making an access hole through the stone and block so that my dog can pass through? The hole would be through the rear wall of the garage, which is only about 5 ft. high but does support the roof rafters. An irregularly shaped hole would be fine. My worry is that if I start chipping

away at the mortar joints, the whole wall may come down.
—*Alden Andersen, Deer Park, Md.*

Stone mason Stephen Kennedy replies: There are no specific rules in dealing with something as variable as stone masonry. Each situation is different and deserves careful examination. In the wall that you describe, I see no structural problem with making a dog-sized hole anywhere you want, except too near the ends of the wall or directly under a rafter. If the opening you need isn't any wider than the rafter spacing, you could make a narrow opening all the way to the top of the wall, aligned between two rafters. Then you wouldn't have to worry about supporting the stones or block above.

If the opening isn't going to run all the way to the top of the wall, there will be masonry above the hole that could fall down. Usually, the masonry is hemmed in by surrounding masonry and doesn't have enough horizontal slack to fall. In a large stone wall, you could make a small hole anywhere and natural vaulting would keep stone from falling. The rocks are wedged against each other. Probably only one or two stones above the hole may shift, and these can be replaced after a wooden framework is made for the opening.

Since you can choose the spot for the opening, you might look for a long stone that will act as a header, and locate the opening beneath it. Or better yet, look for a natural arch in the masonry and remove the stones under it. If you do this, make sure there is enough masonry on either the side of the hole to buttress the new weight. In other words, don't make the opening near the end

of the wall because the force from above could push out the corner.

Your biggest problem might be the heavy smacking of hammer against chisel, which could loosen some of the veneer stones. You can probably cut through most of the mortar with much less shock to the facade. You might try a masonry bit in a drill or a masonry blade in a circular saw, or you could check the local rental yards for concrete-cutting tools.

If you cut a hole from the stone side, chances are it won't align exactly with the masonry blocks. You can chip the block out with a hammer and chisel, but it might not break where you want it to. It's easiest to remove full blocks along the mortar joints and make the opening in the block wall larger than the stone hole. Then, after your opening is framed, the irregular space around it can be filled with concrete, brick or block scrap.

Support for a brick opening

My building department wants me to widen an exterior door from 2½ ft. to 3 ft. The house is built with 8-in. bearing walls of brick. The angle-iron lintel that supports the doorway isn't long enough for the new opening. How can I support the masonry above the door while installing a longer lintel?
—*Craig Davalos, East Chicago, Ind.*

Richard Kreh, a mason and author in Frederick, Md, replies: This kind of underpinning work is fairly common in renovation where wood lintels are being replaced by steel. To support the masonry while you are installing the longer lintel, use a needle beam. This is a horizontal

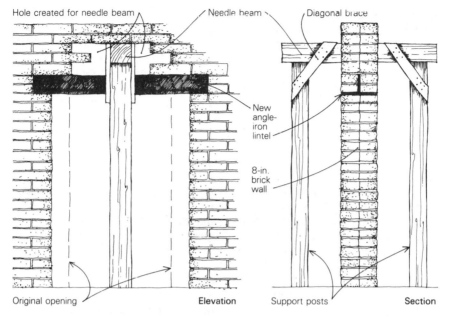

Hole created for needle beam — Needle beam — Diagonal brace

New angle-iron lintel

8-in. brick wall

Original opening — Elevation — Support posts — Section

beam that temporarily carries the load of a column or wall, and is supported with posts on both ends, as shown in the drawings above.

Following the brick bond carefully, break out enough bricks three courses above the present lintel to insert the needle beam in the center of the doorway. Remove as few bricks as possible, and try not to break adjoining bricks, because replacing these takes a lot of time and patience. The supporting posts for the needle beam should rest on either a concrete slab or a wood floor that is fully supported to the ground. Use flat braces or pieces of plywood as gussets to hold the posts and beam together.

Once the beam is in place, cut the door opening to 3 ft. and rebuild the new brick jambs in position. The new angle-iron should extend at least 4 in. onto the jambs on each side for good bearing. The last step is to remove the needle beam and

brick in the wall above the door. Pack the mortar tightly in the bed joints under the old work with a steel slicker, a flat steel tool used for pointing in tight places.

Cutting a door in concrete

We are renovating a 1912 poured-concrete garage with a flat concrete roof. The concrete walls are 8 in. thick with a heavy, rubble-like stone facing. The rear wall, 30 ft. long and 8 ft. high, has two 3-ft. wide by 6-ft. high windows, one on either end. In the large space between them, we'd like to add a door for easy access from the back of the house, and to even up the symmetry of the facade. How feasible is it to break through such a thick wall? Would the opening compromise the integrity of the wall itself?
—*J. M. Whaley, Burke, Va.*

Consulting editor Tom Law replies: It's hard to tell what's inside those concrete walls and why anyone would want to build a garage like that in the first place, especially with a concrete roof. I wouldn't hesitate to cut into the walls, and would not worry about destroying strength.

First you'll have to remove the stone facing around the proposed opening. A brick chisel and a hammer are the best tools for this. Work on the mortar joints, and try not to damage the stone since you'll need it later to patch in around the door. Remove the facing all the way to the roof, and remove a little extra on the sides to give yourself plenty of room to work.

Bashing the hole out with hammers or jackhammers would create lots of vibration in the surrounding wall and possibly enlarge some hairline cracks. Also, the irregular sides of such an opening would be hard to repair and frame against.

Instead, cut out the opening with a gas-powered diamond saw, similar to the type used to cut away damaged sections in concrete roadways. You can rent these saws, but if you've had no practical experience with them, you might want to hire someone to do the job. A diamond saw's depth of cut is limited to about 4 in., so whoever does the work will have to measure carefully and cut from both sides.

I'd cut the door opening straight up the full wall height, as shown in the drawing below left. You don't need to do this for structural reasons, but it will probably be easier than leaving a narrow section intact across the top. Next cut an 8-in. by 8-in. lintel seat on both sides of the opening. Cast a new lintel in place, with a couple of pieces of ³⁄₈-in. dia. rebar thrown in to tie the two sides together again. When you replace the stone facing over the door, you can support it with a steel angle.

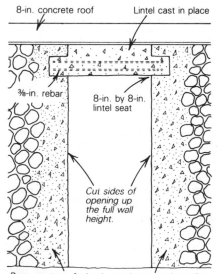

8-in. concrete roof   Lintel cast in place

³⁄₈-in. rebar   8-in. by 8-in. lintel seat

Cut sides of opening up the full wall height.

Remove stone facing beyond proposed opening.

Cracking in V-cap tiles

I have a problem with setting ceramic V-cap tiles. Occasionally a crack will develop along the right angle of the V-cap and may extend through several tiles. I used to apply caps with thinset to a mortar bed, as shown in the drawing on the facing page. I've been told that the cracking is due to shrinkage of the thinset and that the caps should be set in mastic, which I now do. If so, why is thinset shown as the adhesive in ANSI standards and other publications?
    —Ken Morrill, Los Gatos, Calif.

Tilesetter Michael Byrne replies: Let's begin with the V-cap. First of

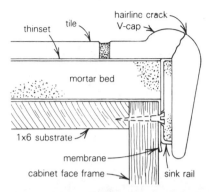

thinset | tile | hairline crack | V-cap

mortar bed

1x6 substrate

membrane

cabinet face frame | sink rail

all, the "V" stands for vitreous, and does not represent a cross section of the tile. The first V-cap tiles were thick, tough, resilient tiles designed to hold up to the pounding that the edge of a counter has to withstand. Modern V-caps are much thinner, can be non-vitreous and may not be as tough as the old style.

A wide crack, caused by something bumping into the face of the cap, would result from a lack of support behind the face of the cap.

With hairline cracks that you can see before you can feel, either the wooden substrate is expanding from water leaking into it or the mortar bed is shrinking.

By lapping the membrane over the edge of the counter as shown in your drawing, you should have eliminated the expanding-substrate problem, leaving the mortar bed as a possible cause. To keep it from shrinking, there are a number of things you can do.

First, use a latex or acrylic additive in the mortar mix and use only enough moisture to hydrate the portland cement. This should give you a mortar with a "dry-pack" consistency.

When floating the mix, don't just spread it around. Use a wood float or trowel to ram the stuff, leaving a bed that, once screeded, is uniformly dense with no air pockets. Then let the bed set up at least overnight. If the bed is going to shrink, most of the movement will occur during this period.

Set the tiles with a latex additive or acrylic thinset mortar, and use an additive in the grout as well (allow about 24 hours for the tiles to set before grouting). These materials have a fair amount of give that will allow some movement between the tiles and setting bed, thereby further reducing the chance of cracking. In spite of all this, you may need to do more.

Chapter 6:

Chimneys, Fireplaces and Stoves

Sizing a flue

I'm planning a large "cooking fireplace"(6 ft. wide, 5 ft. high and 2½ ft. deep) on an inside wall with a 25-ft. chimney. The fireplace opening is 4,320 sq. in., and using the usual 10% formula, it will need a round flue with a diameter slightly more than 24 in. or a larger flue if it's rectangular.

I question the need for such a large flue. The firebox and the products of combustion will be the same if the height is reduced by half. Of course, the larger opening in theory will allow more room air to enter the flue, but at a much lower velocity than the hot gases from the fire, and the total volume may not be much greater than that in a small opening.

We know that a cold flue and a large start-up fire will smoke re-gardless of the flue size. In other words, the efficiency of the flue is not static but varies directly with the temperature of the flue and its height. This is not taken into consideration by the 10% formula, and while it works for the average fireplace, I don't think it can be applied to my large fireplace.

I've seen fireplaces 100 years old with openings about the size of mine. They have no damper, and are on outside walls with 20-ft. chimneys. All of them have 12-in. flues. They are used daily for cooking demonstrations. Unless carefully tended, they do smoke on startup, but once the masonry is warmed up there is no problem.
—*A. M. Burka, Toronto, Ont.*

Mason Dick Kreh of Frederick, Md., replies: Most tables for determining flue size stop at an opening of

70 in. by 40 in. by 22 in. deep. Although you seem familiar with the standard rule of thumb, let me repeat it for others. The size of a flue opening is determined by the area (sq. in.) of the fireplace opening. For a conventional fireplace (one side open), the cross-sectional area of the flue lining should be at least $\frac{1}{12}$ of the total area of the fireplace opening. For multiple-opening fireplaces, the cross-sectional area of the flue lining should be at least $\frac{1}{10}$ of the total area of all open sides.

All fireplace experts agree that the height and width of a fireplace opening have a definite effect on its operation. If there is a question as to the size of the flue lining required for a fireplace, or if its determined size is on the borderline, then by all means use the next larger size.

In my opinion, the correct-size flue for your fireplace based on the rule of thumb is a 24-in. by 24-in. square shape. An 18-in. dia. round flue would also work. I arrived at this by dividing the total square inches by 12, yielding 360 sq. in. If you could buy a 20-in. by 20-in. flue, it would be very close (342.25 sq. in.). I'm sure this would suffice, unless some unusual condition impeded the draft, like a high hill or tree nearby.

You ask about large, open old fireplaces that have only 12-in. by 12-in. flues but seem to work okay. I have seen and remodeled such fireplaces. If you want to use a smaller flue, that's up to you. But if it doesn't work, you'll have to redo it, and I don't think it's worth the risk.

Your other points are well taken. One, a cold flue should be heated up slowly by a small fire; if the flue size

is correct, the fire should not smoke. Also, the fire should be built to the back of the firebox for best results. It is also true that the narrower the opening, the quicker the draft.

Two other factors influence draft in a fireplace. First, a fireplace should be in proportion to the room size. According to the *Donley Book of Successful Fireplaces* (a turn-of-the-century classic, now out of print), a fire that would fill a fireplace could be too hot to suit the size of the room, and the larger chimney and fireplace opening would cause too much air to be exhausted from the room, resulting in a forced indraft from doorways, windows and crevices. This also wastes fuel. A 300-sq. ft. living area is well served by a fireplace 30 in. to 36 in. wide. Wider fireplaces should be built only in larger rooms. Again, there is no set rule for this.

Also, every fireplace should have a smoke shelf and a damper. This is not the case with many of the old, large fireplaces. The lack of a damper contributes to the smoking problem because the draft cannot be controlled. If a fireplace has no damper or if the damper is left fully open, a great amount of the heat in the house will be sucked out, and this can be expensive.

Flue clearance questioned

What's the story on insulating around Metalbestos woodstove flues? Having insulated my house heavily and carefully, I now have a large hole in both the fiberglass and the vapor barrier left by my stove installer, who says that building inspectors and manufac-

turers of pipe and fiberglass all insist on a minimum 2-in. clearance around pipes. Is this true? How risky is zero clearance? Isn't a 2-in. break unacceptable in supertight, superinsulated houses?
—*Brent Harold, Hartford, Conn.*

Albert Barden III of Maine Wood Heat replies: I had to hunt for the information you need. First I called a local distributor of a Metalbestos pipe called Pro-Jet, which is manufactured in Canada. He assured me that the manufacturer insists on the 2-in. air space around the pipe, with no compromises. The U.L. standard and the manufacturer's warranty also require this.

Then I spoke with Bill Bibbins of Bow and Arrow Stove Shop in Cambridge, Mass. He told me the story of someone who had bought a stove that had a Metalbestos flue. He had included the 2-in. air space, but later sold his house to someone who then had cellulose insulation blown in. Some of this cellulose made contact with the Metalbestos pipe and ignited, causing a serious house fire. Bibbins says the safety provided by a 2-in. air space is a lot more important than heat loss. Remember that we are talking about a dead air space, not a vented air space.

Next, I called B. & B. Specialties in Wilton, Wis., and talked with their president, Jerry Bauer, who invented a device called Insul-Flue (available from Facsa Inc., P.O. Box 147, Spencer, Wis. 54479). It's installed in a stud wall and allows a stovepipe connection to pass through the wall to an outside chimney. U.L. approved his device for use with a 2-in. air space as well, but he's so confident in his product that he may go back for a 1-in. or zero-clearance approval.

The National Fire Protection Association has recently amended its #211 standard to disallow a prefab chimney pipe to pass through a combustible wall regardless of clearances. With a solid masonry through-wall connection (still with a 2-in. clearance), the masonry-wall thickness around a flue has been increased from 8 in. to 12 in. So it looks like a 2-in. clearance is the bare minimum required for fire protection.

Metal-chimney corrosion

I am heating my home with anthracite coal, but I've heard that sulfur gas will corrode my Metalbestos chimney. What can I do to prevent this? One suggestion was that I swab the chimney in the spring with a 3:1 solution of vinegar and water. —*Karen Ross, South Burlington, Vt.*

Larry Gay, who writes on wood heat and energy conservation in South Yarmouth, Mass., replies: Since the reintroduction of coal stoves several years ago, there have been scattered reports of severe corrosion in insulated stainless-steel chimneys caused by smoke from anthracite as well as lower grades of coal. The problem is associated with low stack temperatures. Oxides of sulfur dissolve in water in the stack to form sulfurous and sulfuric acids, which attack the steel. The simplest way to prevent the formation of these acids is to keep the stack temperature high. Generally speaking, water won't condense above 300°F.

Chimney manufacturers have become aware of the problem, and several have already introduced new chimneys especially for coal. These have inner liners of more corrosion-resistant steel than the standard No. 430 stainless used in chimneys intended for wood. These more resistant steels, Nos. 304 and 316, contain nickel as well as chromium, and cost considerably more. The new Selkirk Metalbestos Model SC chimney, for instance, is about twice as expensive as the standard Metalbestos SS chimney.

There is no point in swabbing the chimney with vinegar, since it is a weak acid. You might try to neutralize residual acids in the chimney with a weak base, such as baking soda, but burning your coal at a higher temperature to keep water vapor from condensing would be a better cure. One strategy would be to burn coal only during the coldest months and to burn wood in the fall and spring when the stove is apt to be damped more of the time. Damping the stove like this may lead to creosote deposits in the chimney, but it should slow down the corrosion problem. Also, when buying a coal stove, take care to size the stove. If it is too big for the area it's heating, it will have to be damped much of the time, and acid soup is likely to form in the chimney.

Downdrafting

I have a downdraft problem with my gas-fired, on-demand hot-water heater in the basement. The heater requires a 5-in. exhaust pipe. I used double-wall pipe, run on the exterior of the house and through the roof overhang. The vent ends about 2 ft. above the roof. The downdrafting occurs on the coldest and calmest winter evenings. So much cold air rushed down one evening that it actually froze water in the heater's coils. Because this is an on-demand heater, it doesn't run at all during the night, except for the pilot light.

Our basement is unheated and hovers around 50°F. In addition to our furnace, we also heat with wood and have a fairly tight home, so the stove's air demand may contribute to the problem (although I closed the stove down several cold nights and this had no effect on the air rushing down the vent). How do I solve the problem?
—Bob Eichenberg,
New Marshfield, Ohio

Jay Stein of Fine Heating Design in Denver, Colo., replies: Downdrafting will occur when there is a negative pressure in the basement. This negative pressure is no doubt caused by your furnace and woodstove. Even when they are not operating, warm house air in their vents will cause what is called the chimney effect. House air will be drawn into the flue, rise up the vent and be expelled out of the house. Since the water-heater vent is run outside, on cold nights no chimney effect is developed because there is no warm air in the vent. It provides an ideal source to replenish the warm air leaving the house through the furnace and woodstove vent pipes.

You can relieve the negative pressure in the basement by providing outdoor combustion air to your furnace and woodstove. This is usually accomplished by running a duct from the outside to a point near the burners or firebox. Natural-gas appliances require at least 1 sq. in. of free vent area for every 5,000 Btu input. For a thorough treatment of venting techniques recommended by the National Fuel Gas Code, I suggest you get a copy of "Introducing Supplemental Combustion Air" (#DOE/CE/15095-7). This publication is available from the U. S. Department of Energy, Washington, D. C. 20585. For woodstoves there is no universally recognized code. Although 4-in. round ducts are frequently used for this application, I strongly suggest you check the manufacturer's specifications as well as your local building code.

Finally, vent pipes for intermittently operating gas appliances should not be run outside in cold climates because flue gases tend to condense in them and corrode the pipe. Building an insulated chimney around the pipe, with a minimum of 1-in. clearance to the vent pipe (assuming it is Type B vent), will be an improvement. Another technique that is popular with retrofitted instantaneous water heaters is to vent them directly through a sidewall with an induced-draft fan. Simply put, a small fan draws in flue gases and forces them outside through a vent hood. Tjernlund Products Inc. (1601 9th St., White Bear Lake, Minn. 55110) manufactures fans, vent hoods and a special control kit for instantaneous water heaters. Best of all, no chimney is required.

Stovepipe for a high ceiling

What is the most appropriate stovepipe for an airtight woodstove where the pipe rises 25 ft. before exiting through a cathedral ceiling? Should the pipe be shielded all the way up? Should it be triple wall or Metalbestos? Also, does a barometric damper really prevent the accumulation of creosote in a flue? Apart from cooling the stack, it seems that this doggie-door device in a "T" connection above the stove would allow more air into the firebox. —*Peter J. Profant, Garberville, Calif.*

Gary Scatterfield, technical director for the Wood Heating Alliance in Washington, D. C., replies: There is no reason to shield the 25-ft. run of connector pipe (stovepipe) unless it is closer than 18 in. to combustible material (wood, drywall, etc.). The use of Type L connector pipe, which is a double-wall design, reduces this clearance to 9 in.

The pipes you refer to are really chimney sections intended for use near combustible materials, through unheated spaces, or outside. Triple wall is an air-insulated design, and Metalbestos is a trade name for a particular brand of solid-pack insulated chimney (Selkirk Metalbestos, 3070 Universal Dr., Mississauga, Ont. L4X 2C8). These chimney sections usually have listed clearances to combustibles of 2 in.

The important characteristic for these chimneys is that they be listed to the Underwriter's Laboratory Test Standard UL103 "Type HT." This ensures that the design has been tested to accepted safety standards including tests at 2,100°F, which approximates the temperatures commonly measured in chimney creosote fires. Both triple wall and Metalbestos chimneys are listed to that standard.

There are two types of shielding: protective wall shielding reduces the minimum clearance to combustible materials; decorative shielding for connector pipe or chimney sections blends the pipe with its surroundings. Your local stove retailer can provide further information.

Don't use a barometric damper unless one is specifically provided for in your stove installation/operations manual. In general, if you have a high-efficiency, airtight stove, I would not recommend the installation of a barometric damper. Properly set, dampers do not allow more air into the firebox; the stove damper does that. They do, however, draw air into the chimney, adding cool air to the hot flue gases. The cool air may result in more creosote buildup, and if a chimney fire starts, it will be more intense because of the draft.

For more information on chimney safety, contact the Wood Heating Alliance (1101 Connecticut Ave. N.W., Suite 700, Washington, D. C. 20036) for the free brochure, "How Does Your Chimney Stack Up?"

Tom Oyen, of Bellingham, Wash., also replies: Here's some more information about what kind of connector pipe to install between a woodstove and a cathedral ceiling 25 ft. above.

Chimney pipe, which is used outside the house, is insulated to keep the flue gases as hot as possible and thereby minimize the buildup of creosote, which condenses out of wood smoke as it cools. Connector pipe (stovepipe), which connects the appliance to the chimney, isn't usually insulated because it is closer to the hot stove and is surrounded by the room-temperature environment inside the house. The connector pipe in most installations is less than 7 ft. long, so the smoke doesn't have

much time to cool before it enters the insulated chimney.

However, smoke that has traveled through 25 ft. of single-wall stovepipe, as in Profant's installation, is cool indeed. This leads to excessive creosote formation and the increased risk of chimney fires. On the other hand, insulated chimney pipe makes poor connector pipe because it keeps the gases too hot at the point where they exit the stove. These high temperatures will damage the chimney pipe, necessitating frequent replacement of the lower sections.

The best connector pipe in this case is double-wall, Type L pipe, which keeps the flue gases warmer than single-wall pipe does, while at the same time allows air to circulate to prevent excessive temperatures near the stove.

M. Felix Marti, of Monroe, Ore., also replies: I've seen quite a few single-wall stovepipes corrode in one year of use, usually where two joints connect (a joint is a length of pipe). I now use only stainless-steel pipe. It's more durable than standard steel pipe, and stainless will turn beautiful colors, going from purple-blue near the stove to straw blonde farther up.

I'd recommend that any joints going through floors or roofs incorporate slip joints. Stovepipe expands and contracts considerably. I once built a house in Colorado that needed approximately 18 ft. of pipe between the stove and the roof penetration. We assembled all the single-wall pipe and fit it snugly to the insulated pipe for the transition through the roof.

We had a nice fire that afternoon while we finished working, and later we checked the stove before going home. Arriving the next day, we found the single-wall pipe completely disconnected and leaning to one side. Heat expansion had forced the last length of single-wall pipe up into the insulated pipe, which firmly held it while the lower sections shrank away as they cooled.

Be sure to wear gloves when handling stainless steel. The natural oils from your hands can brand themselves onto the pipe after firing.

Chimney settling

What can I do about settling in a massive stone fireplace at the gable end of a house? Settling appears to be occurring on the side of the chimney farthest from the house, since there is a 2-in. gap at the ridge where it has pulled away.
—Dale Busse, Sonora, Calif.

John Hilley, a masonry contractor in Brewster, Mass., replies: Begin by eliminating all above-the-footing causes. For instance, it's possible that the house is moving away from the chimney, rather than the other way around. Too, a straight chimney can actually be bent by the the action of a house moving into it. Or an expansive force inside the masonry could be lifting its inside wall. A heated flue can create this problem. I've even seen a badly rusted angle-iron lintel heave a fireplace. Usually this kind of flexure is accompanied by horizontal cracks—widest next to the house—on the fireplace's sides. Inspect the chimney on all sides for these stresses, but ignore any small fissures at the very top.

If these causes can be dismissed, you may indeed have footing settle-

ment, or subsidence. And you also have a big headache. Gross footing subsidence means the soil can't support the imposed load, and there are myriad causes. The tonnage involved leaves only one solution— consult an experienced engineer, preferably one associated with a construction company interested in tackling the remedial work.

Stopping chimney drips

I have recently finished building a log home with two fieldstone fireplaces; both of them drip water badly during long rains. I have had the joints on the exterior chimneys repointed with a 2-to-1 portland mix, replaced the washes on top, completely reflashed the roof around both chimneys and experimentally sealed one of them with Val-Oil. None of these solutions has even slowed the flow of water. What should I do?
—J. A. Michael, Leesburg, Va.

Jeff Gammelin, a stonemason in Ellsworth, Maine, replies: The best way I've found to seal masonry is to apply a clear epoxy paint (Epoc 5, Epoca Co., 5 Lawrence St., Bloomfield, N. J., 07003) which contains an ultraviolet filter to prevent yellowing. We use it to seal our stone hot tubs and stone bath and shower units. However, it gives the stone a slight "wet look," which you may not want on your chimney.

But before you resort to using a sealer, there are a few other things you should consider. First, make sure your chimney has been fitted with a cap above the top of the flue. This seems like an obvious point, but it's surprising how many chimneys are built without caps these days, and a lot of water can come in through large-diameter flue tile.

If the chimney is capped, then it's possible that the fireplace and chimney were built in such a way that the flue tiles have no room to expand during a fast, hot fire. Under these conditions, the masonry will crack. If this has happened in your chimney, water could be seeping in through the cracks and running down the tiles into your firebox. Since the cracks radiate from deep inside the chimney and subsequently act as expansion joints for future fires, repointing or stuccoing the exterior of the chimney would not really solve the problem.

A suggestion to remedy this problem is to build a long, hot fire in the fireplaces and after a couple of hours, carefully check the chimneys and note where the cracks appear. While the chimney can show a long winding vertical crack to the top of the flue tile, it's more likely that these expansion cracks show up starting about 3 ft. or 4 ft. above the lintel or 2 ft. above the thimble for a woodstove. You can try sealing the cracks with a flexible caulk compatible with masonry.

Tiling a fireplace

I would like to edge a brick fireplace opening with a single row of delft tiles. These are very special tiles, and I'd like to be sure that they remain attached and undamaged when the fireplace is in operation.

What should I use between the tile and the brick? Some books recommend plastering the brick and then attaching the tiles with fireproof epoxy. Others recommend sheathing the opening with ½-in. to ¾-in. fire-resistant wood, fastening the sheathing with screws in lead expansion shields and then gluing the tiles to the wood. I haven't seen any recommendation for simply setting the tiles in mud.

What should be done around the edge of the opening? The sides of the tiles are unglazed. Which of the options shown below will

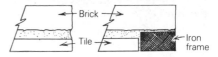

minimize damage to the tiles? The option on the right uses a wrought-iron frame, which I've seen in some pictures, but I'm worried that the metal will conduct more heat to the tiles and pose greater problems.

—*Joan S Kelley,*
Highland, N. Y.

Tilesetter Michael Byrne replies: Expansion and contraction of the masonry portion of the fireplace will eventually cause a failure in any installation using "fire-resistant" wood. Heat may also release undesirable fumes from such products and from organic mastics, which, in any case, should never be used around heat.

First clean all the soot and grime off the face of the bricks. One useful product for this is Sure Klean fireplace cleaner (Technical Services, ProSoCo, Inc., P.O. Box 1578, Kansas City, Kan. 66117).

There are three ways to attach the tiles. The first is easy. Knock down any high spots on the brickwork with a cement rubbing stone and use thinset mortar to attach the tiles directly to the bricks. I use Bon/Don mortar (Garland-White and Co., P.O. Box 365, Union City, Calif. 94587). If the brick face is too irregular, a mortar bed can be floated using a layer of thinset brushed over the bricks to act as a bonding agent. For the mortar mix, use 4 parts sand, 1 part portland cement, and ½ part lime moistened to a thick, spreadable paste. Gauge the thickness by using float strips at least ½ in. thick, tacked in place with nails driven into the mortar joints of the brickwork. Trowel on the thinset and screed off with a straightedge (drawing, below). When the bed has set up, attach the tiles with more thinset.

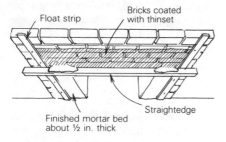

Float strip

Bricks coated with thinset

Finished mortar bed about ½ in. thick

Straightedge

If you lack the skill or experience with mortar, you can still form a solid, flat, fireproof setting bed by using cement backer boards. They come in various sizes (I use Durock, by U. S. Gypsum Industries, Inc., 101 S. Wacker Dr., Chicago, Ill. 60606). To install, cut the board into pieces that correspond to the tile layout and attach to the bricks using thinset. A straightedge will help align the pieces in a single, flat plane. Additional filling with thinset may be required to compensate for low spots.

Different rates of expansion between metal and masonry make tile a better candidate than wrought iron

for trimming the edges of tilework. The drawing below shows several ways to handle the tiles at the firebox corner. Cobalt blue trim tiles are often used as trim.

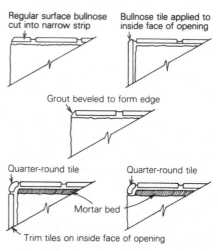

Regular surface bullnose cut into narrow strip

Bullnose tile applied to inside face of opening

Grout beveled to form edge

Quarter-round tile

Quarter-round tile

Mortar bed

Trim tiles on inside face of opening

Even with careful installation, your delft tiles may still show some crazing (visible yet minute cracks in the glaze) after the fireplace is in use. This crazing is practically a tradition with this type of tile and may even occur on delft tiles mounted on frames and hung for decoration.

Heat shield for walls

I am planning to use quarry tile set in mastic on ¾-in. plywood on the wall behind my woodstove. It will match the raised platform of tile on plywood that I've already built for my old potbelly beauty. I am thinking of using two sheets of drywall between the tile and the plywood to slow down the heat transfer to the plywood, which is flammable. Will the drywall buffer make enough of a difference to be safe? —*Joseph Gillette, Butler, Pa.*

Larry Gay, who writes on wood heat and energy conservation in South Yarmouth, Mass., replies: Certainly the drywall would help, but there are a number of other variables that affect the danger of overheating besides how you cover the wall. These include the distance between the stove and the wall, the size of the stove, and how hot it gets.

Standard wall clearances set by the National Fire Protection Association (NFPA, Batterymarch Park, Quincy, Mass. 02269, ask for Bulletin 89M-1976) are 36 in. for radiant stoves and 12 in. for jacketed stoves. These may be reduced if the wall is protected in various ways. The most common method of heat shielding is a sheet of copper or galvanized steel that is held out from the wall 1 in. This 1-in. airspace should be open at the top for ventilation. The required clearance from the wall to the stove is then reduced to 12 in. for radiant stoves and 4 in. for jacketed ones. For more on wall protectors and clearances, see *Wood Heat Safety* (Garden Way Publishing Co., Charlotte, Vt., 05445) by Jay Shelton.

Mark Feirer, of Eugene, Ore., also replies: The addition of two layers of drywall will help to reduce fire hazard, but remember that codes call for a non-combustible surround. Technically, the introduction of a combustible material (plywood, in this case) to the non-combustible drywall makes the entire lamination combustible, because the two layers of drywall can still conduct heat. It may sound as if I'm splitting hairs, but where the possibility of fire exists I figure it's best to avoid unnecessary risks.

A double layer of ⅜-in. drywall screwed to a metal spacer makes an adequate non-combustible base for tile setting without a plywood backing. Hat channel works well for the spacer and can be purchased, at least in my area, from tile suppliers. Gillette might also consider using heat-resistant mastic to set the tile or, better yet, one of the various types of cement mortar. According to the *1981 Handbook for Ceramic Tile Installation:* "Organic [as opposed to epoxy] adhesives are not recommended in areas where the temperature exceeds 140°F."

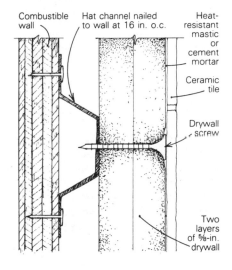

Combustible wall

Hat channel nailed to wall at 16 in. o.c.

Heat-resistant mastic or cement mortar

Ceramic tile

Drywall screw

Two layers of ⅝-in. drywall

Chapter 7:

Insulation and Ventilation

Roof ventilation

I am drawing plans for a solar home with a roof of laminated wood planking 3 in. thick, covered with 4 in. of polystyrene insulation. I specified a vapor barrier and asphalt shingles on the plans, but the building inspector redpenciled the drawings, stating that the roof required at least two ventilation points between the roof sheathing and the insulation. He said if it were not done, the ceiling could collect vapor, resulting in some staining and maybe even rot. I was under the impression that no ventilation to outside air was required with this type of roof.
—*Ben Raterman, Fredricksburg, Va.*

Dan Desmond, a specialist in restoration and energy conservation, replies: It's possible that your inspector is under the constraint of

building codes that don't address less conventional types of construction. Even so, his advice has merit, and the restrictions on your roof are based on reasonable precautions.

Moisture can never be totally eliminated in situations such as yours. A vapor barrier, like insulation, is not a container, but merely a means of slowing down the rate of transmission of moisture.

At first glance it appears that your roof wouldn't experience condensation, even with the inevitable moisture present, because a steady-state of heat loss would occur from the roof, and the underside of the sheathing would always be above the dew point of the air in the insulation above it.

There are two problems with this conclusion. First, in the real world, steady-state conditions are the exception. Also, roofs are especially prone to radiational losses. Researchers at the National Bureau of Standards' Center for Building Technology report that under windless and cloudless conditions, radiation exchanges between a roof and a night winter sky can lower the roof temperature as much as 20°F below that of the surrounding air. Under these conditions, condensation could form on the underside of your sheathing, causing stains and potentially greater damage.

Fire blocking and ventilation

I have been told that I should nail 2x fire blocks between my rafters at midspan to prevent flames from spreading through the ceiling. I want this safety feature but I don't understand how I can ventilate my cathedral ceiling between the top of the insulation and the bottom of the sheathing if these blocks obstruct the passage of air halfway between the soffit vents and the ridge vent. —Shane Webb, Highlandville, Mo.

Engineer Bill Lotz, who specializes in moisture and insulation problems, replies: I can't figure any way to have fire blocking and soffit-to-ridge ventilation either. But assuming that you've carefully installed a 6-mil polyethylene vapor barrier, I'm of the opinion that you probably don't need to go to great lengths to vent your cathedral ceiling. I think venting was a more critical issue a few years ago when there was no thought of installing a vapor barrier, or the covering on fiberglass batts was relied on to do the job.

I can understand your concern for fire safety, and in fact, it might offer one more argument against venting in this case. I have investigated fires where the flames and gas pressure broke the windows and the fire entered the attic through the soffit vents. I would suggest that the rafters be filled right up to the underside of the sheathing with a fire-resistant insulation such as rock wool or fiberglass batts. You could then establish a line of fire blocking between the rafters if you wanted to.

Tom Bender, of Nehalem, Ore., also replies: Most model-code agencies require fire blocking at the junction between the wall and ceiling structure. Until recently, the Uniform Building Code further required that soffit vents on all non-residential structures be offset from windows by 3 ft. to prevent the transfer of fire from the interior of the building to the attic. This provision has now been replaced by a limit on attic area without draftstops.

I think that offsetting soffit vents or using other means of roof venting are much better ideas than eliminating roof ventilation altogether. In addition to preventing moisture-caused structural deterioration, roof ventilation prolongs the life of the roofing material by keeping it from overheating. An insulated roof that isn't properly vented can lose up to two-thirds of its expected life. In most climates, unvented insulated roofs should be used only with slate, tile, metal or similar materials.

Super rafter

I'm building a 1½-story superinsulated house. I plan to use 2x12 rafters, the deepest I can get. How can I insulate the roof to R-60 to

keep the upstairs bedrooms warm without using a drop ceiling or filling the kneewalls full of fiberglass, since I want to use this space for storage? *—Carolyn Gibbs, Brockville, Ontario*

Oliver Drerup, the general contracting partner in an engineering/design firm in Toronto, replies: In the great insulation sweepstakes, the central issue is how the builder can cost-effectively incorporate insulation without hopelessly compromising the air/vapor barrier. Our firm has been using what we call a super rafter. It is simply 2x4s held apart with 16-in. gussets of ⅜-in. plywood or Aspenite and filled with 1½-in. thick beadboard as a thermal break for the wood members (see the drawing below). This gives enough

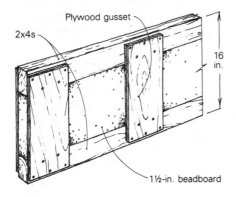

Plywood gusset
2x4s
16 in.
1½-in. beadboard

space for two layers of R-20 fiberglass batts with their joints staggered, and a 4-in. air space above the insulation. These rafters need to be engineered for the span.

For the Brockville area, I think that R-30 walls and an R-40 roof assembly, if combined with air tightness and residential forced-air heat exchange, will perform creditably. You might rethink insulating the roof to

R-60. This would also dictate R-20 between the foundation and soil as well as triple glazing. If the reason for building a 1½-story house is a tight budget, the extra insulation probably wouldn't be cost effective.

However, if you still want to exceed R-40 with the super rafter, interior 2x2 strapping—always a good way to create an electrical chase without involving the air/vapor barrier—can be added to the underside of the rafters and insulated with rigid insulation, or clad with foil-backed drywall. Using 1½ in. of semi-dense Glassclad will give you an additional R-6, while the foil-backed drywall would contribute R-2.65. Bear in mind that the foil forms an effective barrier to the passage of radiant heat whether it faces the room or faces away from the room, if the foil is next to an air space.

When insulating on the interior of an air-vapor barrier, one cardinal rule must never be forgotten. Fully two-thirds of the R-value of the wall must be placed outside the air-vapor barrier. This will ensure that the air-vapor barrier will always be on the warm side of the insulation, thereby preventing any likelihood of condensation forming on the humid interior side.

Mark Ledvina, of Perkinsville, Vt., also replies: The rafter shown should be used only where the span and pitch permit a 2x4 rafter, since the upper member must bear all of the load. The lower 2x4 is really not much more than a drop ceiling suspended from the upper 2x4. If these rafters are used in this manner, they are basically safe; but lower pitches and longer spans must be engineered, as Drerup suggests.

By using standard truss configurations, 2x4 rafters could be used on longer spans and still achieve the depth of this superinsulating rafter. These trusses would have compression members built in just as a floor truss does. These trusses, however, would be much more difficult to insulate with a polystyrene thermal break. Whichever system is used, an architect or engineer should be consulted to avoid assigning insulation values to a trussed timber that it may not have.

Low-cost roof insulation

What's the least expensive roofing system that incorporates R-30 insulation? My house will be post-and-beam framing with decking over 4x8 rafters 4 ft. o. c. and a tin roof. —*Bill Stephenson, Denver, Colo.*

Architect and author Alex Wade replies: The most thermally efficient, low-cost roof system I know of for

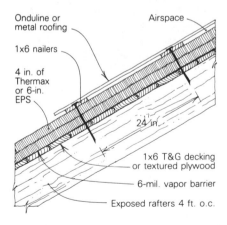

Onduline or metal roofing
Airspace
1x6 nailers
4 in. of Thermax or 6-in. EPS
24 in.
1x6 T&G decking or textured plywood
6-mil. vapor barrier
Exposed rafters 4 ft. o.c.

exposed rafters uses two layers of 2-in. thick Thermax-type rigid polyurethane insulation board. You

could substitute 6 in. of expanded polystyrene foam for the urethane for about the same R-value and less than half the cost, but anchoring the nailers that sit on top of the foam into the rafters below would require some very long barn spikes.

As the drawing at left below shows, you could use either 1x6 tongue-and-groove decking across your beams at the 4-ft. spacing you mentioned (use 2x6 decking for 8-ft. centers) or an inexpensive plywood like Texture 1-11. However, if you use grooved plywood, use a solid board at the edges of the roof or you'll get a serious amount of air infiltration from these channels.

Over the decking, I'd apply a continuous 6-mil vapor barrier and then nail the two layers of Thermax over the barrier, staggering the seams in both directions. Over the Thermax, apply 1x6 nailers spaced on 2-ft. centers. These nailers are very important because they provide an airspace to prevent condensation on the bottom of the roofing. They are anchored into the structural beams with long barn spikes. For roofing, I would use either Onduline or galvanized roofing, both of which can easily span the nailers.

Air leaks at outlets

I put 6-in., R-19, foil-faced insulation in the ceiling of our new home, sealing every tear in the foil. The walls are 3½-in. R-11. All cutouts were face-taped, and insulation was placed behind them to seal out drafts. I still have major drafts at electrical outlets. I have about 11 recessed closet lights and combination ceiling and fan

lights in the two bathrooms, with about 3-in. openings around each fixture, as required by the code. The closets are cold, and the fan/ light combinations are really leaky, especially in windy weather. I have caulked and sealed to no avail. Where did I go wrong?
—*Robert J. Antal,*
New Middletown, Ohio

Larry Gay, who writes on wood heat and energy conservation in South Yarmouth, Mass., replies: The design stage is where the mistakes were made. It's possible to track down and plug air leaks after a house is built, but the surest and easiest way to minimize infiltration is not to cut holes through the vapor (and air) barrier in the first place. This means confining electrical outlets and switches to interior walls and floors or surface mounting them on outside walls, possibly concealed behind furniture. Surface wiring can pass through baseboards with grooves cut into the back. If you insist on wiring inside exterior walls, then run the wiring along a notch in the sole plate so it won't compress fiberglass in the stud cavities and thus introduce channels through which air can move freely. Likewise, light fixtures should not be recessed in ceilings below attics, since this, too, invites serious heat loss. Light fixtures in closets, of all places, should be surface mounted, since appearance is presumably not an issue.

John Stewart, of Alameda, Calif., also replies: Larry Gay's answer to Robert Antal about infiltration around electrical devices suggested something that wouldn't pass muster where I live. The National Electric Code requires that fixtures, except in very large closets, be recessed. This requirement prevents fire caused by heat buildup in clothing or other combustibles on closet shelves.

Although the surface-mounted unit that Gay suggested would violate code, a new type of fixture is becoming readily available. These are labeled IC for Insulation Contact, and as the name implies, they can be covered by insulation up in the attic with no risk of fire.

Ceiling vapor barriers

Vapor barriers are routinely specified for the walls of newly constructed homes. But there seems to be some controversy over placing a vapor barrier between the drywall and the attic. Without the barrier, insulation may become wet with condensation and lead to rotting of structural members. With the barrier, I am told, the drywall will become soggy and fall from the ceiling. If there is sufficient insulation above the drywall to keep its temperature above the dew point, why would it become soggy? I would really like to see an explanation of the dynamics of this situation so I can design around the problems.
—*Drake Dingeman,*
Springfield, Ohio

Jon Eakes, an energy consultant in Montreal, replies: Your question holds its own answer. If the temperature is high enough, you're correct in thinking that the drywall will not get soggy. It's important, though, that the vapor barrier and not just the drywall be above the dew point. The dew point is determined by a combination of temperature and relative humidity (a psychrometric chart will give you the exact relationship between dew point, temperature and relative humidity). If the relative humidity is kept around 30% to 45% in a cold climate, it should be relatively easy to keep the temperature of the vapor barrier high enough to avoid the dew point.

The problem with ceilings, and especially with cathedral ceilings, is that the structural members above the ceiling often serve as thermal bridges. Sometimes there is only the thickness of the wood between the vapor barrier and the cold attic. In worse cases, poorly installed batt insulation can leave gaping air channels between the batts and the structural members, directly exposing the vapor barrier to the cold attic air. This thermal bridging will create a cold line along the ceiling joists where water will condense on the vapor barrier, soak into the drywall and create rust on the nails.

There are several ways to eliminate thermal bridging: insulate the cold side of the ceiling joists; fill the gaps between batts and structural members with loose fill insulation; or attach rigid insulation to the underside of the ceiling joists before installing the vapor barrier and drywall. The ceilings will then function as well as the walls. But you could still have problems if the indoor humidity is too high while the temperature outside is very low. Take steps to keep indoor humidity under control.

Insulating cathedral ceilings

I am building my home in Lancaster County, Pa., and I have reached a point where I need some professional help. We have cathedral ceilings in the house with 8-in. rafters. I already have 6¼ in. of fiberglass insulation between the rafters, but I know I need more. Would the best way to add more insulation be to nail foam panels to the bottoms of the rafters, then add furring strips and drywall to that? —*Anthony L. Tafel, New Castle, Del.*

Consulting editor Bob Syvanen replies: When rafters are not deep enough for adequate insulation, I scab on 2x stock to the underside of each rafter, as shown in the drawing below, to give 11 in. of space. I nail 1x3 cleats 24 in. o. c. to the side of the rafter and 2x4. Nail the cleats to the 2x4 first, while it's on the floor, then nail it to the rafter.

The thicker the scab under the rafter, the higher the R-value. To prevent condensation in the rafter

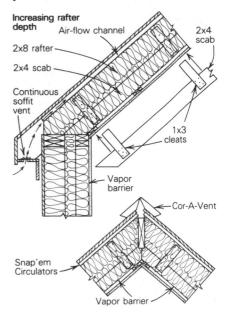

Increasing rafter depth

Air-flow channel

2x8 rafter

2x4 scab

Continuous soffit vent

2x4 scab

1x3 cleats

Vapor barrier

Cor-A-Vent

Snap'em Circulators

Vapor barrier

spaces when insulation is a tight fit (12 in. of insulation in an 11-in. space), I install Snap'em Circulators (Branch River Foam Plastics, Inc., 15 Thurber Blvd., Smithfield, R. I. 02917) between insulation and roof sheathing. Snap'em Circulators are corrugated sheets that create air channels from soffit to ridge. Along with these, soffit and ridge vents must be used. I use Cor-A-Vent (16250 Petro Drive, Mishawaka, Ind. 46544) at the ridge and a screened continuous vent strip at the eaves.

Vapor-barrier placement

Is there an effective way of applying a vapor barrier in a two-story house where second-floor joists intersect with the roof's rafters over the wall (drawing below)? We are building such a structure and

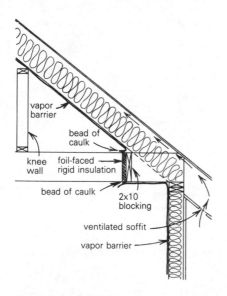

so far have applied the vapor barrier down the rafters and up the first-floor walls and part way

across the ceiling. The R-19 fiberglass insulation in the roof extends over the wall and there is a soffit-to-ridge ventilation space above it, but this envelope cannot be covered with a continuous vapor barrier because of the location of the floor joists. Furthermore, the kneewall built upstairs would seem to keep this vulnerable area cool and encourage condensation. We have not applied any wall or ceiling covering on the first floor, and have noticed considerable condensation on the surface of the vapor barrier on the first-floor ceiling and on the 2x10 blocking. How can this condensation be avoided?
—*Cherlynn Risch, Healy, Alaska*

Gerry Copeland, an architect and builder in Spokane, Wash., replies: The way to provide a continuous vapor barrier in this situation is to cut ½-in. or 1-in. thick foil-faced rigid insulation to fit snugly between the joists right against the 2x10 blocking. Rigid insulation is easier to work with and can be sealed more effectively than if you were to use small pieces of polyethylene between the joists. Cut it exactly flush at the tops and bottoms of the joists. Bring the vapor barrier up the first-floor wall, turn it along the ceiling joists and seal it to the line of rigid insulation with acoustical (non-hardening) caulk. Also caulk the joints on both sides where the pieces of insulation meet the joists. On the second floor, bring the vapor barrier down the rafters and seal it to the rigid insulation the same way. This will provide a continuous vapor barrier.

The condensation that you noticed was probably caused by cold air from the soffit vent leaking through gaps in the insulation batts above the walls. Just a small amount of air passing here would cause an untempered meeting of the cold outside air with the warm inside air at the vapor barrier.

One way to ensure complete filling of voids between framing members is to use blown-in insulation, maintaining ventilation space at the eaves with cardboard baffles. Also, your condensation problem may be aggravated by inadequate insulation. You mention R-19 insulation for a structure in Alaska. Here in eastern Washington state, R-30 is considered a minimum.

Radiant barriers

I am interested in draping a foil-faced radiant barrier over the rafters in my roof designs to minimize attic heat buildup in the Florida climate. The problem is that I've heard horror stories about premature plywood and shingle failure due to excessive heat. Is there any truth to these rumors? —*Mike Paule, Venice, Fla.*

Philip Fairey, a technical consultant at the Florida Solar Energy Center, replies: Rumors about excessive temperatures in plywood and shingles over a radiant-barrier system are just that—rumors. We have tested temperatures in these materials when used in a roof over a radiant-barrier system. On peak-temperature summer days, temperature increases were between 2°F and 5°F. Given that roof temperatures without radiant barriers may reach 190°F, it does not seem logical that an increase of a few degrees will be significant. Our tests show that the color of the shingles themselves will probably make a bigger temperature difference, with lighter colors showing smaller temperature increases due to solar exposure.

Insulating block walls

We're building a new home and plan to use walls consisting of a 6-in. cinder-block core, faced on the outside with 2 in. of rigid insulation and brick veneer, as shown below.

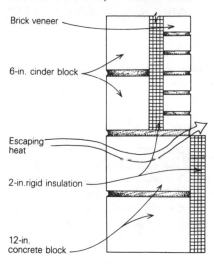

Brick veneer

6-in. cinder block

Escaping heat

2-in. rigid insulation

12-in. concrete block

We want to create a thermal break between these 6-in. walls and the 12-in. block foundation walls below them. The only suggestion we've had has been to place a pressure-treated 2x6 at the bottom of the 6-in. wall with rebar running through it into the 12-in. wall every 4 ft. to 6 ft. The voids in the blocks that contained these rods would have to be grouted solid. Would this work?

—*C. and B. Gregory,*
Binghamton, N. Y.

Charles Lane, an earth-shelter consultant in St. Paul, Minn., replies: Creating thermal breaks is an important part of energy detailing because once the walls, floors and ceiling are heavily insulated, the areas where conductive materials join become a major source of heat loss. But unless you add a good deal more insulation (your proposed 2 in. would yield an R-value ranging from 6 to 10), I wouldn't worry about a thermal break. The R-value of the wall could be increased in several ways (replacing the block with thickly insulated stud walls, for instance), but all of them would require rethinking your wall system. In any case, using a 2x6 as you described represents poor construction detailing, and shouldn't be considered.

Double-wall insulation

I'm thinking of using a double wall of 2x6s and 2x4s for my home in the Yukon. The insulation between the 2x6s will not have a foil back, but the 2x4 insulation will (drawing below). I will leave a space between this foil and the vapor barrier inside the wall to reflect heat back into the house. How wide should this space be?
—*Evan Haynes, Auke Bay, Alaska*

Peter Mann, who teaches passive-solar house design at Mohawk College in Hamilton, Ont., replies: For the foil to function properly there must be at least a ½-in. airspace between it and the nearest surface, including the vapor barrier. However, I would not recommend the use of this particular detail for several reasons. First, you will be establishing a double vapor barrier. Second, you will need some form of strapping to support the inside finishes, and you will have to penetrate the vapor barrier for the plumbing and electrical boxes. Third, the foil will not add significantly to the thermal efficiency of the wall.

The design shown below will be more efficient and has the advantage

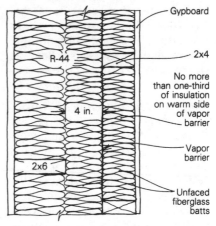

of being well proven in practice. Note that the double studs have a 4-in. space between them, allowing for an additional R-12 insulation batt that should be installed horizontally.

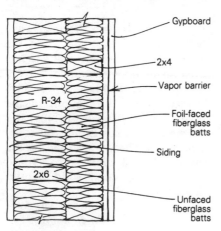

In this design, the vapor barrier is placed on the outer face of the inner 2x4s. This is quite permissible, provided that no more than one-third of the insulation is on the warm side of the vapor barrier. To maintain a complete seal, run all plumbing and electrical inside the 2x4 wall without penetrating the vapor barrier. This detail gives the wall an R-44 value, which can be increased by enlarging and adding insulation to the space between studs.

Insulation retrofit

I purchased a small home and have removed the rock lath from the entire house. It is now time to insulate, and we need to do it properly. I feel that here in northeast Ohio, 3½ in. of insulation for the walls and 6 in. of insulation for the ceiling are no longer adequate.

For the walls, I could install 3½ in. of kraft-faced fiberglass, glue and nail rigid polystyrene over the studs, and finally hang the drywall. This combination of materials will certainly increase the R-value, but will it trap moisture?

I have been told that if the insulation comes into contact with the sheathing, the efficiency of the insulation is greatly reduced. Any truth to this?
—*Pat Hoynes, Moreland Hills, Ohio*

Bill Lotz, a consulting engineer in Acton, Maine, replies: Your proposed insulation system doesn't have a proper vapor barrier. I would suggest a more effective approach, now that you have the interior finish removed. First, fill the stud space or ceiling-joist space with plain fiberglass batts and then install a 1-in. or

2-in. thickness of foil-faced Thermax or other foil-faced polyisocyanurate rigid-foam board. Tape all of the joints with an approved foil tape. The foil then becomes your vapor barrier. It should be as continuous as possible. Use 6-mil polyethylene film to bridge over any holes in the foil. Use acoustical sealant to bond the poly film to itself and to the foil. As long as the vapor barrier is installed with care and you use the bath and kitchen exhaust fans, you should not have problems with trapped moisture.

The stud space should be filled with the fiberglass. Don't worry about old carpenter's tales of the insulation in contact with the sheathing.

Insulation over plaster

I'm redoing the interior of my 41-year-old home. The walls, outside to inside, are brick, 4-in. masonry block, ½-in. wood strips and ¾-in. plaster. No insulation has been added to the walls. I would like to install ½-in. drywall over the plaster with some kind of insulation behind the rock. I need something that will give me good R-value and take up a minimum of space, since the house is small. I was thinking of rigid insulation, perhaps something with foil on both sides. Do you think this would be the right thing to do?
—*Kenneth E. Simon, Hatboro, Pa.*

Energy consultant Dan Desmond replies: Adding only ½ in. of insulation would be one of the least cost-effective things you could do. It's a relatively expensive proposition for the amount of insulation you'd get. Better options, at least to begin with, would include house-doctor services to control infiltration losses, or the installation of a higher-efficiency heating system.

Venting after insulating

I live in a 50-year-old, two-story frame house with lap siding covered with innumerable layers of paint. The exterior walls have no insulation. I have heard a lot about problems with moisture after new insulation has been blown into the walls. Yet reputable insulation contractors have told me that they see no cause for concern. I want to add insulation, so how should I proceed?
—Gerard Peer, Charlotte, N. C.

Dale McCormick, of Cornerstones, an educational owner-builder center in Brunswick, Maine, replies: Go ahead and blow in the insulation, and as you remodel and paint over the years, apply vapor-barrier paint or vinyl wallpaper to the inside of your exterior walls. Also buy an inexpensive hygrometer from the hardware store so that you can keep the relative humidity in your house at or below 35%, the point under which vapor-barrier paint is most effective. Two manufacturers of vapor-barrier paints are The Enterprise Companies (1191 South Wheeling Rd., Wheeling, Ill. 60090) and Gliddon Paints (900 Union Commerce Building, Cleveland, Ohio 44115).

Another common remedy for moisture in the walls is increased ventilation. Tests conducted by the Forest Products Laboratory in Madison, Wis., have demonstrated that the moisture content is reduced substantially on the side of the house where the prevailing wind aids the ventilation. However, on the other exterior walls, the only effect of the vents is to move the dew point toward the interior face of the wall, causing increased moisture levels there. This fact offsets the marginal effect that increased ventilation may have in preventing damage to your exterior paint.

Urethane-foam insulation

In an attempt to insulate my 200-year-old stone house, I am thinking of having a contractor spray 2½ in. of urethane foam over the exterior, which has a stucco finish. The foam will be protected from ultraviolet light by a coat of latex paint. Will this work? *—Timothy Murray, Birdsboro, Pa.*

Pat Hennin, director of the Shelter Institute in Bath, Maine, replies: You can proceed with the urethane foam if you take two precautions. First, make sure that your foam contractor adds a fire-resistant chemical to the mix. Also, treat the interior of your stone walls with a clear sealer, such as silicone, and caulking to prevent moisture generated on the inside of the house from reaching the urethane.

Something else to consider is whether the finish on your stone walls has sufficient texture to create a mechanical bond with the urethane. Urethane sprayed on smooth surfaces, such as steel storage tanks, can literally fall off after a few years. If you think that bonding may be a problem, attach chicken-wire mesh to the exterior of your building before the foam is sprayed.

F. Neale Quenzel, a restoration architect in Newtown Square, Pa., also replies: Pat Hennin's response to Timothy Murray regarding spraying urethane foam on the exterior of a 200-year-old stone house could lead to some serious problems. Houses this old don't have parged, waterproofed foundations, and ground moisture can climb a masonry wall by capillary action as high as 20 ft. or more. Applying silicone to the inside face of the wall and caulking the cracks could create an artificial dam, drawing moisture to the top of the wall and out through the joists, leading to rot.

The major source of heat loss in older stone masonry buildings typically isn't the walls. It would make more sense for Murray to concentrate on insulating the attic, sealing windows with thermal shutters or shades, and weatherstripping doors and windows. Trying to keep moisture out of a stone building this old is a losing battle.

Insulation quandary

I am debating the merits of blowing insulation into the walls of my 100-year-old clapboard house before I repair the plaster. We were sent product information recently on Thermal-Krete (Omni Tech Energy Products Inc., 1515 Michigan N.E., Grand Rapids, Mich. 49503-2085), which is a "foam-type" product. Can you recommend it? Also, is it possible that blown-in insulation will give us a serious condensation problem?
—David R. Morris, Sunbury, Ohio

Dan Desmond, an energy consultant in Lancaster, Pa., replies:

I don't advise using any new product in a virtually irreversible installation like insulating wall cavities without documentation of truly independent testing. Verification from agencies such as the National Bureau of Standards Center for Building Technology or USDA's Forest Products Lab is the kind of assurance I would be looking for.

Thermal-Krete is not really much like concrete, as the name seems to suggest. It is similar in texture to urea-formaldehyde foam, although the manufacturer states that there is no formaldehyde in the product. It is based on a magnesium compound (magnesite) that is extracted from seawater, mixed with a chemical binder and installed in liquid form. With Thermal-Krete, very careful chemical mixing and installation procedures are a must. This product may prove to be a great idea, but without independent testing and proven success in widespread applications, I would be cautious in endorsing any claims.

Because this product can be pumped into stud cavities, it is natural to compare it with blown fiberglass and mineral wool. It is not true that only the liquid product will give adequate insulation because of the tendencies of the other two to hang up on obstructions. A good installer with the right equipment can pack the stuff in so tight as to pop the drywall or plaster off the wall.

As to potential moisture problems, an insulation retrofit results in reducing several thousand small infiltration paths to several dozen large ones. Warm moist air will still exchange with cold, dry air. Moisture problems usually show up near areas where there is a thermal bypass—windows, doors, chimney or stack openings or baths. Differences in lifestyle (how much moisture is produced inside the house) are often the factor that determines whether or not you'll have a moisture problem. The best protection in an existing house is to seal off thermal bypasses by applying caulking and installing weatherstripping, to disconnect any mechanical humidification you might now be using, and to prime walls and ceilings with a vapor-barrier paint.

Venting walls

While researching superinsulated building techniques, I noticed that everyone stresses the importance of adequate attic ventilation. But no one recommends ventilation for side walls. One designer did

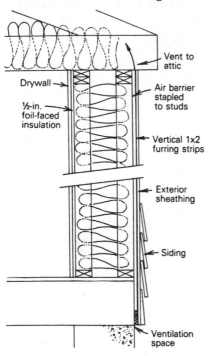

Vent to attic

Drywall

½-in. foil-faced insulation

Air barrier stapled to studs

Vertical 1x2 furring strips

Exterior sheathing

Siding

Ventilation space

mention that plywood or foil-faced insulation boards commonly used as exterior sheathing are impervious to the migration of water vapor through the wall. This could cause moisture to be trapped in the walls.

I am considering a double-wall building technique that would provide an air space between the insulation and sheathing, as shown in the drawing below left. Would this kind of system be superior to standard wall construction? Can you recommend any improvements to my plan?

—*Mark Helling, Cincinnati, Ohio*

John Hughes of Passive Solar Designs Ltd. in Alberta, Canada, replies: The wall, as drawn, would be more than adequate, considering the climate in Cincinnati. By making a few changes though, you can improve its energy efficiency and even lower the cost (drawing below). You've created a "vented rain

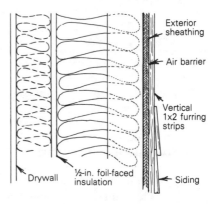

Exterior sheathing

Air barrier

Vertical 1x2 furring strips

Drywall

½-in. foil-faced insulation

Siding

screen" by strapping the wall with vertical 1x2s before putting on the siding. This is an excellent way of stopping rain from getting through the siding and into the wall, should there be any holes in the siding.

However, I would suggest putting the sheathing directly on the studs, then the air barrier, the 1x2s, and finally the siding. There are three reasons for this. First, the sheathing will provide greater racking strength if it's attached directly to the studs. Second, the air barrier alone might not be able to resist the pressure of the fiberglass batts. Since batts are meant to fill a wall cavity completely, they're slightly oversized, and this extra thickness could push the air barrier outward, filling the ventilation space. And third, the sheathing will protect the insulation from wind-washing, which will occur as air moves through the air space. Wind-washing decreases the effective R-value of the wall, increasing heat loss.

Sealing the foil-faced insulation will create an excellent vapor barrier as well as an air barrier, but you should move it to the outside of the inner 2x4 wall. Then all the electrical wires can be run in the inner wall, and there's no need to seal the boxes. However, using the foil-faced foam simply because of the foil is an expensive way to achieve a rigid vapor barrier. Since you already have plenty of R-value in the wall, you might consider using foil-faced hardboard, which costs less and would still serve as an effective air-vapor barrier.

By building the inner wall first, you will be able to get at the outer face to seal the rigid insulation. Be sure to seal the insulation to the top and bottom plates with a bead of caulk. There's at least twice as much insulation on the cold side of the vapor barrier as there is on the warm side, so no condensation should occur on the foil.

If walls were vented the same way attics are—with the insulation exposed in the vent space—it would reduce the effective R-value of the insulation. Air would enter at the bottom of the wall, be warmed by heat loss from the house, rise and exit into the attic. In doing so, it would draw more air into the wall cavity, robbing even more heat from the house.

Attics are vented to carry off moisture escaping from the house, but the air enters the attic above the top of the insulation and doesn't pass through it. As the outside air temperature drops, the effectiveness of attic ventilation is reduced, since cold air can't carry off as much moisture. If you find frost in the attic, don't increase the attic ventilation—stop the flow of moisture from the house to the attic by tightening the air/vapor barrier.

Choosing insulation

I am considering blown-in insulation for my turn-of-the-century home. Will I have moisture problems using this kind of insulation in the absence of a vapor barrier? Also, which is preferable, fiberglass or rock wool?
—Robert C. Morrison,
Voorheesville, N. Y.

Bill Lotz, an engineer specializing in insulation and moisture problems in Acton, Maine, replies: There is a big difference between how well blown-in insulation works in one installation and how it works in another. In some houses, it proves to be an excellent way to provide retrofit insulation; in others it becomes a wet, ineffective disaster. What determines success or failure is the construction of the house itself, the occupants and the climate.

If the house has a wet basement or crawl space, an unvented bathroom and kitchen, or a clothes dryer that is vented indoors, you must dry up these sources of moisture before insulating the walls of the house. You can then retard the remaining moisture that is produced by the occupants by applying a vapor-barrier paint, since installing a polyethylene film isn't practical in your case. If you can get these sources of moisture under control, you shouldn't have any problems with condensation in your walls.

The choice between rock wool and loose fiberglass is not a critical one. If price quotes for each work out to be about the same, I'd choose rock wool because of its greater fire resistance.

Wall vapor barriers

I would like to revive my 20-year-old (and badly weathered) cedar board-and-batten siding by replacing the battens and some of the boards. As long as so much of the siding will be taken down, I'm wondering if I should take it all down and put up a layer of plywood sheathing before reinstalling the siding.

I am thinking about nailing and gluing either ¼-in. or ⅜-in. exterior plywood to the studs for the sheathing and stapling a sheet of plastic over it for an additional air-infiltration barrier. I don't expect that this will make the house too tight because the double-hung windows are single glazed, and plenty leaky. Does all of this sound like a good thing to do?
—Dave Landgraf, Benbrook, Tex.

Consulting editor Tom Law replies: The job you propose is a lot of work, but it can be done. Since the house is just 20 years old, it may have plywood sheathing under the siding already—a little bit of investigation should uncover this. Installed properly, plywood makes a reasonably good infiltration barrier. If the house has board sheathing with lots of gaps between the boards, and your main concern is air infiltration, you'll definitely want to take steps to reduce the infiltration. In either case, you should consider covering the sheathing with a vapor-permeable sheeting product such as Tyvek (Dupont, Wilmington, Del. 19898). Staple it directly to the sheathing, and it will be a lot easier to install than plywood.

Framing for superinsulation

I am thinking of using 2x8 or 2x10 studs to build my house so that I can superinsulate. I have been told that I can also use a staggered stud frame that is really two separate framed walls. Is this cheaper and more effective?
—Keith Reingold, Ithaca, N.Y.

Eyrle Brooks, a professor of mechanical engineering at the University of Saskatchewan at Saskatoon, replies: It is cheaper and more heat-efficient to build the outside walls of a low-energy house with staggered 2x4 construction rather than 2x8 or 2x10 studs. The outside row of studs can be load-bearing, and the inside row supports the drywall and insulation. The increase in cost of materials over a standard frame is basically only one extra row of 2x4s and the extra stock required for framing and finishing around the deep windows and doors.

One advantage is that this system can accommodate any thickness of insulation. Also, if 10 in. or more of wall insulation is used, the vapor barrier can be replaced on the outside edge of the inside row of 2x4s, making the installation of wiring much easier.

Building to beat moisture

I hear dire predictions about moisture buildup in superinsulated walls. I would appreciate some information on proper construction and venting procedures. At left below is a diagram of the wall as we plan to build it.
—*Robert K. Searles, Union Center, Wis.*

Wayne Schick, research professor emeritus of architecture at the University of Illinois, replies: Since damp wood develops fungus, mold or rot and wet insulation insulates poorly, the wood and insulation in any wall—thick or thin—should be kept as dry as possible. There is no practical way to stop all water vapor from getting into a wall, but polyethylene sheeting behind the interior drywall makes a good vapor retarder (barrier). Or you can paint the walls and ceiling with three coats of low-permeability paint. Potentially large moisture sources, such as crawl spaces or basements, should be well sealed against moisture penetration. Good builders have used these techniques for at least two decades. Incidentally, when the electric wiring has been done in the outside walls, you can spray urethane onto the outside of the outlet boxes to seal the holes.

For superinsulated walls, a double-framed (Lo-Cal) wall can be made any thickness suitable for the climate. This wall provides a gap at the top of the insulation-filled cavity that allows what little moisture that penetrates into the wall to be vented to the attic. For example, the 10½-in. cavity has a 3½-in. gap between the double framing. For other thick walls, the top plates can be drilled with ¾-in. dia. holes at 8-in. intervals in order to vent the wall to the attic. For more specific information and construction details, the Small Homes Council-Building Research

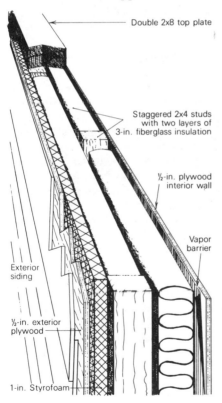

Double 2x8 top plate

Staggered 2x4 studs with two layers of 3-in. fiberglass insulation

½-in. plywood interior wall

Vapor barrier

Exterior siding

½-in. exterior plywood

1-in. Styrofoam

Council (University of Illinois, 1 E. St. Mary's Rd., Champaign, Ill. 61820) has three publications you may find helpful in your effort: "The Illinois Lo-Cal House," 8 pp., $.50 ppd.; "Details and Engineering Analysis of the Illinois Lo-Cal House," 109 pp., $8.50 ppd.; and "Moisture Condensation," 8 pp., $.50 ppd.

Insulating an attic ceiling

I am turning the attic of my home into a living area. I would like some advice on how best to insulate the ceiling. I live in a hot, humid climate and am most concerned about keeping the heat out of the upstairs living area. Headroom is at a premium. I would like to put as much rigid insulation as possible between the rafters and then install ½-in. drywall or some sort of insulated panels directly to the rafters. I understand the rigid insulation with the highest R-factor is unsafe for ceiling application. If I must, I will fur down and install 6-in. fiberglass. What is the minimum distance to fur down and still leave enough room for air flow next to the roof sheathing?

Second, I am considering installing vent registers or a power ventilator in the ceiling to remove interior heat. I am concerned that this may interfere with the flow from soffit to ridge vent.

I will be putting on a new roof soon. Should I insulate under the new fiberglass shingles? Downstairs I have 1,500 sq. ft., and the living area upstairs is 500 sq. ft., so insulating the whole roof may not be cost effective.

—Robert D. Dyer, Ponchatoula, La.

Bill Lotz, a consulting engineer in Acton, Maine, replies: About rafter insulation: I suggest 2 in. of good-quality foil-faced foam insulation board with an R-value of 13 or so. When the foil faces an air space, you can add a value of R-3 for a total of R-16. In your climate, that should be adequate.

This insulation should be cut to fit snugly between the rafters, as shown in the drawing below, with 1½-in. by ¾-in. wood (or foam scrap) spacers. This results in a 1½ in. air space between the foil-faced insulation and the roof sheathing.

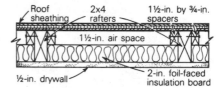

Fire codes vary from state to state, but ½-in. drywall is usually an acceptable fire barrier between foam insulation and living space. Check your local building codes, since ⅝-in. type X (fire-resistant) drywall may be required.

I see no reason why a house ventilation fan would have any adverse effect on air flow in the soffit-to-ridge vent corridor. When the fan is on, the natural air flow reverses, but it should cause no problem. However, it would be better to install the fan in an outside wall with a good louver-damper system that will resist rain penetration. There is some chance that warm, moist air from the house could condense at night in the attic and cause staining.

You may wish to consider installing one of the many foam/panel laminates (these have rigid insulation bonded to a structural sheathing) as a roof insulation system and forget about using foam between the rafters. Remove the old shingles, use ring-shank nails to attach the foam/panel product to the rafters and nail the new shingles to the structural panel. Several manufacturers make insulated structural panels: among them are the Homasote Co. (Box 7240, West Trenton, N. J. 08628) and Koppers (1901 Koppers Building, Pittsburgh, Pa. 15219).

Vacation-home insulation

In my area, most supply houses seem to carry only foil-backed fiberglass insulation. Should I use a polyethylene vapor barrier over the foil? The home I'll be insulating is a summer vacation cabin that I don't heat in the winter.
—*John Hoard, Kalamazoo, Mich.*

Pennsylvania energy specialist Dan Desmond replies: I think using a poly moisture barrier over foil-faced insulation is unnecessary if you install the insulation with a tight friction fit and if you are careful in stapling the tabs over the studs. In older homes, however, the stud spacing may be irregular, and you may have to staple the tabs to the inside faces of the studs. This situation could require the adddition of another vapor barrier.

In the case of your cabin, I would use a very light moisture barrier such as kraft backing on your insulation, or none at all since the possibility of moisture damage is greatly reduced by two things. The first is the fact that you won't be in the cabin generating moisture (showers, cooking, respiration) during the winter. Second, because you aren't

heating, the dew-point temperature differential required to induce vapor diffusion is very low. Still, you will get some interior condensation in the fall and spring. For this reason, I wouldn't concentrate on getting the shell too tight, and I would use galvanized nails and rustproof hardware throughout.

Condensation concerns

Foil-faced sheets of rigid urethane foam are increasingly popular for exterior sheathing applications. I fear that the foil will act as a vapor barrier on the outside of the wall and result in condensation forming in the wall. Will an efficient vapor barrier inside prevent this? Also, what interior vapor barrier do you recommend—polyethylene plastic or the asphalt-layered kraft-paper barrier that comes on most fiberglass insulation? Here in the South, I'm concerned with the effects of air conditioning as well as with winter heating on condensation. —*Ben Erickson, Eutaw, Ala.*

Peter Mann, who teaches passive-solar house design in Hamilton, Ont., replies: Because the foil facing on rigid urethane foam is a barrier to water vapor, any vapor present in the stud cavity will condense on the cold foil surface. This water can then cause a variety of problems, notably a drastic loss of insulation efficiency and rotting of the studs. As the weather gets colder, the problems increase.

An efficient interior vapor barrier will help reduce this phenomenon, but complete vapor tightness can never be guaranteed. Hence further precautions must be taken, such as slitting the foil face of the foam sheets before putting them up or venting the stud cavities through the top plates. In some areas, foil-faced foam insulation sheets are banned by code. Check with your local building inspector.

The best approach is to use an exterior insulation panel that will allow water vapor to pass, such as a compressed, semi-rigid fiberglass type. The best inside vapor barrier is 6-mil polyethylene sheets, carefully taped or caulked at all joints. It is vastly superior to the now outdated kraft-paper facing.

Your concerns about condensation in the summer are groundless. Air conditioning does not create a significant enough temperature difference for water to condense inside the house.

ADA remodel

I'd like to use the airtight drywall approach in remodeling my house. The walls are 2x4 construction, and I'd like to add rigid insulation on the inside. What type of insulation should I use? Should I do anything different with the caulking back? —*Jeffrey L. Ellis, Meadville, Pa.*

Architect Tom Bowerman replies: I suggest using polyurethene foam because of its high R-value per inch. This permits interior application without losing much interior space. I'd use 1½-in. foam and fur out the top and bottom plates with 1½-in. spacers to give the drywall a firm backing. Fire-rated drywall is probably required in your area, because foam insulation is flammable.

The backer rod would be used in the same manner as in new construction, and the furring strips would be gasketed to the floor as well as to the drywall. It might be a good idea to use vertical furring strips on the studs and install the foam between them. But you could avoid this by using long drywall screws that would pull both the drywall and the insulation up snug to the studs. This would eliminate the possibility of movement and joint cracking. With the latter method, I'd definitely use fiberglass-mesh joint tape.

Attic insulation

My two-story house is insulated to R-28 in the walls and R-40 in the kneewalls and roof of the attic. The attic isn't part of the living space and is kept cool. I wonder if I should install insulation (R-19) in the floor of the attic to keep heat from rising above the second-floor living space. If so, should this installation also include a vapor barrier? —*Jim Dunham, Lincolnville, Maine*

Dan Desmond, an energy consultant in Lancaster, Pa., replies: In principle, insulation in the second-floor ceiling with a vapor-barrier paint on the ceiling below would have been your best option. Now that you have R-40 in the attic, though, trading off for R-19 is questionable if by "cool" you mean outdoor ambient temperature. If the attic will be maintained above 40°F, however, you could install the floor insulation you mentioned. If you do, be sure that the attic has some ventilation. Its effectiveness can be observed in how much condensation you find on the attic windows.

An alternative to insulating further is to install a ceiling fan controlled by a differential thermostat that would dump attic air to the second floor whenever there was a temperature differential of, say, +10°F in the attic.

Backdrafting in HRVs

In the use of heat-recovery ventilators there is a problem created by exhaust fans in the bathroom and kitchen, as well as by clothes dryers. These fans, when used in tight houses, would cause the flow through the HRV to be into the house only, or would cause backdrafts through chimneys. Until the air entering and exiting the home under all conditions is considered, the HRV is an expensive and marginally effective item. Is anyone trying to solve this problem?
—*G. Watcrous,*
Manhattan Beach, Calif.

John Hughes replies: It's important to realize that a properly installed HRV is a balanced system, bringing in as much air as it exhausts, and is not intended to replace house air being exhausted by other appliances, such as range hoods or clothes dryers. Having an HRV in a tight house will neither increase nor decrease the likelihood of furnace backdrafting caused by dryers, fireplaces or other air guzzlers.

The concern about backdrafting is valid, though, and I agree that air movement into and out of a house should be considered at the design stage. Fortunately, since all really "tight" houses are new, it's quite easy (though not necessarily cheap)

to build in backdraft prevention. Most conventional forced-air furnaces have a make-up air duct to bring in fresh air when the furnace is running. At other times, this duct could (and should) be designed to allow enough air to enter the house to replace any air being exhausted from the house. The R-2000 program (research and standards on energy-efficient construction sponsored by the Canadian Home Builders Association and the government of Canada) now requires that all fuel-fired appliances be either induced-draft or condensing-type units. And fireplaces and woodstoves should have combustion-air ducts to the outdoors. I don't think range hoods move enough air to cause backdrafting. Even in a tight house, there is some natural air infiltration.

As to your comment that HRVs are expensive and marginally effective items, I agree that they're expensive. But so are cars, stereos and many other items we seem to think we need, and most of these won't improve the air quality in your house. The air filter only needs to be washed monthly, and the core removed and cleaned about twice a year. Total time required—maybe an hour or two a year. Marginally effective? Detailed testing of 280 R-2000 houses showed that they had lower levels of radon, formaldehyde and nitrogen dioxide than conventionally built houses. What price do you put on clean air?

Chapter 8:

Flooring

Installing end-grain flooring

Please advise me on how to install end-grain blocks as a floor covering over a concrete slab. What thickness should the blocks be? What adhesive should be used? Can they be stained or bleached? And what finish would be best? Are there any problems I can expect that don't occur with a regular wood floor? —*John Chapman, Lexington, N. C.*

John Couch, owner of Oregon Lumber Co., which manufactures end-grain flooring in Lake Oswego, Ore., replies: New concrete slabs must be at least 50 days old. Be sure the slab is dry and protected with a dependable vapor barrier underneath. If the vapor barrier is impractical or, in the case of an older slab, is uncertain, then damp-proof the top of the slab with two layers of

#15 felt paper applied with asphaltic primer and mastic. You could also use Moist-Stop (Fortifiber Corp., 4489 Bandini Blvd., Los Angeles, Calif. 90023), a three-ply polyethylene membrane, or its equivalent.

Block thickness will depend on the degree and sharpness of potential impact. End-grain fir will take over a million pounds per square foot before it will dent. I use 1-in. blocks under lift trucks, so they will certainly do for most residential applications. However, if there might be heavy or sharp impact, go to a thicker material (1½ in. to 2½ in.) to avoid splitting.

All wood floors are susceptible to dimensional change if the temperature and humidity vary enough to change the equilibrium moisture content. A very high or very low E.M.C. is okay, providing the subsequent change is minimal. Be sure to let the blocks acclimate (at least four days) and install them in the same environment as will be expected in the future. Do not install and later turn on the heat or air conditioning. I recommend using a solvent-base adhesive that will remain pliable. Avoid asphaltic-type mastics because there is a danger the finish will wick solvent in the mastic to the surface. Spread the mastic with a ¼-in. notched trowel and wait 45 to 60 minutes before setting blocks. I suggest ½-in. to 1½-in. cork expansion joints at all walls and columns.

End-grain wood is extremely absorbent and will take eight to ten times more finish than a conventional floor. It can be stained or bleached. Use a flooring-grade penetrating oil, pigmented to your choice of color, either sprayed or applied with a lamb's-wool applicator. Continuously apply and reapply evenly in saturation quantity to large checkerboard sections. First-application coverage is approximately 100 sq. ft. per gallon. Allow solvent to escape for at least six hours, then apply a second coat of oil at a rate of approximately 200 sq. ft. per gallon. Be sure to remove any excess oil with rags or steel wool.

The final step is to apply two coats of D-503 Futura (Bowen Jiffy, P.O. Box 216, Mamaroneck, N. Y. 10543) or other Swedish finish.

Silencing a subfloor

I've been thinking about installing hardwood flooring on the second floor of a 20-year-old house. Presently, carpet is laid over a pad and a ¾-in. plywood subfloor. The existing subfloor squeaks, and noise

from the ground floor is objectionable in spite of the sprayed acoustic ceiling below. How can I eliminate the squeaks, improve the acoustics and install a finish floor and any additional subfloor (1,000 sq. ft.)? I'd also like to minimize total material costs. —J. B. Bazley, San Jose, Calif.

Consulting editor Bob Syvanen, of Brewster, Mass., replies: The simplest way I can think of to eliminate squeaks in an existing subfloor is to remove the subfloor and reinstall it using screws and subfloor adhesive.

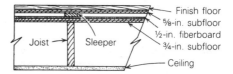

As for the acoustic problems, the trick is to separate the floor above from the ceiling below. The drawing shows a system I've used. Nail down ½-in. fiberboard carpet underlayment board like Homasote over the existing subfloor. Then nail down 1x3 sleepers 16 in. o. c. parallel to the joists. Follow this with a second layer of subfloor—⅝-in. plywood is good. Finally, install the finish floor atop the plywood.

Leveling an old floor

I am remodeling the second floor of an old farmhouse. Because of water leaking from the bathroom over the years, the floor joists have sagged. The sagging was compounded by plumbers who cut through two floor joists to install large cast-iron supply and waste pipes. While remodeling the first

floor, I repaired the severed joists and made sure the others were sound and had adequate support. What is the best and most economical way to level the floor upstairs? At the worst spot, the sag is about 1 in. to 1½ in. Should the flooring be removed and the joists leveled by sistering 2x stock onto the sides of the joists? Or should I cut shims for the tops of the joists to produce a level surface? I understand there is a product that can be mixed, poured and leveled on the old floor, but wouldn't this add too much weight?
—*Caroll Callaway, Barrington Hills, Ill.*

Dan Rockhill, a contractor and professor of architecture at the University of Kansas, replies: Your suggestion to use a product that can be poured and leveled upstairs is good. You want self-leveling underlayment, a cement-based product. It is available from several different companies, including Thoro System Products (7800 N.W. 38th St. Miami, Fla. 33166). I don't think the extra weight is significant enough to worry about. A 1-in. layer in a 12-ft. by 12-ft. room might add 150 lb. of uniform load across the floor—about the weight of a bureau loaded with clothes.

Start by locating the low spots with a transit, water level or spirit level. The entire floor should be coated with a special primer (available from Thoro), and the low spots, or big holes, should be filled with a mixture of underlayment and sand. Bring this to within ¼ in. to ½ in. of your proposed finish elevation. The next day, mix a soupy version of the same underlayment and pour it over the floor, letting it seek its own level. The material sets up in a few hours (it will be hot to the touch as it does) and is ready for carpet or other floor coverings in 24 hours. If you'll be laying a wood floor over it, you can set sleepers directly on top of the underlayment, then nail down your finish floor. Leveling the average 12-ft. by 12-ft. floor that has a deflection of ¼ in. would cost about $150 in materials.

Curved floor boards

I'm having a home designed that contains a 90° segment of a circle. The center of the circle is about 2 ft. away from two of the library walls. The radius to the outside of the farthest wall is about 24 ft.

I need advice on making curved boards for hardwood floors that follow the arc of the circle. At a minimum, I would like to do the hallway and library floors this way. —*Joseph L. Todd, Flint, Mich.*

David Mulder, a stairbuilder in Battle Creek, Mich. replies: First you need to decide what kind of wood you want to use and how wide you want the floor boards to be. The most common manufactured flooring is oak, 2¼ in. wide. But because yours will be a custom floor, I'll use a width of 3 in. as an example. Shrinkage may be a problem on a curved floor, because the grain is running in various directions. So make sure the stock you use has been dried to at least 8% moisture content. Then try to get the house as close to its final humidity level as possible (i.e., make sure it's closed in, most interior work is complete and the furnace or air conditioning is running) and store the stock on site well ahead of time.

Rip a strip of wood for a layout stick, or story pole, that will be a guide in laying out the floor. Make sure the strip is long enough to reach from the center of the circle to the farthest outside radius (in this case, the outside edge of the hall-way). Also make sure the wood is thin and without any knots—you don't want it to break.

On the layout stick, work out and mark the measurements that you will need. Strip flooring has a ¼-in. long tongue along one edge and a ¼-in. deep groove to accept a tongue along the other. So mark

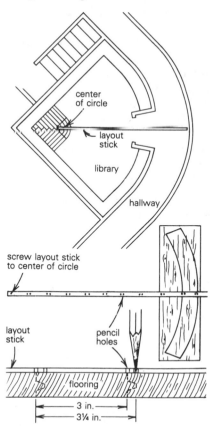

center of circle

layout stick

library

hallway

screw layout stick to center of circle

layout stick

pencil holes

flooring

3 in.

3¼ in.

points at 3 in., 3¼ in., 6 in., 6¼ in., 9 in., 9¼ in. and so on, until you reach the outside radius. Drill a small hole, big enough for a pencil point, in the center of the layout stick at each of your marks, so you can make a tracing on the floor boards.

Because you need a lot of room to swing the arcs, your best bet is to work on site, which means it will be easier if you don't put up any interior walls until after you lay your floor, or at least until you get all the boards laid out. It might be possible to frame the interior walls, then run the layout stick through the opening for the library doors (top drawing at left).

In either case, screw the end of the layout stick to the plywood sub-floor at the center of the circle and begin marking your boards. Keep in mind that you don't need to lay out each board exactly in place. As long as it has the proper radius, any board will fit at any point in a particular course of flooring, which is why you might get away with running the layout stick through the library doorway.

Each board needs two radiused lines scribed on it, representing the inside edge (bottom drawing at left), which will receive the groove, and the outside edge of the tongue. The first few courses of flooring can be done in one piece. As you move farther out from the center, though, successive courses will need more and more boards. It will save some time if you cut your flooring from the widest stock available, probably 1x10s or 1x12s.

While you're laying out the radiuses on each board, you should also mark the ends. You can use the lay-out stick for this as well. The exact angle for the end cuts would be down the center of the layout stick. But if your stick is fairly narrow, you can get away with drawing a line along its edge on both ends of the flooring. Otherwise, you'll have to mark the center line, top and bottom, and connect them with a straightedge.

The curves in each board can be cut with a bandsaw or with a jigsaw, either stationary or handheld. Cut first along the inside edge (the 3-in. mark, for instance). Once the piece is cut, it needs to be sanded to the layout lines, and the edges should be sanded square to the face.

The last step is shaping the tongues and grooves. A perfect setup would be to have two shapers, one with knives to cut the tongues and the other with knives to cut the grooves, or a shaper with two spindles to do the same. If you don't have a shaper, you could do this with a pair of routers that have ½-in. collets. With just one router you would have to keep changing bits back and forth for each piece, which would be a pain in the neck.

Several companies make router bits that will work. The Amana Tool Co. (1250 Brunswick Ave. Far Rockaway, N. Y. 11691) makes a tongue-and-groove bit; you need two sets if you're using two routers. They run about $50 a set. Freud (218 Field Ave., High Point, N. C. 27264) makes a wedge-and-tongue set of bits that would also work.

If you are using a router, I strongly suggest using a good router table to get the same results as on a shaper. Cutting the tongue on the outside edge will dress the face of the board down to the 3-in. finished width. Once your pieces have been laid out, cut and shaped, they're ready to install.

Hardwood/softwood floor trim

I bought 1,000 bd. ft. of sugar pine. The planks are up to 16 ft. long and 16 in. wide, 1⅜ in. thick and absolutely clear. I'd like to use them as the floor for my master-bedroom suite. In order to accentuate the planks, I would like to trim each one in a contrasting hardwood, such as wenge or bubinga, as shown in the drawing below. The subfloor is ⅝-in. CDX

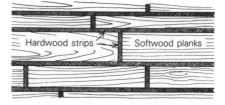

nailed on 24-in. centers (that's stretching it a bit, I know). How should I fasten the planks to the subfloor to allow for movement in that size plank? What's the best way to do the hardwood trim to allow for movement of the planks? What finish should I use?
—Charles Suggs, Norman, Okla.

Paul Fuge, owner of Dimension Hardwood in Shelton, Conn., replies: Such a floor will be a strong visual statement, and it should be laid out with colored tape on the subfloor of the master bedroom before any sawdust flies. Live with it a while and let the infatuation wear off until you have the courage to lift the tape and change a few lines to make it exactly right.

Think of the floor as a frame-and-panel surface with the hardwood strips as the fixed stiles and rails, and the floorboards as the panels. So that the softwood planks will slip under the hardwood strips, rabbet

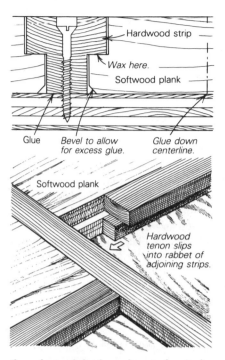

Glue   Bevel to allow   Glue down
        for excess glue.   centerline.

Hardwood strip

Wax here.

Softwood plank

Softwood plank

Hardwood
tenon slips
into rabbet of
adjoining strips.

the edges of the boards, as shown in the drawing above, The hardwood strips should be screwed and glued firmly to the subfloor so they hold down the edges and ends of your floorboards. The centerline of the floorboards can be held down with a good solvent-based flexible construction adhesive like Rexnord PL 400 (Rexnord Inc., P.O. Box 2022, 5103 West Beloit Rd., Milwaukee, Wis. 53214) and/or screwed from the bottom through the subfloor. Don't glue the edges of the floorboards.

Sugar pine is a very soft wood and will dent, so you must use an oil finish on the floor. Surface finishes like urethane will crack when dented. The floorboards must go across the joists because your subfloor is like al dente linguini hanging between two forks. How about some solid bridging every 6 ft.?

Oak over linoleum

I am planning to cover my kitchen and breakfast-room floor with 2-in. wide, tongue-and-groove white oak strip flooring. The subfloor is 1x4 T&G boards over joists 16 in. o.c., and doesn't have any squeaks. Should I use ½-in. or ¾-in. thick flooring? What length fasteners do I need? Can I lay the oak perpendicular to the joists? The floor is covered with linoleum now, but it is perfectly smooth and solidly glued down. Should I remove it first?   —Mark Smith, San Diego, Calif.

David Kloss, a hardwood flooring contractor in Los Angeles, replies: Laying a hardwood floor over linoleum is a very common practice, as long as the linoleum is in good shape. You could use either ½-in. or ¾-in. oak, and with the sound subfloor you describe, you could lay the boards parallel to or perpendicular to the joists. Ask a flooring supplier or rental yard to supply you with the correct fastener for the thickness of floor you decide on. When you are finished sanding, make sure to seal the floor immediately and thoroughly. Getting water on a kitchen floor is unavoidable, but the results can be disastrous. Spills will soak into the new wood, and cause it to swell and discolor.

Quartersawn oak planking

I will soon be installing 600 sq. ft. of native burl oak planking that I've had air-drying for over two years. It is quartersawn in random widths from 6 in. to 12 in. I will thickness-plane the boards to

¾ in., and lay them butt-joined. My subfloor is ¾-in. T&G plywood, glued and nailed to floor trusses 19¼ in. o. c.

How do I fasten the planks? I don't want to screw and plug the flooring because I'm afraid the plugs will detract from the planks. I'm leery of using glue because my air-dried boards may crack or warp badly and require replacement. This leaves me with face-nailing and the question of what kind of nail to use. Am I proceeding correctly?   —Ron W. Smyth
Good Thunder, Minn.

Hardwood-floor specialist Don Bollinger replies: I advise strongly against the use of such wide boards. Planking wider than 6 in. to 8 in. (especially if it is only ¾ in. thick) is extremely difficult to control even after careful drying and sealing. I would recommend cutting wider planks down to pleasing "random" combinations such as 3 in., 5 in. and 7 in. or 4 in., 6 in. and 8 in.

If you don't tongue-and-groove your boards and blind-nail them, you'll need either to screw and plug, face-nail or glue them down. If you do not end-match, I recommend keeping all butt joints on the joist layout so that you can nail or screw into them. I also fear your subflooring is a bit too light for the span across your joists. The bare minimum I recommend for wide planking is ¾-in. plywood with tongue-and-groove edges over joists set 16 in. o. c.

Nail selection is more a matter of personal choice; however, I do recommend some additional holding strength such as that provided by ring-shank or galvanized or cut-shank or even twist-shank flooring

nails if you decide not to use screws. Modern cut nails manufactured specifically for use in power nailers have very narrow rectangular heads and do not show themselves readily when set, filled and finished over. If you are a real perfectionist and have lots of time, you may want to hide your face nailing by lifting a narrow strip of wood using an in-cannel carving gouge, driving the nail under this piece and then gluing and sanding the strip back in place.

Although quartered oak will not move as much as typical flatsawn or plainsawn oak, you can still expect to get a lot of lateral movement across your floor during the course of the year. The wider the planking, the less space you have for absorbing this between planks. You might also watch for loose or nearly loose pieces of butterflies or tiger rays detaching themselves from the surrounding grain. These rays are particularly praised in quartered oak but can become a wood-flooring finisher's nightmare.

Large-crack fillers

I rented out my house and the people didn't take very good care of the floors, which are made of pine. There are cracks ranging in size from ¹⁄₁₆ in. to ³⁄₁₆ in. I will sand the floors and take up all the varnish, but what can I put in the cracks so they will not show when the floors are finished?
—Adrian Krause, Caldwell, Kan.

Simon Watts, a master woodworker and author in Putney, Vt., replies: Cut some pieces of dry pine with about a 15° taper, staining the pine to match the floor if you wish.

Make them of differing thicknesses so you can choose the right one for each crack. Scrape loose dirt out of the cracks and vacuum, then glue a piece of pine into each crack and lightly tap into place. Wipe off the excess glue and plane the piece flush with the floor. The best time to do this is when the cracks are largest—probably in mid-winter.

Hardwood hints

I'm getting ready to lay a hardwood floor on ½-in. CDX plywood, which is nailed to joists on 16-in. centers. The flooring is quartersawn red oak, ¾ in. thick, which I milled myself and have had stickered for a year. What moisture content should the wood be before I lay the floor? The boards are 3 in. to 12 in. wide. Would grooving these boards and using plywood splines be better than tongue-and-grooving them? If I spline them, can I use a power nailer? Should I screw the wide planks to the joists? —*James Ryan, Putnam Valley, N. Y.*

David Kloss, a hardwood-flooring contractor in California, replies: Before installing your oak flooring, you should definitely put down another layer of ½-in. CDX plywood. In Los Angeles, the moisture content of wood used in interiors runs about 6% to 8%. In your area, your safest bet is to ask a local hardwood-flooring contractor, although the figure shouldn't be too much higher than this. Most boards that are warped can be straightened as you nail them, but it's hard to do this with boards 12 in. wide. As a matter of fact, don't use boards wider than

7 in. or 8 in. Extra cross-grain width means unruly wood movement after the boards are laid. And getting them down in straight, tight runs isn't easy.

I wouldn't use plywood splines. Oak splines from the same planks would create a stronger flooring and would have the same contraction and expansion as the rest of the boards. You'll have to experiment a bit with a power nailer to make sure that you are cutting splines that will fit the lip profile of the tool.

Using screws on the wide boards is a good idea, but don't just put screws in wherever there is a joist. Also put some screws in the narrow boards to keep a pattern that's pleasing to the eye. Look closely at a plank peg-and-groove floor that you think is attractive to get an idea of how to stagger the screws. Use #10 common wood screws, 2 in. long. First surface-drill (counterbore) a hole, sink the screw and plug it with a ⅝-in. dia. peg. You can use pegs from the same stock or from a darker wood, like walnut, for contrast. Remember, though, that the entire floor will have to be sanded to get the pegs smooth and flush with the surface of the planks.

Fasteners for hardwood

I'm going to be laying a wide-plank hardwood floor soon, and it will require some screws as well as nails. What kind of screws should I use, and what is the best way to plug the holes? —*Ralph Dornick, Altoona, Pa.*

Don Bollinger, a flooring specialist in Seattle, Wash., replies: There are two considerations in using screws and plugs with hardwood flooring: structural and aesthetic.

On the structural end of things, if your boards are not end-matched and your subfloor and underlayment together are less than 1 in. thick, you should cut all joints to fall on a joist and use at least one screw to anchor the end of each board. If your planks are fairly wide (4 in. or more) I recommend more than tongue-nailing to keep them down. If your planks are long (6 ft. or more), then a screw every other joist is usually sufficient, but this is where aesthetics comes into play. Depending on the different widths of your boards, the kind of wood you are using and whether or not the plugs will be made of a contrasting wood, you may want to put at least one screw and plug in every joist.

I use #10 or #12 square-drive flathead wood screws for most of my work. They should be long enough to pass through the finished flooring and the underlayment and penetrate the joist. I seldom use a screw shorter than 2 in.

I use a combination tapered bit and counterbore to make the pilot holes for the screws and the plugs at the same time. But where the boards butt, I often drill the pilot holes on an angle so they penetrate the joists better. This means drilling the counterbore separately, because it shouldn't be at an angle.

You can buy plugs, but I make most of mine by using a ½-in. plug-cutter on face-grained or edge-grained boards. I glue the plugs in, setting them cross grain to the surrounding wood. This makes for a nice contrast and spares me the impossible task of trying to match the grain with every plug.

Recycled boards for flooring

Two years ago I bought 2,000 bd. ft. of mixed red and white oak that had been earmarked for drawer sides. Once I thickness-plane the boards, which range from 3 in. to 10 in. wide, they'll be about ⅝ in. thick. Is this too thin for flooring? If not, how wide should I rip the boards? How should their edges be treated, and how should they be fastened? —John Shoneman, Hillsborough, N. C.

Don Bollinger, a flooring specialist in Seattle, Wash., replies: Mixing red and white oak makes a delightful combination of grain and color patterns for a floor, and the ⅝-in. thickness isn't a problem. In fact, one of the most popular types of flooring used from the turn of the century through the 1930s was ⁵⁄₁₆-in. by 2-in. oak slat flooring, which was face-nailed to the underlayment with 2d or 3d brads. This takes a very heavy underlayment, though, and the slats often work loose with traffic and structural settling.

Tongue-and-groove your oak stock (we have even milled ½-in. oak flooring this way). There is no substitute for tongue-and-groove in allowing wood flooring to move with seasonal variations in moisture content while still holding its relative position. However, because you'll be using wide boards, you cannot rely solely on nailing the tongue to secure the flooring.

I would use a random-width pattern of 3-in., 4-in. and 5-in. boards. End-matching the boards would be best (a tongue or groove milled on each board end), but if not, I'd make sure that each butt joint fell over a joist. This way the ends could be secured with a screw and the counter-bore plugged. If a lot of the boards were over 6 ft. long, I would probably screw and plug to every other joist (or even every joist) in addition to nailing the tongues with a power nailer, using 2-in. cut nails.

I don't recommend gluing plank flooring, especially if you live in a climate where there is a good deal of moisture variation between seasons. In my experience, gluing will produce at least a slight degree of curling at the edges of the wider planks, or a slight upwards bow in the middle. This cupping can be a problem even if you don't glue, so I seal my wide boards thoroughly on all six sides before installing them if I anticipate a problem. I even reseal boards during installation that have been cut to length or ripped to width. I use Benite for this, a generic sealer popular around here for everything, including siding.

Southwestern air drying

Is it possible, here in the desert Southwest, to use air-dried lumber for flooring, as kiln-dried stock is hard to come by in our sparsely populated area?

I am considering using ponderosa pine. Would this be okay? And if I used 8-in. planks 8 ft. long, how many screws (and plugs) should I use per piece? If I use three on each end, should I also use some in the middle? Also, is three too many on the ends? I want to use a tung-oil finish, cutting it 50/50 with turpentine. Would this be satisfactory in a low-traffic area?

From what I've seen of wide plank flooring, the boards don't need to have tongue-and groove joints, which makes my job simpler. But I wonder about the cracks. Should I try to fill them before finishing or what? What did the builders do in the early homes in the eastern U.S.?
—*Charles Collins, Virgin, Utah*

Millworks owner and operator Paul Fuge replies: A little common sense and the Southwestern desert will dry lumber, especially softwood lumber like ponderosa pine, in a reasonable amount of time for use in interior finish work. If you buy freshly sawn green lumber, you must sticker it properly and wait until the boards stop shrinking. Use one board as a sample that you check periodically, measuring to $\frac{1}{32}$ in. or less. When the wood stops shrinking during hot, dry weather, it is cured.

Milled lumber from a retailer should also be handled the same way, because it may not have been dried to a specific moisture content or to one low enough for interior finish work. It may also have been stored outside.

Three screws on each end and two or three spaced 16 in. to 24 in. apart in the middle would fasten the boards securely. If the boards are T&G and blind-nailed during installation, fewer screws are needed along the edges.

Tongue-and-grooving, contrary to popular myth, does nothing to reduce shrinkage. Only proper drying, straight boards and careful installation minimize cracks.

I strongly prefer an oil finish on soft woods like pine, fir and spruce to a hard-surface finish like urethane, which builds a film on the wood that's hard to renew when worn. A polymerizing tung oil would work, but my favorite is DuraSeal (Minwax Co., 102 Chestnut Ridge Plaza, Montvale, N. J. 07645), an oil/resin combination designed specifically for floors. Oil finishes can be rejuvenated periodically simply by sanding the worn areas and applying the oil.

Storing used flooring

Last summer I removed several rooms' worth of ⅜-in. thick oak flooring from a house built around 1920 that was being demolished.

I now have the flooring stored in a detached, unheated garage with a concrete floor, and it could be several years before I am ready to install it in my own house. Will I have to dry the flooring before I install it? And if so, will it help the wood to dry if I bring the boards into my house for a couple of months during the cold season just before installation?
— *Leonard Hollman, Eudora, Kan.*

Paul Fuge, owner of a millwork shop in Shelton, Conn., replies: Salvaged flooring usually comes from abandoned unheated buildings. The moisture content of the wood can run from 10% to 18% and more, depending on how much dampness managed to get into the building. Removing the flooring to an unheated garage will maintain the wood at a moisture content too high for installation. Your idea of moving the wood indoors during the cold winter months will work, providing that the following conditions are met.

The flooring should be stacked in piles 4 ft. or 5 ft. wide, with spacers between layers. Spacers can be pieces of flooring placed about 2 ft. apart, perpendicular to the length of the flooring piles. The room must be kept at 70°F day and night, perhaps with a supplemental electric heater. The air should be stirred up and circulated with a small oscillating fan.

Shrinkage of wood flooring

When my wife and I built our home, we bought 1x4 and 1x6 T&G fir flooring from a reputable distributor of building materials. This distributor also handles hardwood flooring and is familiar with the drying requirements for wood flooring. The floor was laid by a professional contractor, who nailed and glued it to a 1⅛-in. subfloor over a full basement. He did an excellent job, as did the finisher, who applied a Glitsa finish.

During the first winter and over the next year, the flooring dried and shrank. It now has gaps between the boards that range in width from ¹⁄₁₆ in. up to ⁵⁄₁₆ in., averaging about ⅛ in. The contractor who laid the floor says it's the worst shrinkage that he has ever seen.

We are asking the distributor for damages with the belief that the lumber that was supplied, which came from a local mill that dries to 15% moisture content, was not suitable flooring material. It is my understanding that flooring should have a minimum of 9% moisture. Is that true?

Are there tables that would show me, based upon the amount of shrinkage in the lumber and present moisture content, what the moisture content was when the

flooring was purchased and laid? Do you think this much shrinkage should be expected?
—*Grover C. Ligon, Condon, Mont.*

Paul Fuge, a millworks operator in Shelton, Conn., replies: Yes, there are tables that show the relationship between shrinkage and moisture content. Wood movement is usually expressed as a percentage of maximum dimension related to moisture content. When wood has been cooked to remove all moisture it is said to have 0% moisture and be at its minimum dimension. At 30% and higher moisture content by weight, wood is at its maximum dimension. The graph below (from the USDA Forest Products Laboratory Handbook, Forest Products Laboratory, Box 5130, Madison, Wis. 53705) depicts a moisture content/shrinkage curve for Douglas fir.

The predictability of the relationship between moisture content and dimension should make the business of providing wood at the correct moisture content for a specific application easy. Wood intended for residential flooring applications should be between 5% and 12% equilibrium moisture content (EMC)—6% to 8% for hardwoods, 10% to 12% for softwoods.

The rub is that wood at 3% moisture content looks and feels very much like wood at 23% moisture content, or any percentage in between. The only way to be sure of the moisture content of a particular board is to measure it with a moisture meter or to know positively that it was dried to 5% to 10% moisture content and maintained in storage conditions similar to its final application.

I suspect that your flooring was supplied at too high a moisture content. Selling properly dried and maintained dry wood is the responsibility of the building-materials distributor; however, the fault for poor flooring performance is often traceable to factors beyond the control of the manufacturer and dealer. Job-site moisture problems frequently cause shrinkage and swelling. Think objectively about the actual conditions on your job before assigning blame.

One of the most dangerous places to store finish lumber is in an unfinished, unheated or uncooled house. Framing lumber, plywood, insulation, concrete, plaster, drywall and joint compound all absorb many gallons of water during processing, storage and installation. Once the house is enclosed, the hundreds of gallons of moisture in the building materials evaporate inside the house and, if allowed, share their water

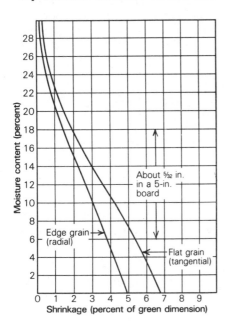

Shrinkage (percent of green dimension)

with finish lumber. Short of allowing several months for the project to dry out after construction, something must be done to protect the finish lumber before and during installation. Flooring installed well before final occupation will shrink or expand, and the problem may not be the manufacturer's fault.

Wood species for flooring

I have been harvesting trees on my land to mill into wide-board hardwood flooring. Unfortunately I have no oak, but I was planning to use beech and hard maple for major traffic areas and red maple for areas that get lighter use. My other choices include ash, black and yellow birch and hickory, but I've heard that some of these species can warp and twist worse than others. I am thinking of cutting the boards 5 in. wide. Do you foresee any problems with this, and should I relieve the backs of the boards? —*Vince Amoroso, New Albany, Pa.*

Paul Fuge, a millworks operator in Shelton, Conn., replies: Few hardwood species are unacceptable for use as flooring provided they are properly dried and precisely milled. The problem is usually that the moisture content of the flooring is too high when it's laid, or that the conditions of the installation are extreme, such as a damp crawl space under the flooring or a sunspace that heats and dries the air excessively.

Hardwood flooring should be dried to 8% moisture content before it's milled. Then spread it out in the room where it will be laid for a week or so before installation. All the framing,

plastering and drywall work should be completed and allowed to dry before the room is stocked with flooring.

A 5-in. milling width will work nicely. Back-relieving the material will provide air channels for removing seasonal moisture. Although this is a good practice anytime, it is particularly important in applications where the basement or crawl space below is likely to remain moist.

Not having oak isn't a tragedy. Beech and hard maple are excellent flooring materials. Beech, however, tends to twist and warp as it dries; double the number of stickers you normally use for better results.

Ash and hickory are both ring-porous woods like oak, but they have a more interesting heartwood-sapwood relationship. And pignut hickory is hard to beat for flooring. It is tough like oak, but machines well and has a delicate grain pattern like walnut and butternut. Don't count out soft maple, either. It is easy to work and often has interesting mineral coloration and curly figure. The birch, however, should be used for trim and cabinet work.

Removing linoleum

We are trying to remove linoleum and its glue from a tamarack wood floor in our 50-year-old house. Some of the stuff came up by just peeling. Then we tried an old iron and a putty knife, but that just turned into a sticky mess. Please give us an economical way to remove the linoleum. —*Tim Boden, Sandpoint, Idaho*

Wood-flooring specialist Don Bollinger replies: I don't have any quick-fix methods for removing sheet vinyl, linoleum or VAT (vinyl asbestos tile) from wood flooring. I don't know anybody who does. There was a time when many hardwood flooring companies would do this type of work. They simply did the best they could with scrapers and heat guns or blowtorches, and then revved up their floor sanders. That was before anyone was aware of the dangers of asbestos poisoning. A high percentage of existing vinyl and linoleum contains asbestos.

It would be a delightful surprise to find genuine linoleum at the bottom of numerous layers of vinyl or VAT. Linoleum was made of dried linseed oil and wood flour over burlap or canvas (no asbestos). It was rarely glued to the floor and should lift up (taking all succeeding layers with it) rather easily by slipping a stiff putty knife between it and the wood floor.

The best recommendation I can give anyone who's about to remove vinyl, linoleum or VAT is to test it first for asbestos. Your local EPA authority can do it for you or tell you where you can have it done. It will only take a few days and cost around $25 to $30. Be sure to test both the sheet goods and the adhesive for asbestos.

If the report comes back negative, have at the floor with dry ice, torches or sanders. The fastest method I've ever heard of for removing the vinyl, linoleum or VAT is by freezing, though you should still count on doing some scraping or sanding to remove adhesive residue.

Freezing is best done with dry ice. My favorite approach is to use an old metal flat-bottomed tray with wooden handles. Don't use an aluminum tray; it's a poor conductor. Wood handles provide excellent insulation against the cold. Place a chunk of dry ice in the tray and set it on the material to be removed. Very shortly the sheet goods will freeze solid and pull loose from the wood. You will be able to shatter it or chip up the pieces.

If the report comes back positive, get all the information you can on asbestos removal. Probably the safest way to proceed (to remove and dispose of it) is to hire a contractor who has been certified by local environmental authorities. Do not, under any circumstances, have an uncertified mechanic do the job or do it yourself without the proper training. Asbestos fibers can stay airborne for incredibly long periods of time, even in rooms with almost no air circulation.

If you decide to remove it yourself, first take any courses or training available in your area for asbestos removal. Wear a respirator with particle catchers for trapping asbestos fibers, as well as disposable gloves and coveralls. And you should dispose of all outer clothing (including gloves and the mask's filter) in the same manner as the material removed from the floor. Proper disposal of asbestos fibers is crucial. Contact your local EPA authorities for the recommended procedures. For additional information, call the Consumer Products Safety Commission (800-638-2772).

Noisy stairs

What can be done to quiet extremely noisy wooden stairs on a 40-year-old home? Is it possible that finishing nails driven into the treads would help? How about screws and plugs, or glue?
—Martin Jelenc, Madison, Wis.

Consulting editor Bob Syvanen replies: The solution for fixing a noisy stairway depends on how it is constructed. Surface nailing the treads would be a cheap quick fix, but you would eventually hear the squeaks again. Screwing the treads to the carriages and plugging the holes is a better fix, but the stair may also squeak again. A first-class job can best be done by exposing the stairway construction to find the problem causing the noise. Whatever part of the stair that has failed can then be easily repaired, and any weak spots can be strengthened to prevent future breakdown.

In carriage stairs (drawing below), squeaks occur when the tops of the carriages that the treads rest on are not in the same plane, allowing the treads to shift when weight is applied. When I use this type of construction, I make sure that I shim the

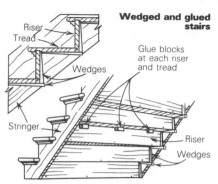

Wedged and glued stairs

was not meant to be nailed—the wedges, blocks and glue are what holds it together.

When nailing hardwood, predrilling is a must. I use a sharpened finish nail, the same size as the nails to be used, as a drill bit. Cutting the head off the nail makes it fit better in the drill chuck.

Leveling a subfloor

I'm building a house from used materials. The subflooring of the upstairs bedrooms and bath consists of weathered 2x6s laid across 6x12 beams on 4-ft. centers, and exposed below. The 2x6s are not T&G, and their thickness varies by as much as ¼ in. I plan to cover them with ¾-in. plywood as a base for carpeting. How do I deal with the swales in the floor, and how should the plywood be fastened?
—*Jo Anne Garrett, Baker, Nev.*

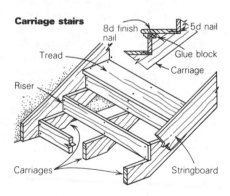

Carriage stairs

treads so they're equally supported at all bearing points, or shave down the carriages to do the same thing.

The routed, wedged, and glued stairway (drawing, above right) squeaks when the glue blocks and wedges have loosened. The remedy, of course, is to reglue all blocks and wedges. This type of construction

Doug Amsbary, a contractor in Franconia, N. H., replies: If you have not already laid down the 2x6s, separate them into two piles—thicker ones and thinner ones. Then when you nail them down, use the thicker pieces for every other course so that the ¾-in. plywood will rest on these and span the thinner boards between. You can minimize the variation in height with this approach.

If the 2x6s are already down, you will have to find the dips and humps with a straightedge and correct them. Use a straight 6-ft. board or level at right angles to the 2x6s. Check for extreme high and low spots. Fill the low spots with shim strips ripped out of 2x material. Glue and nail them down. Plane down the high areas. If the situation is really bad, you could use either a rented floor sander equipped with open-coat sandpaper or a portable power planer. Either way, watch out for embedded nails or you'll be buying yourself new sanding discs, a new set of knives or a sharpening job at the very least.

Once the floor is relatively flat, lay the long edge of the plywood at 90° to the 2x6s, and stagger the end seams by several feet. You could also use thinner plywood if it isn't spanning any serious dips in the floor.

Using a Phillips bit in a variable-speed electric drill, screw the plywood down with 2-in. drywall screws placed on a 10-in. grid. Gluing the plywood down using an adhesive that has a filling capacity is also good practice. Continental Chemical 3C Brand's #202 construction adhesive works well. Run a ¼-in. bead on the centers of the highest 2x6 planks.

Brownstone breakdown

Our bow-front brick attached townhouse has steep brownstone entry stairs that lead up from the street to the main (second) floor. Although the exterior walking surface of the stairs appears to be in good condition, the underside silts constantly, creating a terrible mess in the lower vestibule. I've tried using Val Oil and Thompson's Water Seal on it, but gravity is against me. What do you recommend? —*Virginia Glennon, Boston, Mass.*

F. Neale Quenzel, a restoration architect in West Chester, Pa., replies: Not only is gravity working against you, but so is the brownstone, which is highly absorptive. First, you should check the walking surface of the stairs. Make sure that the stair treads slope away from the house and the risers.

Next, check the joints between the stair parts and the house for leaks. These joints should be caulked. The outer mortar pointing, which cracks more often than not when exposed, should be raked back to a depth of half the width of the joint. Then the joint should be caulked. This will keep the water out of the interface between the joints.

Next, before you apply the water barrier, scrape off all of the loose material on the underside of the stair. This should be done with a wood scraper followed by a natural-bristle scrub brush. Then apply the sealer to all exposed surfaces, inside and out. The finish you use needs to repel weather, but also allow the stone to breathe. The best sealer we've used is Chem-Trete (Dynamit Nobel of America, Inc., 10 Link Drive, Rockleigh, N. J. 07647).

Radiant heating under bricks

A low-temperature water radiant-heating system, using plastic tubing in the floor and a conventional hot-water heater, seems ideal for comfort and for adaptability to solar hot-water systems.

In New Mexico, a common floor system is full-size brick pavers with butted joints, laid on a 1-in. to 2-in. sand bed directly on grade. It is an attractive floor that is really quite economical. Can radiant tubing be placed in such a sand bed? Would the conductivity of sand be adequate? Would the tubing be sufficiently protected from damage? —*Isaac Benton, Albuquerque, N. Mex.*

Michael Luttrell, a solar consultant in Napa, Calif., replies: Polybutylene pipe can certainly be placed in a sand bed beneath brick pavers. We have conducted a few tests of such an installation, and found that sand, with air voids, provides only half as much heat transfer as concrete. We generally get five to ten times as much heat as is actually required to heat a house (100 to 150 Btu/sq. ft.) with pipe in concrete. If the heat load is modest, then sand might be adequate. If not, consider doubling up on the amount of pipe and running the system at higher temperatures. In preparing the bed, moisten the sand and use a mechanical compactor to reduce the number of air voids.

I'd be concerned about heat loss into the ground. We generally use a well-drained gravel base under a 4-in. slab on grade, and cover the edges of the slab with 2 in. of rigid insulation. If you install the pipe on grade and have moist soil and cold winters, the heat loss into the ground and to the perimeter could be high.

There will also be the challenge of holding the springy pipe in place while installing the sand and bricks. Remember that the system works best when the pipes are close to the surface. We always anchor the pipe at 2-ft. to 3-ft. intervals by tying it to the reinforcing steel, or (over wood) nailing it down with plastic clips. Clearly, the pipe is best installed in concrete. You needn't worry about leaks; they are extremely rare.

Radiant-floor systems work well with solar, but not necessarily with batch-type solar systems. The reason is that radiant-floor piping needs flow, thus a pump. However, with the pipe in concrete and a masonry floor surface, the floor will deliver heat with water temperatures as low as 85°F, practically doubling the efficiency of a solar collector compared to baseboards or fan coils, which require 120°F to 140°F. But a pump system will still be necessary.

Radiant-floor heating system

We have a compacted-rock floor with 1 in. of rigid insulation about 8 in. from the surface. We plan on putting a vapor barrier on the rock and 1½-in. brick on top of another 2½ in. of rock or grout. Our plan is to install hot-water pipes in this floor system. What is the state-of-the-art approach? —*Mick Lamont, Portland, Ore.*

Michael Luttrell, a solar consultant in Napa, Calif., replies: Consider using polybutylene, a plastic pipe developed by Shell Oil Co., with a rating of 100 psi at 180°F, in a ½-in. I.D. size. The pipe is superior to copper and EPDM in numerous ways—it won't corrode, has a low head drop, requires no connectors in the floor, is hand-bendable into a 6-in. radius, and has a high abrasion resistance. It also costs much less than copper.

Polybutylene is available from most plumbing-supply houses. Be sure it is stamped "100 psi @ 180°F" and "ASTM D-3309." It is available in 100-ft. or 1,000-ft. rolls. We use brass insert fittings with copper-alloy rings, but since that requires a special calibrated crimping tool, you might want to use any of several types of compression fittings or hose clamps. Ask your supplier what's available.

Install the tubing within an inch or so of the surface, pressurize it to 60 to 100 psi and check for leaks. Hold the pressure while you cover the tubing with rock and compact it. If the rocks have sharp edges, cover the tubing with a little concrete and chicken wire, or encase it in coarse sand. Polybutylene tubing doesn't conduct heat well into the air, so contact between the tubing and a solid material is important. Don't make the runs (loops) longer than 200 ft. to 300 ft. Attach parallel loops to a manifold in a convenient space with balancing valves. You should not have tubing joints in the floor. Flow rates can be very low, 1 gal. per min. per 1,000 sq. ft. of floor area.

This application is an innovative and experimental approach that doesn't yet have the approval of model-code agencies, to my knowledge. Many states now approve polybutylene for various uses, including potable water, but since the material is gaining acceptance slowly, you should check with your local building department. You increase your chances there if you have the tubing on a low-pressure closed loop with a heat exchanger.

If you couple this system directly with a solar collector so you can use "low-grade" heat at 80°F to 85°F to charge the mass and heat the space, you will nearly double the efficiency of the collectors, as compared to the 160°F to 180°F required for baseboards or fan coils. This method provides a natural and "invisible" form of heat at below-body temperatures; you cannot feel the heat, but it heats the space nonetheless.

Radiant-heat requirements

I would like some information on placing radiant-heating pipes under 140 sq. ft. of ceramic floor tile, which we are planning to install in our superinsulated timber-frame home. We plan to use gypcrete below the tile about 1 in. to 1½ in. thick, in which we will embed the pipe, placed on plywood on 2x6 T&G decking. The heated water will be pumped from the coils in our wood cookstove.

We need to know the type and pressure classification of the pipe and its spacing and diameter, as well as the pump size and water temperature.—*William H. Goodhue, Nordland, Wash.*

Michael Luttrell, a solar consultant in Napa, Calif., replies: For your floor consider polybutylene, a plastic pipe developed by Shell Chemical Co. It has high temperature and pressure ratings (180°F at 100 psi) and is available in 1,000-ft. rolls (no joints in the concrete). It is non-corrosive and can be easily bent by hand. Use ½-in. I.D. tubing, and vary the spacing from 6 in. o. c. by windows and outside doors to 12 in. o. c. in the center of the room. Lay out a spiral or zigzag pattern so tubing will not cross over itself in the floor. Keep each pipe loop of equal length, and from 200 ft. to 250 ft.

long; connect all the pipes to a manifold outside the concrete.

Fasten down the tubing with plastic clips to the plywood decking, pressure-test to 100 psi, and maintain 50 psi to 60 psi during the pour. Watch the pressure gauge carefully while placing concrete for any indications of leakage or damage to the tubing. Do not allow water to freeze in the tubing; it may expand and crack the concrete. Once the concrete has set, release the pressure and connect the manifold to the permanent system.

Using a woodstove for a system like this is tricky. Woodstove combustion temperatures can go above 1,000°F and can generate steam. Be sure to install a pressure and temperature relief valve close to the stove and vent to a safe place outside. In order to handle temperature surges, install a 20-gal. or 30-gal. surge tank in the line to the floor. For pumps, we prefer ⅓₅-hp bronze or stainless-steel pumps.

To mix the water going into the floor to the proper temperatures (90°F to 100°F, depending on heat loss) use a 1-in. tempering valve. You might also consider installing some temperature-monitoring equipment that would allow you to fine-tune the whole operation.

Wood over a radiant slab

I am bidding a renovation job that has a radiant-heated concrete slab. The present flooring is carpet over asphalt tile. The owners would like hardwood flooring. Is this feasible? I'm afraid that the wood would shrink and crack because of the heat; and, second, **that it might lower the effectiveness of the heating system.**
—*Paul Mahany, Bethesda, Md.*

Michael Luttrell, a solar consultant in Napa, Calif., replies: Wood flooring can be used quite successfully over radiant slabs, with several important reservations. If it is an older floor with copper or steel tubes, the system will have a distinctly limited life. In my experience most of these floors develop their first leak within 25 years, and they are often no longer usable after 40 years. Putting a wood floor down over such a slab would be foolish.

Another consideration is the operating temperature of the system. Many older radiant floors were designed for 120°F to 150°F. In this temperature range, I too would be concerned about the durability of a wood floor. Newer floors are often designed to operate at 80°F to 100°F, a range in which wood floors and their finishes survive nicely and don't inhibit the radiant effect. The conductivity of wood even when kiln-dried is quite high. Thin parquet or tongue-and-groove strip flooring works best, although I have also had excellent results with 1⅛-in. oak planks. Always use kiln-dried wood with a low moisture content (7% to 8%), and fit it as tightly as possible to reduce the chance of big shrinkage gaps appearing once the heating system dries out the wood even more.

If the floor is operating at high temperatures and you still want to put down hardwood, there are two possible solutions. If the renovation also includes heavy insulation, super-efficient windows and other conservation features that drastically reduce the heat loss from the house, then you might be able to lower the operating temperature of the present system. Or you could abandon the present system, lay new polybutylene tubing over the existing slab, install sleepers and lay a floor over the new tubing.

In order to run the floor at low temperatures, consider using a variable temperature control to maintain the lowest possible water temperature in proportion to outside temperature. There are many controls of this type on the market. A high-temperature safety aquastat, like the Penn 19-ABC-4 (Johnson Controls Inc., Control Products Div., 1302 E. Moore St., Goshen, Ind. 46526), can be set to turn off the pump should the floor temperature exceed the limit set on the aquastat.

Coverings for radiant floors

I will soon be building a house on a south-facing spit of land on Chesapeake Bay, and I plan to have radiant-slab floors. I was hoping to use wood over the concrete, with Oriental rugs for accent in other areas. Is this a good idea? —*Robert C. Livingstone, Petersburg, Va.*

Dennis Adelman, a hydronic consultant and systems designer in Durango, Colo., replies: In theory, any floor covering over a radiant slab will make it more difficult for heat to reach the room. In practice, a floor covering with an R-value of up to 1 is allowable over a 3-in. to 4-in. slab. This means that most tile, marble or stone won't be a problem. Even carpeting is possible, as long as it isn't excessively thick or underlaid with a heavy rubber pad.

This rule of thumb lets you use a wood plank, strip or parquet that is ¾ in. thick. It should be bonded to the slab with a mastic that will withstand radiant-floor heating (RFH) temperatures (tar-based adhesives will not work). The wood should be well seasoned, with a moisture content less than 8%.

You will need to figure in floor coverings when you size your RFH system. Basically, you have to modify the emissivity coefficient of the slab, and then multiply that figure by the heat output that the system needs to supply. For example, the coefficient of a 4-in. slab is 1; a ¾-in. wood-parquet covering adds .75 for a total of 1.75. If your room-by-room heat-loss calculation says that 2,000 watts are needed to keep the house warm at design conditions, then you would multiply 2,000 by 1.75 to get a total of 3,500 watts. This figure represents the system capability that is needed in the loop at the bottom of the slab. Ceramic tile over a slab (with a coefficient of 1.15) would require 2,300 watts in the same room.

As a general rule, I even allow for furniture, throw rugs and appliances by using a correction factor that slightly oversizes the system. It's easy enough to turn the heat down if you decide to sell the furniture later on.

Adhesive for a solar floor

I'm setting tile on a concrete pad to maximize solar heat absorption in a greenhouse. I was planning to use mastic, but something just didn't feel right about it. The mastic would seem to be an insulator, impeding heat transfer between

the tile and concrete. Is a mortar bed recommended? Will a layer of mastic affect efficiency?
—*Neal W. Thielke, Llano, N. Mex.*

Tilesetter Michael Byrne replies: Because the adhesive layer is so thin (³⁄₃₂ in. to ⅛ in.), the R-value for whatever adhesive you use is insignificant. Few studies have been made, but I think most manufacturers would assign the R-value of masonry to any thinset adhesive. The main issue on a solar-gain floor installation is suitability. Since floors of this type require a thick concrete slab or mortar bed as a base and heat sink, thinset mortar wins out over ready-to-use mastics by providing a stronger, more compatible bond and higher compressive strength.

Finishing a teak floor

We have teak flooring in our entry, hall, dinette and kitchen. Someone told me that ship decks are made of teak because it "takes care of itself." What kind of finish should I use, and how frequently will it need to be renewed?
—*Barb Bechtler, Mansfield, Ohio*

Don Bollinger, a wood-flooring specialist in Seattle, Wash., replies: One of teak's most prized qualities is its high resistance to deterioration, even from salt water. I particularly like to see it used in entries, where a good deal of moisture is likely to accumulate.

Generally, the higher the oil content of wood, the greater its resistance to deterioration. I have found Burmese teak to be the best on this account. Unfortunately, this high oil content can also make teak a poor recipient for surface finishes, such as urethanes, varnishes and Swedish finishes, because the natural oil keeps the film from bonding to the wood. This doesn't mean that you can't finish the stuff, but you do have to take longer preparing the surface.

The person who told you that ship decks made of teak take care of themselves is very nearly correct. The folks I know who work on teak decks use three basic methods for cleaning and restoring. The first is sanding, recaulking between the boards and then refinishing with a good marine spar varnish, urethane varnish or a penetrating sealer. I like teak oil or tung oil for this step. The other two approaches don't use a finish. One is to scrub the teak with bleach or other caustic liquids to make it uniformly white, and the other uses high-pressure hot water for cleaning.

The last two approaches remove most stains but are totally dependent upon the teak's natural resistance to retard the deck's deterioration; I wouldn't suggest using them inside a house.

I have three favorite finishes for interior teak floors. All require careful sanding. The first is the so-called Swedish finish. As with any finish that builds up on the surface, it's important to "rake" teak with rags dampened with lacquer thinner or denatured alcohol to remove excess oil on and right below the surface of the wood. As soon as these solutions have dried, apply the first coat of finish. You can continue with a second or third coat without any further preparations. Swedish is not a good finish for Burmese teak because of its high oil content. Even when the floor is thoroughly raked, the finish can lift after·a while.

The second finish that I like is a penetrating sealer and wax. I generally use Dura-Seal and Dura-Finish, which are made by the Minwax Company (102 Chestnut Ridge Place, Montvale, N. J. 07645).

The final and most natural method of finishing teak is penetrating oil, such as teak oil or tung oil. I find at least three to six coats are necessary. You will probably have to re-coat every three to six months, especially in high-traffic areas.

The last two finishes can be spot-cleaned quite easily by light hand-sanding, using the same grit sandpaper as the final sanding in the refinishing process. When you've gotten rid of the stains or soil, use the sandpaper to feather in on all sides so that there's no abrupt line between the repaired area and the surrounding floor. Then simply re-peat the finishing process from the beginning. Whether your final coat is Dura-Finish or a penetrating oil, it's a good idea to coat the entire floor with it. The Swedish finish doesn't spot-repair well, but it is very flexible and durable, and should require less maintenance.

Refinishing an old teak floor

Our house has a teak plank floor in the living room and dining room; rumor has it that the wood came off an old battleship that was scrapped after World War I. The varnish finish is worn and dull. I'm sure that thorough sanding and refinishing would restore the highlights of the wood. Is this a job I could do myself? I've used a big floor sander before, but never on teak. Is teak sawdust harmful

to inhale, and must a finer grade of abrasive paper be used before finishing? Lastly, what kind of finish should I use to duplicate the original battleship finish?
—*Paul Martin, Lakeville, Conn.*

Ted Ewen, a restoration specialist in Scarsdale, N. Y., replies: Unbelievable as it may seem, teak from scrapped naval vessels did find its way into many houses after World War I. You can refinish the floor yourself, although some people are allergic to teak dust. Use a good filter mask. Coarse belts, usually 20-grit, should be used only to remove the finish quickly. Next, use 36-grit to smooth the surface of the wood and take out any deep scratches left by the coarse abrasive. A final sanding with 80-grit should give you a surface that is ready for a new finish.

Once the sanding is done, vacuum the floor thoroughly. Also vacuum dust from walls, windows, doors and shelves in the room. For your finish I'd recommend a good-quality varnish like Benjamin Moore's Benwood one-hour varnish. For the first coat, thin the varnish by adding three pints of pure gum turpentine to each gallon of varnish, about 37% turpentine by volume. Give the room good ventilation, but don't use a fan except as an exhaust in a door or window. Map out your course so you can complete each section of floor without boxing yourself in.

Use a 4-in. wide varnish brush with long bristles and let the finish flow on generously and evenly. Always brush with the planks, not across them. If you have to stop, finish out the plank you're working on to avoid causing a lap mark.

Allow the first coat to dry for at least 48 hours, then sand it lightly with 200-grit paper. The easiest way to do this is with an orbital electric sander. Sand with the grain of the wood and go over the entire floor; all you want to do is remove any small particles that have dried on the surface. Vacuum the floor and you're ready to apply the second coat. This time cut each gallon of varnish with 1½ pints of turpentine. Apply in a generous, even coat as before.

Repeat the sanding operation, this time using 220-grit paper. Then vacuum thoroughly and wipe the entire floor with a tack cloth, a clean rag impregnated with varnish to make it tacky. You may need several tack cloths to complete the job. Now for the final coat. Apply the varnish full strength. Once it dries, you should have a finish that will stand up beautifully for many years.

New-floor protection

For my new floors, I would like to apply a hardener or sealer that will take the abuse of construction traffic, but also be easy to finish at the end of the job. The floor will be tongue-and-groove Douglas fir. What would you recommend?
—*Thomas Hanson, Lakeside, Ariz.*

John Leeke, an architectural woodworker in Sanford, Maine, replies: The general practice in the construction industry is to lay finish floors as one of the last phases of work on a structure. This saves the wear and tear of traffic and mechanical abuse. If there is a compelling reason to lay the finish floor early in the project, the following procedure should be used.

Seal the finish floor with two coats of sanding sealer. Sand lightly after the first coat to cut off any raised grain. This will keep plaster, paint spills and most of the fine white particles of joint-compound dust out of the pores of the wood. Sanding sealer, as the name implies, is easily removed by sanding before finishing the floor. I use an oil-extended alkyd-resin spar varnish for my finish because polyurethanes do not adhere well if any sanding sealer is left in the pores of the wood.

To protect the floor from scuffs and dings, it should be covered with overlapping double layers of heavy building paper or cardboard. Taping the edges may seem like a lot of trouble, but it will keep the tradesmen from tripping over them and tearing up the paper. Even with all this effort, workers on the site should take some precautions when using the floor. Keep a barrel of sawdust handy to soak up spilled paint. However if sawdust is used to clean up any spills, sweep it up and get it outside immediately. Such a mixture can burst into flame by spontaneous combustion.

Water-based floor finishes

I applied a Swedish (Bacca/Glitsa) finish on a new oak floor, and after 15 months I am very pleased with it. However, I don't like endangering my health to install and finish a floor. Recently I've been hearing about water-based urethanes, which are supposedly safer to apply than solvent-based products. Can you tell me more about them? Also, there is talk of eliminating the use of solvent-based

finishes here in California. Do you know anything about this?
—*Gunnar Alquist, Santa Rosa, Calif.*

Don Bollinger, a flooring specialist in Seattle, Wash., replies: The folks at Glitsa American Inc. (327 S. Kenyon, Seattle, Wash. 98108) assure me that their Bacca/Glitsa floor finish is no more toxic than any other solvent-based finish on the market. N-butanol, or butyl alcohol, is the ingredient that prompts concern over the product's health hazard. The Glitsa folks say butyl alcohol has about the same toxicity as rubbing alcohol. Glitsa now has a water-based line of floor finishes, called Artesian Finishes.

Water-based coatings use water as a substitute for some of the solvents (which act as carrying agents for the solids) that they would normally contain. Therefore these coatings contain fewer volatile organic compounds (VOCs) than solvent-based finishes. VOCs are gaseous byproducts of industry that, when released into the atmosphere during the curing process, combine with oxygen in the presence of sunlight and create low-level ozone (smog). Some formulations of water-based finishes have eliminated up to half of the solvents normally used. Although water-based coatings have been around for a long time, most manufacturers are still trying to overcome quality-control problems. Usually these problems are related to drying times, film thickness and durability.

Water-based finishes are less noxious than solvent-based finishes, but they still contain VOCs and you must take adequate precautions when applying them. The absence of offensive odors in most water-based

products creates a false sense of security among many unwitting users. This lack of odor has led some applicators to dispense with proper respirators. In reality, many toxic yet commonly used compounds in coating products (glycol ethers, for example) have little or no odor. Additionally, the odors of many solvents are masked because they have been diluted in water.

In answer to your second question, states that have not complied with ambient air-quality standards set by the Environmental Protection Agency (California is one of them) must develop a state implementation plan to bring their areas into compliance. This plan must meet or exceed standards set by the EPA.

Perhaps because it's one of the worst polluting states, California has taken a very aggressive stand during the past few years. A number of other states have used California's policies as models for their own programs. This past year, California began a test program in major metropolitan areas, targeting architectural coatings for compliance enforcement. Because these coatings are applied at job sites scattered all over the state, the EPA decided to monitor manufacturers, not users. Each product they sampled was rated based on the level (in grams per liter) of VOCs found in it. The EPA recommended a maximum allowable level of VOCs in floor finishes (whether solvent-based or water-based) of 350 grams per liter. California authorities took it upon themselves to enforce a maximum level of 250 grams per liter.

These policies have affected most of the solvent-based finishes and many of the water-based finishes as well. It is interesting to note that finishes sold in quart-size containers or smaller are exempt from the standards. At the present time, most of the finish manufacturers who want to sell in California find themselves reformulating or modifying their products. Some have even resorted to repackaging in quart containers to avoid the standards. Still others are dodging the laws by renaming their products to get them classified into categories with higher VOC allowances.

EPA officials tell me most of these loopholes will be addressed in some fashion in the near future. Meanwhile they are hoping these manufacturers will be spending the additional time they have gained with these practices in developing more efficient coatings.

Gap fillers

Last year I laid a floor of 2x6 yellow pine that was quite green. Now that the wood has dried out, there are lots of cracks between the floor boards. I am planning to stain and varnish (polyurethane) this surface, but I need a good gap filler first. What would you recommend? *—Sarah Chabot, Blacksburg, Va.*

Don Bollinger, a flooring specialist in Seattle, Wash., replies: The problem you're having with shrinkage is common with 2x softwood flooring, and it's a difficult one to avoid. Most 2x flooring needs at least a year of drying before it's stable. In my experience in the Northwest with hemlock car-decking, I've found two or three years is better. But few builders can hold the ma-

terial that long under ideal drying conditions before laying it.

The filler you need has to meet several requirements. First, it has to be able to stand up to floor traffic. It also needs to take stain evenly, sand well and have a similar texture to the wood you are using. It must be flexible enough not to break up during the seasonal expansion and contraction of the wood flooring. I don't know of a filler that does all this. I have tried many products over the years with varying success. Adding the very fine dust that the final sanding of a floor produces to a lacquer base is my favorite. This filler is reliable for texture and sanding qualities, but the dried filler and the flooring will take a stain differently. This produces a less-than-perfect color match, and requires you to keep an ample store of fine sawdust of each of the wood types you might need to fill.

Commercially available pigmented acetone-solvent wood fillers are made specifically for floors and are usually quite durable. There are many brands of this kind of wood filler, and they are all about equally effective. Match the color of the filler to a scrap of flooring that has been stained. Keep the lid on the wood-filler can and keep the can upside down when you are not using it, because the acetone will evaporate very rapidly. Good ventilation is necessary when you work with this stuff.

One comment about using polyurethanes on softwood floors. These plastic finishes, though they are very hard, create a thick film over the surface of the floor, obscuring the grain. They also remain rigid, though bonded to flooring material that is constantly moving. I prefer some of the new Swedish finishes. These products come in gloss, semi-gloss and matte finishes. They help maintain the look of the wood at the same time they seal and protect it. Although the Swedish finishes are not quite as hard as some polyurethanes, they are more resilient and durable. They won't yellow with age, nor will they ever need waxing. I use a single coating of Glitsa over one or two heavy float coats of Bacca. These finishes are made by Glitsa American (327 South Kenyon, Seattle, Wash. 98108). Bacca is a two-part process that has to dry for several hours. A light sanding is required after each coat. Glitsa is used straight from the can, and should be allowed to dry for at least 12 hours.

Chapter 9:

Doors, Windows and Interior Trim

Seam problems with laminate

I built my own kitchen countertops of ¾-in. fir plywood and plastic laminate, and ran into a couple of problems. My counter is L-shaped, with the edges thickened with plywood strips to make 1½-in. thick nosings. The plywood substrate had to be seamed, which was done

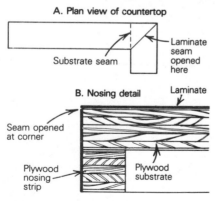

A. Plan view of countertop

Substrate seam

Laminate seam opened here

B. Nosing detail

Laminate

Seam opened at corner

Plywood nosing strip

Plywood substrate

with glue and draw bolts. This seam is strong and has not moved at all. The counter's 12-ft. length (drawing A, at left) made it awkward to move around. The laminate work was done with the counter in place on the cabinets, so stress due to movement was not likely.

I used contact cement and with a paint roller applied one coat on the laminate, two coats on the plywood surface, and three coats on the porous edges of the plywood. My problems occurred a day after I applied the laminate. The laminate edging apparently pulled away from the plywood slightly, leaving part of the top edge of the nosing strip visible (drawing B, at left). This is not very noticeable, but the diagonal seam in the laminate at the corner of the countertop, which I had so carefully made by overlapping the pieces and cutting with my router to get a perfect fit, has now separated almost ¹⁄₁₆ in.

Does the porous edge of the plywood make it a poor substrate, and was it a bad idea to seam the laminate over solid plywood instead of over the seam in the substrate, where it could be drawn together with draw bolts?

—Doug Lewis, Portland, Ore.

Cabinetmaker Paul Levine of Sherman, Conn., replies: Seams are always a problem with plastic laminates and should be avoided whenever possible. Remember that sheets of laminate come slightly oversize (a 4x12 sheet often measures 49 in. by 145 in.). I can't tell from your drawing if the return portion of the counter is less than 49 in. But if it is, and the main counter is less than 145 in. long, one piece of laminate would have covered the whole surface without a seam.

Many times a seamless surface isn't possible. Although it can be risky because of potential water problems, I have centered seams under a sink so that only an inch or so of seam, in front and in back of the sink, is visible. But wherever you locate the seam, you need to be very careful with the core preparation. Never use fir plywood for the substrate. It is expensive, and its wavy surface interferes with a good bond for laminates and veneers.

Particleboard offers a superior bond at about half the cost, and also is available in 12-ft. lengths. If you can't find 12-ft. sheets, use the 4x8s, but don't pull them up with a draw bolt. Bricklay (half-lap) full pieces for the 1½-in. thickness you want

(drawing C, below). If you must conserve materials and can't double up the entire counter, use a 3-in. wide strip all around the perimeter. Also, reinforce the splice in the corner with a large scab underneath the seam (drawing D, below).

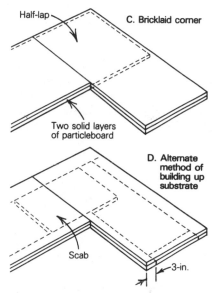

C. Bricklaid corner

Half-lap

Two solid layers of particleboard

D. Alternate method of building up substrate

Scab

3-in.

Your problem is a poor bond. Double-coat everything when laminating plastic. A roller usually lays a thin film of glue. Roller sleeves made especially for contact cement have a short loop-type nap.

Make sure the contact cement is dry before putting the plastic down. None should transfer from the dry surface onto a piece of kraft paper, or onto clean hands. But if you wait too long you can always add another coat.

Good contact must be made when bonding. The best tool for applying pressure is a rubber roller with a handle. If you laminate too seldom to justify buying one, use a block of wood wrapped in felt to protect the plastic. Strike the block with a mallet while sliding it along the surface of the plastic.

Contact cement will sometimes fail to bond properly because it is too cold or too moist. Cold surfaces may partially bond, fooling you, and then lift later. The moisture problem can take two courses. In one the contact cement fails to dry properly, and a poor bond results. In the second, as the contact cement dries, it cools down and causes condensation to form on the surface, preventing a bond. You can usually spot this condition ahead of time. At times I've used a hair dryer (with nonflammable contact cement) to blow off the moisture. If you try this, be careful of overdrying the contact cement, or else you'll have to recoat.

The front edge of the counter must be straight and square to offer a good groundwork for the nosing strip. It's best to double up your countertop thickness first, and then rip the counters to size. This way you're cutting through both layers at once and are assured of a true edge. This ripping must be done before attaching the short side of the L to the main run.

Stress created by laying the counter on cabinets whose tops aren't dead level should not open a well-made seam, but will open up a seam if a poor bond exists. It's also possible that humidity changes in conjunction with a poor bond caused your laminate to shrink and open at the seams. Just like wood, plastic laminate will shrink and swell. Both your laminate and substrate should be stored for several days in the environment where they'll be installed, so they can adjust to the humidity level.

Except for redoing your countertops, I'm not sure there's a solution to your problem. You might try the plastic seam filler available in colors to match plastic laminate.

Hiding finger joints

Do you know of any method of staining or finishing to cover finger joints in a wood handrail and newel post? I recently bought and installed a new handrail and was quite disappointed to find that the birch wood had several finger joints in it. —*Michael Eshleman, Pequea, Pa.*

Wood finisher George Frank replies: Staining is the easiest way to cover the finger joints in your rail and newel post. However, the stain will also mask the grain of the wood. Generally speaking, stain is merely thinned paint, so the thicker you apply it and the less you wipe it down, the more hiding power it has. Another way to conceal joints is to use a very fine pencil brush to paint veining lines over the joint, following the natural grain of the wood as closely as possible. You may want to use this technique in combination with a lighter coat of stain.

New molding on old walls

I have been restoring our old house, trying to retain original materials wherever possible. However, a few pieces of ceiling molding in the living room are missing (in the corner where the ceiling and wall meet). I've sent a sample of the original wood molding out and had new molding matched to it.

When I tried to install the new molding, I found that the old plaster walls are wavy, and that they aren't at right angles to the ceiling. The original molding has shaped itself to this situation, but for the life of me I can't figure out how to install the new molding without gaps between it and either the wall or ceiling. It looks terrible. What can I do? —*John Forrester, Skyland, N. C.*

Ted Ewen, a specialist in historic house restoration, replies: The problem you face in installing the new crown molding is often encountered in old house restoration. From the description of conditions outlined in your letter, I would say you have a choice of two procedures.

The simple route involves cutting the molding to size and nailing it in place as you would for a plumb wall, pressuring it to conform to the wall and ceiling as much as possible in the nailing process. Then fill the gaps carefully with spackle or wallboard compound. Two applications are required, because the compound shrinks as it dries. When the second application is completely dry, sand it until it's smooth.

The second procedure is considerably more work but it results in a more attractive finished appearance and makes new molding blend better with existing molding. Use a carpenter's bevel to transfer the odd wall-ceiling angles to both bearing surface of the molding. Working at intervals along the wall/ceiling intersection, shape the corresponding section of molding with a sharp smoothing plane until the bearing-surface bevel matches the angle of the carpenter's bevel. There will

probably be small variations in the angle at different intervals along the intersection (especially if it is wavy, as you mentioned in your letter). If your molding is slim at the bottom, don't trim off more than about $\frac{1}{16}$ in. (so as not to damage the molding). That doesn't sound like a very large amount, but you'll be amazed at how much it helps the fit.

Test the fit of your beveling work by positioning the molding and checking to see that the trimmed spots match the variations in wall and ceiling surfaces. You can tack the molding in place temporarily, and use a scriber to mark trim areas along the entire length of both wall and ceiling bearing surfaces. When you are satisfied with the fit, nail the molding permanently in place with finishing nails. Any gaps that are still evident can be filled and finished as outlined in the first procedure.

Angling baseboards

I ran into a problem when I tried to install baseboards in my dome house. Most of the corners are not 90°, and to complicate matters, there are also corners where the walls slope and so aren't perpendicular to the floor. I would like to know how to install baseboard on inside and outside corners at angles other than 90°.
—*David M. Levy, Malibu, Calif.*

Consulting editor Bob Syvanen replies: When I have to join baseboard at odd angles, I generally make a few trial cuts until it fits. Outside corners, no matter what the angle, are always bisected bevel cuts. Inside corners should be coped because a mitered cut will open at the joint

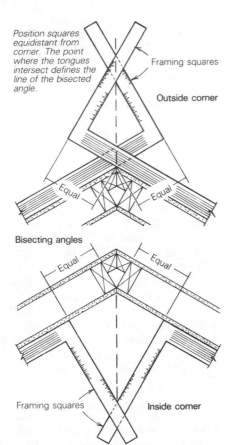

Position squares equidistant from corner. The point where the tongues intersect defines the line of the bisected angle.

Framing squares

Outside corner

Equal Equal

Bisecting angles

Equal Equal

Framing squares Inside corner

As shown below, baseboard on a wall that's not perpendicular to the floor has to be held in the miter

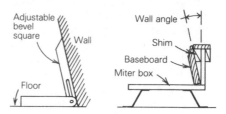

Adjustable bevel square

Wall

Floor

Wall angle

Shim

Baseboard

Miter box

box at the same angle as the wall. Use an adjustable bevel square to pick up this angle. Any means of shimming the baseboard in the miter box will do.

Poplar for trim

I have a lot of poplar trees growing on my land that are large, straight and nearly clear. I am thinking of cutting them for 4x6 floor joists that will be exposed, or I might saw these trees into boards, dry them and use them for trim. I've been unable to find strength values for poplar, so I'm using the figures for white pine because the two species seem comparable. Am I on the right track? I've also noticed that some of my poplar is stained brown at the heart. These areas aren't really punky, but I suspect rot, knowing that poplar is prone to this.

—*Hank Read, Warren, Maine*

Paul Fuge, a lumber dealer and millworks operator in Shelton, Conn., replies: The poplar you have growing on your land is likely *Liriodendron tulipifera,* the tree with the tulip-like flowers in the spring.

Tulip poplar is straight and clear, readily sawn and shaped, accepts

when it is nailed. In either case, an inside corner or an outside corner, you have to begin by bisecting the angle. The reason for bisecting the outside corner is obvious. Bisecting the inside corner reveals the shape of the coping cut.

Bisecting angles by swinging arcs with a pair of dividers is good, but I like to use a pair of framing squares or combination squares, as shown in the drawing above. It's fast, and those are the tools that are usually at hand on the job site. After bisecting the angle and marking its centerline on the floor, I hold a squared-off piece of baseboard in place and transfer the angle to it.

nails without trouble, and holds paint well. It works as easily as pine, but finishes to a greater degree of elegance. Tulip poplar is often used as trim, but I wouldn't use it for beams if there were a readily available alternative like oak or the more typical softwoods. It will work if it's all you've got.

Your idea of comparing it in strength to white pine is correct. Tulip poplar is not very strong, but much more troublesome is the tendency of poplar beams to spring (become very warped) when sawn. This is annoying to say the least if you're trying to use them as joists. Saw extra material and place crowns up and bows opposing each other; hold them in place with props or solid bridging until the floor is nailed off.

The dark brown or black parts that are soft are rot; light-brown coloration is normal and will not affect strength. The beams will have no natural rot resistance, so keep them above grade and dry. If you do decide to mill your poplar into beams, consider taking advantage of its workability to carve some designs in them.

Cutting curved trim

I want to case out a window whose head (or top) is a full semicircle. Its radius is 18 in., and it is trimmed on the inside with molding that has the profile shown in the drawing below. How do I cut this trim and then make the pieces fit? —*Mike Wood, Arlington, Tex.*

Stephan Sewall and David Stenstrom, architectural woodworkers in Portland, Maine, reply: Making casing for a curved window is not an easy task. It involves making a trammel that will suspend the router above the work and allow it to pivot from a single point in order to define a curve. Even with this shopmade setup, a considerable amount of hand work is required.

The trammel consists of a paddle-like base made of 3/4 or 4/4 stock with a slot in the handle that holds a long extension (drawing below). The router is mounted onto the wide end of this paddle. The extension slides in the slot in the handle of the base to allow you to adjust for different arcs and is secured with two small

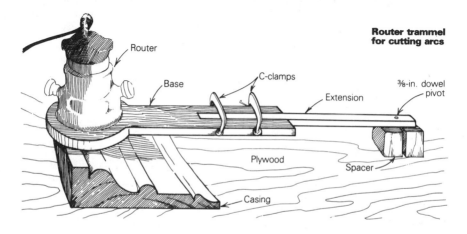

Router trammel for cutting arcs

Router

Base

C-clamps

Extension

⅜-in. dowel pivot

Plywood

Spacer

Casing

C-clamps. You should drill a ⅜-in. hole near the other end of the extension to accept a dowel pivot point later on. Even though it's adjustable, the length of this jig and the location of the hole for the pivot point have to be based on the radius of your circle and the width of your casing.

Use a half-sheet of inexpensive plywood to lay out the outline of the curved casing, as shown in the drawing below. The center of the circle should be marked clearly; it will

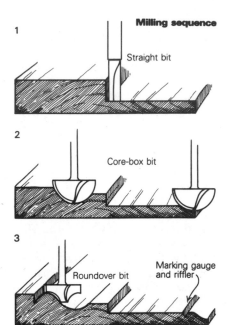

Milling sequence

1 Straight bit

2 Core-box bit

3 Roundover bit   Marking gauge and riffler

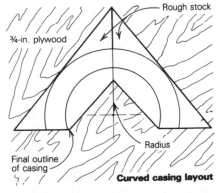

Rough stock

¾-in. plywood

Radius

Final outline of casing

Curved casing layout

be used as the pivot for the router jig. This casing can be made in two pieces with a joint at the top of the arc. You can measure for the pieces of blank stock you'll need for the curved casing directly from the drawing on the plywood. The ends of the casing that meet the straight sections should be left long, but the cuts for the joints can be marked from the drawing when you're ready to make these crosscuts.

Now draw a plumb line from the pivot point up through the high point of the arc. Using this line, the two pieces of raw stock can be set down on the plywood one at a time and marked for the angle of their joint. Once these are cut, they can be screwed carefully to the plywood

from the back. Don't put a screw in any area where wood will be wasted, and make sure that the joint between the two pieces is tight to eliminate tearout by the router bit.

Once the stock is in position for milling, drill a ⅜-in. hole through the plywood at the pivot point and drive a ⅜-in. dowel 3 in. long into the hole. Mount the extension arm on the dowel with a spacer in between to hold the base of the router just slightly above the work. The first router passes will cut the curved outline of the casing (drawing above). A ½-in. straight-edged router bit is best for this. It may take two passes to get through the thickness of the casing on each edge if the casing is thicker than the length of the bit's cutting edge. With the same bit, a flat can be cut in the casing from the center bead out to the inside curve. An appropriate-size core-box bit can be used next to cut the concave curve on the inside edge of the casing. The core-box bit can also be used on the other concave curve on the outside of the center bead.

The only other cut that's practical to make with the router is the convex curve at the outside of the casing. A roundover bit (with the pilot removed) can be used for this. Depending on how much time and money you want to spend and how exact these replicas have to be, you could grind your own router bits to conform more closely to the profile of the original casing.

From now on it's pretty much handwork. A marking gauge can be used to establish the two V-grooves on the casing. They can be deepened with a V-shaped riffler. The rest must be carved freehand. The center bead can be chiseled close to round, then sanded to shape.

Don't remove the casing from the plywood when you have finished milling it. Leave it in place to make the crosscuts on the casings where they will join the side casing. Make any final adjustments in these joints by dry-fitting the side casing to the round head casings, and making sure that the profiles match and the transition is smooth.

Insulating a dome skylight

How much dead-air space needs to be incorporated in a plastic-bubble skylight to reach R-30? Is there a better way to insulate?
—*Gregory Gran,*
Angels Camp, Calif.

Glenn Tucker, a solar consultant in Bethel, Conn., replies: The effective R-value of a 1-in. thick dead-air

space between glazings at a 45° slope ranges from about 0.82 to 1.12, depending on the mean air temperature within the space and the temperature difference from one side of the space to the other. As either the mean temperature or the temperature difference increases, the R-value decreases slightly. Air spaces ¾ in. to 2 in. thick give the best R-value, with performance dropping off noticeably for thicknesses less than ½ in.

To achieve an R-30 skylight with outside air temperature at 0°F, you will need roughly 28 ¾-in. air spaces. While 28 layers of glazing would provide great insulating value, it would be costly, impractical within the depth of the skylight and result in a drastic reduction of incoming solar gain. Even if you use low-iron

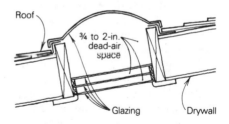

glass, which transmits about 93% of the light striking it, the overall system would block out over 80% of the incident solar energy.

A better system is to use two or three glazing layers and an opaque, high R-value insulating shutter or shade at night. Then you get the best of both worlds—good daylighting when the sun is out and minimal heat loss when it is not. If insulating panels are not practical because of the skylight's location, then consider using three or four glazings as a reasonable compromise.

If your skylight has three or more properly sealed glazings, condensation will not be a problem, except in extremely moist environments. Condensation on the inner surfaces will occur only when the temperature of that surface is below the dew-point temperature of the inside air. As you add more glazings, the innermost surface becomes warmer and warmer, and condensation problems become negligible.

Drafty skylights

A cool draft flows down from the two Velux skylights in my bedroom. I finally realized that warm air in the room was coming in contact with the large glass surface behind the shade (the window covering) at the top, losing its heat, and therefore dropping to the bottom of the shade as cold air. (I believe that this is called reverse chimney effect.)

The window opening could be completely closed off by insulating panels to solve the problem, but I'm worried that installing fabric-covered panels in a living space would be a hazard. Also, some window coverings require a valance secured to the top of the trim. This would cover the woodwork, and I want to leave my beautiful oak trim exposed. Can you offer any other solutions to my problem?
—Blaine Maus, Walpole, Mass.

Larry Medinger, who designs and builds energy-efficient homes in Ashland, Ore., replies: You are right in assuming the problem to be a cascade of cooled room air falling from the cold inner surface of your skylights. However, your concern for

the hazard of fabric-covered panels is unfounded. There are plenty of sources of flammable material in the typical room. Fabric is a lot safer than most of the vinyls and plastics in carpets and furniture. The insulating material of the panel should be a phenolic foam, which is much less flammable than urethane and when burned is no more toxic than wood. Phenolic foam tends to crumble more easily than urethane foams, so build your panels with some kind of backing or support. One of the companies that produces phenolic-foam products is Koppers Company, Inc. (1900 Koppers Bldg., Pittsburgh, Pa. 15219).

If your skylights are beyond arm's reach from the floor, or if they are over an inconvenient area such as a bed or a balcony, consider some method of sealing them that operates by a rope-and-pulley system. There are electrically operated systems that might be adapted; Window Quilt (Appropriate Technology Corp., Box 975, Brattleboro, Vt. 05301) and Four Seasons Greenhouses (425 Smith St., Farmingdale, N. Y. 11735) are two suppliers of such systems. If the skylights are within reach, simple removable insulating panels would be best, as long as storing them during the day isn't a problem.

There is really no surface-mounted, remote-control system that will not cover your oak trim to some extent. If it is practical for you to open the ceiling back to the framing stage, you can install a sliding panel system, where the insulated cover slides into a pocket built in the ceiling. Then you can refinish and retrim the skylight area and enjoy the trim unobscured.

Codes for skylight glass

There is a lack of consensus over the use of tempered versus laminated glass in skylights, and recently the Council of American Building Officials (CABO) voted not to allow unscreened tempered glass in residential skylights. What are the current code requirements for skylight glazing?
—*Fielding R. Bowman, Greenwich, Conn.*

Geoff Cahoon, a glazing consultant in Boulder, Colo., replies: Let me start with a few definitions. Tempered glass is glass that has been heat-strengthened (heating strengthens glass just as it does steel). Once it has been tempered, it cannot be cut. Laminated glass incorporates a layer of plastic or wire between two sheets of glass. It is much more fragile than tempered glass. Tempered laminated glass is also available, but it is very expensive.

Now, on to your question. While CABO (5203 Leesburg Pike, Suite 708, Falls Church, Va. 22041) did indeed take this action a year ago, they changed their minds later in the year following howls of complaint from the glass industry. Tempered-glass fabricators submitted a survey demonstrating that of 1.5 million glass skylights installed over a five-year period, no injuries occurred in the few cases in which breakage was reported. Now CABO has adopted new rules for the use of tempered glass in residential skylight applications. The current regulation allows the use of unlaminated tempered glass in skylight applications less than 12 ft. off the floor, when the individual lights are not more than 3/16 in. thick and when the skylight is less than 16 sq. ft. in total size. Commercial installations are covered under different codes.

In the meantime, the Building Official and Code Administrators (BOCA, Inc., 4051 West Flossmore Rd., Country Club Hills, Il. 60477-5795) have also adopted this code revision, and the International Conference of Building Officials (ICBO, Inc., 5360 South Workman Mill Rd. Whittier, Calif. 90601) and the Southern Building Code Conference International (SBCCI, Inc. 900 Montclair Rd., Birmingham, Ala. 35213) are in the process of adopting it.

As with any code question, specific answers depend on which code authority (if any) is used by your local building officials as the basis of their code. It's always best to check with a local code inspector on acceptable practices in your area.

Slides for casement windows

In order to weatherseal my casement windows properly, I want them to swing outward. How can I make a system that will let me open and close the windows from the inside? The crank system used on commercial windows seems prohibitively expensive and hard to install on home-built windows.
—*Bones Ownbey, Elmdale, Kan.*

Chris Hallstead, a builder in Free Union, Va., replies: If you don't need screens, your hardware problems are over. A number of durable casement slide-bar operators are sold for less than $10. If you do need screens, here's a way to make your own slide bar. Fasten two lengths of steel stock (about 1/8 in. thick by 1 in. wide) with a rivet, loosely enough so they pivot freely (drawing below). The piece you attach to the window sash must be long enough to project through the stop and allow the slide bar to swing parallel to the sill when it's not in use. The joint at the sash must also allow pivoting because the angle changes with the outward swing of the sash. The second piece

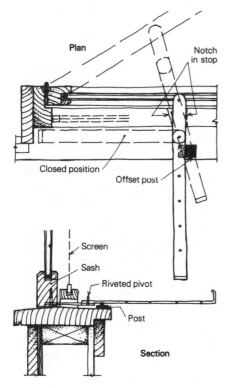

Plan

Notch in stop

Closed position

Offset post

Screen

Sash

Riveted pivot

Post

Section

of steel can be any length that allows the window to open to the desired degree. Holes drilled along its center line provide positive stops. The pivot post can be fabricated from steel, or can be as simple as a finish nail or a wood screw with the head sawn off.

The stop must be notched to allow the slide bar to pass through, and deep enough to allow for raising the slide bar over the post. Ideally, the width of the notch on the inside should be tight to the slide bar to keep insects from entering the window at the mechanism. However, it must flare out at the outside to allow for the angle changes of the slide bar during its operation. For security and weatherproofing, you will still need a casement sash lock mounted on the outboard stile of the sash.

The materials for this system are very inexpensive, but it's long on labor. Another alternative to buying a commercial crank operator is to look around for hardware from salvaged steel casement windows.

Choosing wood for shutters

I need to build interior shutters for a new addition on my home. What wood is best, and what thickness? —*Philip C. Barr, Poquoson, Va.*

Rob Hunt replies: First, concerning the wood, you need to consider the grain and hardness. The clearer and straighter the grain, the easier the wood will be to work, and the less warpage you will end up with. This is especially important for the louvers; if they warp, the project will be ruined. You must also consider the hardness of the wood, since you'll be doing a lot of sanding on shutters that are finished naturally or stained. And the harder the wood, the more difficult it will be to attach the louvers to the dowels with the little staples.

I use white pine and cypress for exterior shutters. White pine, walnut, mahogany or any wood that has a fairly straight grain and is not too hard will do nicely on the interior. As for thickness, I suggest using 1⅛-in. to 1¼-in. thick stiles and rails, if your louvers are to be 1¾ in. wide. If you prefer narrower louvers (say, 1¼ in.), use ¾-in. thick stiles and rails.

Which wood for windows?

I am building a house whose plans call for some custom-made windows and exterior doors. The weather here is changeable and fierce. What type of wood is best suited for this purpose? Would red or white oak be a good material to use? —*Paul Hansen, Salt Lake City, Utah*

John Leeke, an architectural woodworker in Sanford, Maine, replies: I decide what wood will be best for a window and door project in two very different ways. The first, and easier, way is to use the kind of wood that has been used traditionally. If many woodworkers through the years have focused on a certain wood for a particular use, then I trust that collective judgment. Here in New England, the wood for door and window work is eastern white pine, selected for heartwood and straight grain. In Utah the traditional wood of choice might be Douglas fir or redwood. Check at historic-house museums to learn which woods have been used in the past. Then ask at the local millworks to find out what wood is in common use today.

With the second method, I take a completely fresh look at the problem. I consider all of the resources and options to find which wood best suits each situation. This requires a lot more thought and effort, but can result in an additional margin of performance and personal satisfaction (perhaps two of the best reasons for building a custom house).

To begin, consider how the wood must perform. Stability is important because doors and windows must fit closely but be free to move in their frames. In your climate you need a wood that doesn't swell and shrink very much. The softwoods, including the cedars, firs, pines and redwood, are more stable than red or white oak and most other hardwoods, though mahogany and teak are also very stable.

Because paint offers the best protection for exterior woodwork, the wood's ability to hold paint is important. The cedars, redwood and some pines (eastern, western and sugar) are the easiest to keep painted.

Redwood, eastern white pine, Douglas fir, the cedars and white oak are resistant to decay; most western pines and red oak are not.

Next, consider how easy the wood is to work. This is especially important if you're making the windows yourself. If the windows include fancy moldings or curved sections, machinability is important. Machine cuts will be smooth on the pines and mahogany. The cedars, Douglas fir and redwood are splintery. They may require extra sanding and touching up.

Finally, consider cost and availability. Mahogany may be the ideal wood for your window, but its high cost may not fit into your budget. You can get almost any wood on today's commercial market, but the woods used by other woodworkers in your area will be the easiest to get. Special orders may take more time than your schedule allows.

To make the final choice, I often start with a list of available woods. Then I decide which of the characteristics listed are most important. I cross off the woods that don't meet these requirements and end up with one or two woods that have the right balance of properties.

Window design

My wife and I wish to build a comfortable, energy-efficient house on a piece of land that has a fine view to the west. It would be nice to have glass areas overlooking the view, but we are worried about overheating the house in the late afternoon sun. Of course, we could install Venetian blinds or some similar manually operated device. However, the house is likely to be unoccupied just when blinds should be closed. Also, we could extend a porch roof over the west-facing windows, but this is not part of our current plans. Are there any products or techniques that might help?
—David D. Huntoon,
Ridgefield, Conn.

Larry Medinger, who designs and builds energy-efficient, passive-solar homes in Ashland, Ore., replies: It is always better to stop solar radiation outside the skin of the house rather than inside, where, no matter what product you use, some of the energy will be absorbed and re-radiated into the house. The first strategy to look at is limiting the size of the west-facing glass. Windows 3 ft. to 4 ft. high will give as much view of far-off sights as floor-length glass. Also, try to think of your "picture windows" as just that, beautiful pictures of your view that change as you move about the room. That way you can also limit the horizontal dimension of your glass.

Second, consider landscaping and site design. Studies done several years ago comparing the effectiveness of various roof overhangs show that the reflectivity of the ground surface in front of the window has a great effect on the amount of radiation entering the window. You can plant a combination of tall, fast-growing deciduous trees and shrubs that will allow a horizontal "window" between them to your view. The tall trees will shade the wall of the house and the surface of the ground near the house. The shrubs will stop radiation that's reflected off the ground farther away from the house. You want to be able to look outside and see the shady sides and undersides of your shrubs and trees combined with a sunny far view.

Your porch idea would certainly help protect the windows. If your home design is a traditional one, a porch can be a very satisfying part of the overall look of the home. However, be careful to design it in such a way that it does not give you, from the interior, an enclosed feeling and that the floor surface of the porch would not reflect the sun upward into the windows, thus partially defeating your purpose.

You might consider using summer window awnings. Colorful canvas awnings can be very attractive on a home, and they should last at least until your trees are large enough to take over.

We have used a beam-trellis design with removable summer awnings both to protect west-facing glass and as a year-round architectural element. Such a structure will not have the enclosed feeling that a solid porch roof can have and thus can extend farther away from the house to provide more shade from the low afternoon sun. It can be extended far enough to protect the bottom of a patio door or French doors adequately. With the canvas removed, the winter sun will shine in to brighten up the room and give what warmth it may have.

Reflective curtains and blinds are a last line of defense. If you've already planned to install them for winter heat retention, then you can get double use out of them in the summer. It would be reasonable to have them drawn all day while you weren't there, but, if you rely on them solely as a way to block heat gain, you'll still need to deal with weekends and sunny afternoons when you are home and want to enjoy the view.

Holding sash in place

I am upgrading a summer home to make it a year-round residence. The windows are 54 in. high and 45 in. wide, with upper and lower window sash that are not counterweighted. I can't find a source of sash springs or other suitable counterbalance, and there is no room to add sash weights.

—Bruce Smith, Maynard, Mass.

John Leeke, an architectural woodworker in Sanford, Maine, replies: One product I can recommend to get the sash to stay put is Grovco Window Springs (Grovco Sales Co., 537 Easton Rd., Horsham, Pa. 19044). These simple, inexpensive springs are inserted between the edge of the sash and the window frame, as shown above right. They hold the sash in place by pressing against the frame. The springs can

be slipped between the edge of the sash and the frame, and nailed in place without even removing the

Grovco window spring

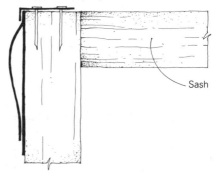

Sash

sash. If there isn't enough room, the edge of the sash can be planed a little. Grovco springs can also be ordered from Sommer & Maca Industries (5501 W. Ogden Ave., Cicero, Ill. 60650). They chiefly supply glaziers, and the minimum order is $20.

If the sash is too heavy for springs, tape balances (drawing below) are needed. Their construction is very similar to a common steel tape measure, or return rule. One is

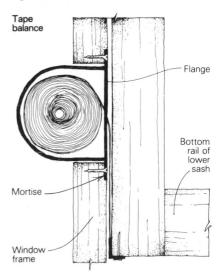

Tape balance

Flange

Bottom rail of lower sash

Mortise

Window frame

mortised into each side of the window frame, flush with the surface, as shown. Its thin steel tape is fastened to the bottom of the sash and reels out between the sash and frame as the sash is lowered. A coil spring inside provides just enough resistance to the weight of the sash to keep it in place. Install each unit by chiseling a mortise a few inches down from the top of the window frame. You will also need to chisel a slight recess above and below so that the flanges of the unit will screw in flush with the face of the window frame. Tape balances are sold by Blaine Window Hardware Co. (1919 Blaine Dr., Hagerstown, Md. 21470).

Two other methods use locally available hardware, and will help keep the wind from blowing in as well as hold up the sash. Spring-brass weatherstripping can be applied to the edge of the sash, if it's not too heavy. Or try aluminum side tracks (drawing below), which have

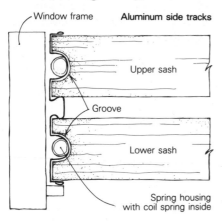

Window frame   Aluminum side tracks

Upper sash

Groove

Lower sash

Spring housing
with coil spring inside

a spring counter balance to hold up the sash. Your sash may already have the wide, round-bottomed groove that is needed to use these guides. If not, you can cut the groove with a router and a core-box bit.

Offset door hinges

In recent months I have been remodeling homes for the disabled. One problem faced by people in wheelchairs is narrow door jambs. This problem can easily be solved by offset hinges that swing the door clear of the jamb. Unfortunately, most of these hinges are designed for doors wider than the standard 1⅜-in. interior doors, or must be ordered in quantity, and even then cost $150 or more. Can you help me locate a source for inexpensive offset door hinges?
—*William Bergstrom,*
Oakland, Calif.

Barbara Winslow, an architect with experience designing for the disabled, replies: One of the easiest and least expensive solutions to the problem of narrow door jambs that I've found is the MED hinge. This off-

MED hinge in open position

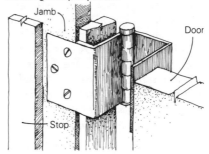

Jamb

Door

Stop

set hinge fits standard 1⅜-in. interior doors, and uses the same shallow mortise on the jamb and the same three screw holes as standard hinges. When the door is open, the hinges swing the door clear of the jamb with an added 2 in. of travel space—enough to make many narrow doors accessible to wheelchairs, as shown in the drawing above.

The hinges (MED hinge model #MO5-6050) are available by mail order in any quantity from Pacific Rents (3031 Beverly Blvd., Los Angeles, Calif. 90057). The current price is $28 per pair, plus tax and shipping.

Etched-glass techniques

I've been investigating etched glass for doors and windows that I'm making. I'd like to know which plastic to use for the acid resist. Which acids are recommended for the novice? I am thinking of making bites from two sides to interrelate figures. Is there one side (normally) that would obviously appear to be the "right" side to a casual observer?
—*David Haynes, Nanoose Bay, B. C.*

Chris Denison replies: There are several approaches you can take to etched glass. First, however, let me say that the process I used to etch the door panels I make is extremely dangerous. The acids used in that project are as bad as they get, and that is why I am unwilling to divulge their names.

Alternative etching or frosting techniques consist of two fairly simple approaches. First is a kit sold in many hobby and stained-glass supply stores. This consists of a cream etching solution, usually ammonium bifluoride, and a resist-like contact paper. If the cream solution is fairly fresh, you can achieve a light, smooth frost on the glass. This is a permanent acid bite into the glass, not an applied paint. If the cream is not fresh, the finish can be streaky.

The resist or contact paper is applied to the glass, and then the area to be etched is cut away with an X-acto knife. These cream solutions can also be silk-screen painted directly onto the glass if you are making multiples of the same design. One such product is Armour Etch, made by Armour Products (Godwin Ave., P.O. Box 56-4100, Midland Park, N. J. 07432).

The other common frosting technique is mechanical and involves sandblasting the glass. This is dangerous because fine glass dust when inhaled never leaves the lungs and will eventually cause a form of emphysema known as silicosis. A good respirator and dust collector are essential for sandblasting.

Sandblasting technique is fairly simple. A rubber resist such as 3M #510 buttercut is applied to the glass, and the design is cut away with an X-acto knife. The glass is then sandblasted with a fine grit (#120 or better) aluminum oxide, garnet or silicon carbide, using a small nozzle (3/16 in. or less) and low pressure (around 40 psi). These tools and techniques are common in the monument and stonecarving industry, so I suggest you look for help at your local tombstone store.

Here are some other sources of information: for acid work, contact Corning Glass Works, Research and Development Dept., Corning, N. Y. 14831; to study all glass techniques (hot and cold), write The Pilchuck Glass School, 107 S. Main 324, Seattle, Wash. 98104. These three publications may be of interest: *Glass Etching* (a small how-to manual by Capp & Bush, available from Dover Publications Inc., 31 East 2nd St., Mineola, N. Y. 11501); *Glass Studio Magazine* (P.O. Box 23383, Portland, Ore. 97223; and *Glass Art Magazine* (P.O. Box 985, Broomfield, Colo. 80020).

With regard to the question of the "right" side of the glass to etch, there are two basic considerations. The etched side of the glass usually faces the light source for the best effect. The etched side also usually faces away from the source of stains (etched glass picks up greasy fingerprints easily).

With regard to the question of making two "bites" into the glass, one on either side, this gives you three shades to design with. If you etch on one side, you will have two shades—clear glass (black) and etched glass (white). If you etch some of the other side of the glass, you will have three shades—clear glass (black), etched on one side (white), and etched on both sides (even whiter).

Exposing gold leaf

We want to strip a modern enamel finish from a raised-relief sunburst design on several old door frames. We're a bit apprehensive about the job because the panels still have their original gold leaf intact beneath the enamel. What is the solution?

—Pat and William DeBonte,
Kent, Conn.

Dr. Leonard Clark, technical director at Formby's Inc., replies: If there is authentic gold leaf beneath the more recent enamel finish, then you should be able to strip the enamel and reveal the leaf without complications. Gold enamel or gold flakes will come off when exposed to stripping compound, just like other finishes. True gold leaf will be unaffected by paint-removing solvents. But it is soft, so you should never take a sharp metal object to its surface. In fact, don't use anything more abrasive than the tools I'm about to recommend. Try the following:

Remove the door from its hinges and position it horizontally in a well-ventilated work area, with plenty of newspaper spread about to catch the debris. Apply a thick coat of semi-paste paint remover over the parts you want to strip and wait for the enamel surface coat to bubble up away from the leaf (oil-base enamels are much more reactive to stripping compounds than the newer latex enamels). Then use an old toothbrush to loosen and remove the finish. If your brush has synthetic bristles, don't be shocked if they deteriorate when exposed to the stripper. Natural bristles will hold up better, but in any case it's best to be prepared with some spare toothbrushes to replace the worn-out or gummed-up ones. A burlap rag is good for removing loosened paint from flat surfaces.

You may have to repeat this application/removal sequence to get all the enamel away from the leaf. I recommend using a paint remover other than the popular water-wash variety (alcohol or mineral-spirits washoff). Water-wash strippers require water rinse-off, and this could cause undue swelling or warpage to certain parts of your door.

Strap hinge for an old look

I am designing batten doors for my new home, and can't find the hinges I want. With strap hinges, or H or H-L hinges, I will have to hang the door from the casing if it is to open 180°. I'd prefer to use

half-surface hinges with a strap or H or H-L on the outside of the door and in a black finish.

—Daniel Driver, Albion, Calif.

Bruce Gordon replies: Consider using a butt hinge to hang the door with a dummy strap mounted on the face of the door next to the butt hinge to give you the traditional look. Make sure to size the butts so that the screws go into the edge grain of the door and not into the end grain of the batten.

Another solution to your problem is to use a strap hinge with a jamb leaf, as shown in the drawing below.

Strap hinge with jamb leaf

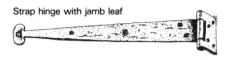

These items are carried by Ball and Ball (463 Lincoln Highway, Exton, Pa. 19341), which offers fine-quality reproduction antique hardware. A catalog is available for $5; a mini-catalog is free. A source I use for inexpensive Colonial hardware is Acorn Manufacturing (Box 31, Mansfield, Mass. 02048).

Brass care

I have just purchased a 40-year-old half-cape home. All of the door hardware is very fine, solid brass. Most of this brass has tarnished. I am in the process of polishing the brass and removing remnants of the old lacquer. This brings back the fine polish and luster of the brass. What should I coat the hardware with to forestall tarnishing, and where can I get it?

—Gary Padley, Kalamazoo, Mich.

William Feist, a wood-finish technologist at the Forest Products Lab in Madison, Wis., replies: This is a bit out of my line, since I generally deal with wood finishes, but I have a couple of tips in my file, so I will pass them along.

You can do a number of things to brass to retain the luster and control tarnish. After cleaning and polishing, consider one of the following alternatives: Coat the brass with varnish or varnish thinned one-to-one with solvent. Polyurethane varnishes would probably work best. Another way is to coat the brass with shellac or lacquer (spray or brush). Spray lacquers are probably best. If you want to avoid finishing products, just coat the brass with liquid or paste wax (use a commercial wax made for brass, like Brasswax). Whatever coating you choose must be applied over clean surfaces.

Here is an oil-finish procedure I recently saw: Clean the brass thoroughly with a grease-cutting solvent. Then polish it, taking care to handle it with clean soft gloves to avoid contamination and finger marks. Rinse the brass with clean lacquer thinner and dry. Next, heat the brass in an oven at 150°F for 20 minutes. Remove it from the heat and rub tung oil into the warm brass with a soft clean cloth, and let it dry at least four hours. Wax if desired.

Straightening bowed doors

I have just moved into an older home. All the trim and doors are solid oak. The stiles on three doors are somewhat bowed. None makes a good fit in its frame. Two of the doors are painted with an oil-base paint, and the other is stained and varnished. Is there anything I can do to straighten these doors? *—Gene Yacura, Fruitland, Ont.*

David Stenstrom, an architectural woodworker in Portland, Maine, replies: The simplest solution is to scribe the bow of the stiles onto the jamb and to plane the rabbet to fit the curve. You'll also probably have to reset the strike plate so the door will close tightly.

Straightening the door is more difficult. Rip about a 2-in. strip off the side of the bowed stile, being careful not to destroy the integrity of the joinery. Find a piece of oak with a bow similar to that of the door. Glue and clamp this strip to the stile with the curve in the opposite direction. Use C-clamps and blocks to get the surfaces flush. The opposing forces

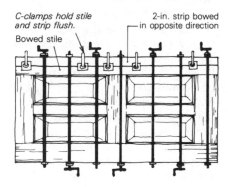

C-clamps hold stile and strip flush.

Bowed stile

2-in. strip bowed in opposite direction

may cancel out and straighten the door. On the stained door, try to match the grain.

When a door is made, the stock for the stiles is face-joined before planing to ensure its straightness. If a good finish is kept on both sides of the door, and particularly on the end grain at the bottom, the door should stay true.

Rising butt hinges

I have been looking for rising butt hinges (also called back-rise hinges) so that I will not have to cut an exterior door. With the installation of these hinges, the door would clear the floor tile that I plan to lay. Can you help me find a supplier? *—E. C. Roireau, Redondo Beach, Calif.*

Kevin Ireton, associate editor of Fine Homebuilding, replies: Heavy-duty rising butt hinges are available from Ball and Ball (463 W. Lincoln Highway, Exton, Pa. 19341). They offer both 3-in. and 4-in. hinges in brass and aluminum. You have to specify right-hand or left-hand when you order them. Prices range from $41.80 for a pair of 3-in. aluminum hinges to $69.30 for a pair of 4-in. brass hinges. I called the company and talked with Whitman Ball about rising butt hinges. He said they first turned up in England around the end of the 18th century. The hinges have a spiral barrel (drawing below) and are used to raise a door as it is

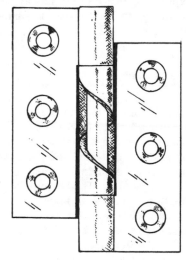

opened so that the door will clear a rug or an uneven floor. When open, the door will be about ½ in. higher than when it's closed. Although they don't exert enough force to latch a door, rising butt hinges are self closing. When you install them on a door, you have to trim the top inside corner of the door. Otherwise, it will rise into the head jamb as the door is opened.

Exterior-door design

Three of our doors open into a courtyard, where they are exposed to rain and sun. They have particleboard cores faced and edged with oak veneer. In less than a year, the doors swelled until they scraped the jambs and thresholds. Soon after, the finish lifted; and finally the bottom edges of the doors bulged, discolored and began to delaminate. How can I build a durable door for this situation? Can a round window, an important design consideration, be included?
—*John Kriegshauser,*
Kansas City, Mo.

Irwin Post, a forest engineer in Barnard, Vt., replies: Sun and rain are very hard on wood doors. On a veneered door, the moisture content of the thin veneer can go from above the fiber-saturation point during a rainstorm to nearly oven-dry when the sun shines on it—unless it is protected by a finish that is very resistant to water.

Particleboard is a poor choice for the core. I recommend using an insulated core incorporating exterior plywood for dimensional stability and energy conservation. Use waterproof glue throughout. Your window design could be included easily. Once the door is built, apply at least three coats of high-quality, exterior polyurethane varnish. At the first sign of failure, generally in five to ten years, strip and refinish the doors.

Chapter 10:

Plaster and Drywall

Outdoor casting materials

What kind of casting material is used for exterior ornaments like capitals, brackets and the like? I am referring to a material that looks like plaster but is a lot harder and water resistant.

—Josee Dunn, Claremore, Okla.

John Todaro, an expert in molding and casting for restoration work, replies: There are several casting materials that will hold up well outdoors. Concrete, of course, can be used. Increasing the proportion of cement in the mix and using a fine grain of sand will provide a smoother finished surface. Hydrostone, available at most art-supply stores, is an extremely hard, dense casting material. Vatican Art Casting Stone is another alternative; it comes in white, brown, grey-green, black and terra-cotta. You can also formulate

your own color by adding pigments. Twenty-five pounds costs about $10. Both these products come in powder form and require mixing with water. They can be ordered from Sculpture House, 38 E. 30th St., New York, N. Y. 10016.

Attaching plaster molds

Can you explain how ceiling rosettes, moldings and other ornamental plaster molds are attached to walls and ceilings? I also need to know if it is difficult or hazardous to remove these items so that casts and molds can be made.

—John Fant, Cleveland, Ohio

Architectural restorationist Jim Boorstein replies: Traditionally, plaster casts, moldings and ceiling rosettes are attached to the wall or ceiling with plaster. The plaster bond is very strong. If your ceiling or wall plaster is old, you will need to moisten it or brush on a coat of a commercial bonding product to ensure that the new plaster adheres to the old. Sometimes I mix a bit of glue into the plaster to attach small plaster casts. This mix bonds well and is a bit stickier. On small ornaments, pilasters for example, or a small area of cornice when there is not a lot of plastering to do, I use white glue straight.

There is no rule about removing plaster ornaments. Some come off easily, while other pieces insist on breaking. Rosettes are dangerous to take down. The best approach is to take them apart in place. If that is not possible on an architecturally important piece, I recommend removing the rosette intact with its surrounding ceiling plaster. For this kind of job, you'll need to work from adequate scaffolding with the help of several people.

Often you can make molds with the ornament in place. I find this is to be the best approach when possible. Strip the paint, seal the plaster surfaces and isolate the area you want to make a mold of. Use a nonhardening clay.

Stains around corner bead

Something that looks like an oil stain has appeared on some outside corners of our drywall. The stain appears around the perforated metal corner bead on interior walls and partitions, but only on some of the corners. For example, the stain has appeared in only one of our two bathrooms. Our house is heavily insulated throughout its perimeter walls and ceilings, as well as within the interior walls. We have also installed a vapor barrier on the inside of the exterior walls and ceilings. Since Maryland's eastern shore has a humid summer and a wet winter, we suspect that moisture is the source of the problem. The walls have already been painted, and we would appreciate any suggestions on how to cover or correct this unsightly problem.
—*Sandy Buchanan, Stockton, Md.*

Craig Stead, a contractor in Putney, Vt., replies: The stains are most likely caused by corrosion of the metal corner bead, which has led to a brown rust stain bleeding through the surface paint. Moisture selectively condenses on the corner bead because the metal corner is cooler than the rest of the wall. It's like the sweating you get on your iced lemonade glass on a humid summer day. This condensed moisture, in combination with the alkaline drywall mud, rusts the steel corner bead. The rust that forms on the corner bead is slightly water soluble and migrates through the mud coating to show up as a brown stain.

High-humidity problems are common in today's tight houses. Adequate ventilation at the source of the humidity is one approach to controlling the problem. Use the kitchen vent fan when cooking, particularly when boiling water. Use the bath vent fan or open the window a crack when showering.

Most likely, your house's stained corner has been painted with a latex primer and overcoat. Since the rust stain is water soluble, you'll find that it will bleed through any latex paint used over it. Any number of coats of latex paint can be applied, and that stain will reappear as the paint dries. The only solution is to seal the stain with a sealer and stain killer before applying the next finish coat of paint. These sealers are specifically designed to prevent the bleed-through of water-soluble stains. They are great not only for problems such as yours, but also for sealing paneling with water-soluble stains before painting it, or for sealing knots on spruce and pine before painting.

Two brands of sealer that I have used with success are Kilz primer/sealer, manufactured by Masterchem Industries (P.O. Box 2666, St. Louis, Mo. 63116) and B-I-N primer/sealer/stain killer, manufactured by William Zinsser & Co., Inc. (38 Belmont Drive, Somerset, N. J. 08873). Both dry rapidly and can be overcoated after an hour or so. Kilz is oil-based, and cleanup can be done with mineral spirits; B-I-N is shellac-based, and cleanup is done with alcohol. Both give off noxious fumes, so work in a well-ventilated space or use a good organic-fume respirator.

Another use for these primers is as a base coat before painting over wallpaper with latex-base paint. In renovation, you often find a room that has many coats of wallpaper over brown-coat plaster, and it's very tempting just to paint over it nad be done with it (in spite of what the purists say). But if you use latex-base paint, you will find that the water in the paint will dissolve the wallpaper glue, leaving curled seams and bubbled spots. Sealing the wallpaper with Kilz or B-I-N will prevent moisture from getting through it, and the delamination problem will be effectively solved.

Resurfacing a plaster wall

We are remodeling a 40-year-old brick house. The interior walls are lath and plaster, and the exterior walls are plaster on hollow tile. While the walls and ceilings are in good condition, they are of a rough sand-type finish and we prefer a smoother look. There seems to be only the original coat of paint throughout. What must I do to prepare the walls and ceilings to ensure a good bond, and what is recommended as a skim coat? —*William Zimmerman, Fayetteville, N. C.*

Dean Russell, who does historic restoration and ornamental plaster work, replies: You have a couple of options. Although it is better to relath over the existing walls and replaster, this is often not the preferred solution since walls increase not only in width, but also in weight. The more practical alternative is to resurface with some kind of skim or veneer coat.

First, determine if the sand texture is in the paint or in the original plaster finish. If it is in the paint, scrape as much of the paint off as possible to remove this sand finish. Then sand the surface with 50-grit or even 35-grit paper. Wash down all surfaces to make sure no scrapings or dust remain—plain water used sparingly will do the trick.

If the sand finish is in the plaster finish coat, you shouldn't try to remove it, but take off as much of the paint as possible with a wire brush and scraper. Now wash with water to remove any dust and residue. Take care in preparing the surface, as this preparation will determine the success or failure of your bond.

Now you are faced with the choice of using veneer plaster or drywall joint compound. If you choose to plaster, first apply a good-quality bonding agent that's designed for use with plaster. Two brands are Thorobond (Thoro System Products, Inc., 7800 N.W. 38th St., Miami, Fla. 33166) and Plasterweld (Larsen Products Corporation, 5420 Randolph Rd., Rockville, Md. 20852). Roll or brush on the bonding agent, avoiding drips and runs, and allow it to dry. Wash off any excess from surrounding areas before the bonding agent dries.

Applying veneer finishes (some brand names are Imperial and Diamond, manufactured by U. S. Gypsum, 101 South Wacker Drive, Chicago, Ill. 60606) requires professional plastering skill, since they have a relatively short setting time and once hardened, they don't sand very well. If you feel you have the skill, try a small closet or other hidden area first Follow the directions provided by the manufacturer.

If you choose to use drywall joint compound, apply a first "tight" coat of compound with a broad taping knife (at least 9 in. wide). Apply a thin, even coat; don't try to smooth out the surface with this first coat. When it's dry, sand off ridges and high spots and skim on a second coat of slightly watered-down compound. Lay on this thin coat by covering a section and then returning immediately to cut off the excess by drawing the knife across the surface with the blade at a right angle to the work. Try to remember that this coat and the ones to follow are designed to fill in hollows, not to add a lot of thickness. Continue this skimming coat until the whole sur-

face is covered. When it is dry, sand and repeat for a third and fourth coat, spot-patching serious hollows between coats. Use progressively thinner mixes of compound and finer grades of sandpaper each step of the way. This will keep the overall thickness to a minimum, and you won't bury your trim and moldings in unsightly compound.

Of these two methods, I would suggest using the drywall joint compound if you don't have some good plastering experience. The multiple coats do take more time, but joint compound is fairly forgiving—it sands well, washes off and doesn't set up or harden like plaster. In homes of historic value, drywall compound is also reversible, whereas the bonding agent/plaster system is not. We have done numerous old houses that date back to about 1830 with this joint-compound system over sound but unsightly plaster and have had good success.

Repairing plaster

I would like some advice on how to repair interior lath and plaster walls and ceilings. The problem is mainly hairline cracks. The plaster is firmly attached to the lath. I'd like to avoid adding more than ¼ in. of thickness to the existing walls and ceilings in order to preserve the molding profiles. One suggestion has been to apply wire mesh with concrete screws, followed by a finish coat of plaster, but I'm afraid that the cracks will reappear. Can you recommend a patching method that will not be visible and will not crack again?
—*Oliver A. Fick, Norcross, Ga.*

Dean Russell, a historic restorationist in Mattituck, N. Y., replies: Over the years, I have tried a number of methods for repairing plaster cracks and have met with varied success. The one I've found most effective, economical and easiest is to prepare the cracks carefully, tape them with fiberglass-mesh tape and finish with joint compound.

First remove all loose paint. Do not remove the white finish coat of plaster unless it's loose and doesn't adhere to the brown coat. Fine hairline cracks should be gouged open to about ⅜ in., filled with plaster of Paris, then taped with fiberglass mesh tape and feathered smooth with joint compound. This usually prevents minor cracks from reappearing.

For slightly larger, more serious cracks where the plaster is still firmly attached to the lath, open the cracks to about 1½ in. Bevel the edge of the cut, as shown in the drawing below, and expose the lath underneath. If the lath is wood, try

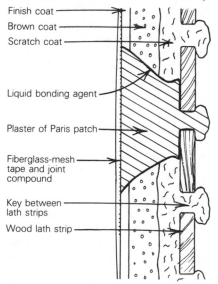

Finish coat

Brown coat

Scratch coat

Liquid bonding agent

Plaster of Paris patch

Fiberglass-mesh tape and joint compound

Key between lath strips

Wood lath strip

to expose some of the gaps between the strips.

If there seems to be too much movement to open up the crack, first secure the plaster with some 2-in. fender washers and 1⅝-in. or 2-in. drywall screws alongside the crack to hold things in place until the repair is completed. Stay back about 9 in. from the crack to allow space to feather out the repair. Space the screws about 12 in. to 18 in. apart. For best results, make sure the screws catch the framing. With care, screws may hold tight to the lath. We use a variable-speed cordless drill or a screw gun with an adjustable clutch. Be careful not to overtighten the screws—this can hurt more than it helps. Leave the screws and washers in place only until the patching process is completed. Then back them out and patch the small holes.

Apply liquid bonding agent to the old plaster edges and lath. Three bonding agents I have used are Plaster-Weld (Larsen Products Corp., 5420 Randolph Rd., Rockville, Md. 20852), Thorobond (Thoro System Products, 7800 NW 38th St., Miami, Fla. 33166) and Elmer's Concrete Bonder (Borden Inc., 180 E. Broad St., Columbus, Ohio 43215). When the bonding agent has dried, patch the enlarged crack with plaster of Paris. Force a good amount of plaster into the cracks and between the lath. This will help to hold the loose "slabs" in place. Cut off the plaster flush with the existing surface. After it dries, butter joint compound over the repair with a 6-in. taping knife and embed fiberglass tape. Follow standard taping procedures.

If the cracks seem more ominous, secure the edges as stated, but space the washers farther back, and cut a 4-in. swath (2 in. on each side of the crack) down to the lath. Attach a strip of galvanized diamond-wire mesh to the lath with 1-in. drywall screws. We don't use nails because the pounding would worsen any problems. Fill with plaster of Paris or high-gauged plaster mix (1 part lime putty to 1 part gauging plaster) and cut flush. When the plaster sets, cover with 6-in. wide tape or cover the edges with fiberglass tape (2½ in. wide) and finish with joint compound.

Another method of repair is a system called Glid-Wall (The Glidden Co., 925 Euclid Ave., Cleveland, Ohio 44115), which consists of fiberglass sheets that are applied over a paint-on primer and then covered with another paint-on coating. It finishes with a light texture, which may or may not be acceptable. It is essentially an updated canvassing technique. I would still recommend patching any large cracks first. Glid-Wall also hides ugly paint and minor surface imperfections, which may be a plus in cases where the wall surface needs only a little help.

If there seems to be no hope for the plaster surface and molding profiles are not a factor, you can build a new plaster wall right over the existing surface. This sidesteps demolition and debris disposal problems. First, be sure the framing can take the extra weight. Then attach self-furring ¾-lb. diamond-mesh lath to the framing with 2-in. drywall screws 6 in. o. c. Apply a scratch coat (2½ parts sand to 1 part gypsum plaster), and a brown coat with the same proportions. Finish with the standard lime putty/gauging mix, troweled smooth.

Replastering dilemma

Should I replaster over existing lath or relath my Greek Revival restoration? —Joe Sherman, Montgomery, Vt.

Dean Russell, a restoration-plaster specialist in Mattituck, N. Y., replies: If your building has historical value, you'll probably want to preserve as much of the original fabric as possible. This might include the lath; the decision is yours. If so, proceed by removing any plaster that is still adhering to it. Then carefully remove some of the lath at the bottom of walls and at intervals across the ceilings so that you can get behind the remaining lath and clean out all broken plaster keys.

To replaster, begin by applying a liquid-plaster bonding agent (I use one by Larsen Products Corp., 5420 Randolph Rd., Rockville, Md. 20852) to the lath with a brush or roller. This keeps the lath from swelling when the wet plaster is applied, which will crack the scratch coat. Originally, this problem was solved by wetting down the lath, but this isn't practical in replastering since finished floors and trim are often already in place.

When the bonding agent is dry, I staple Cornerite (U. S. Gypsum Co., 101 South Wacker Drive, Chicago, Ill. 60606) into all corners and wall/ceiling angles, and Striplath (also made by U. S. Gypsum) to span any breaks in lath and over window and door headers. I can then plaster over the lath with the standard three-coat system. As a scratch coat, I like Red Top Wood Fiber plaster (U. S. Gypsum) with 1 cu. ft. of sand per 100-lb. bag or Red Top Regular Gypsum plaster (2 to 2½ cu. ft. of sand to the

100-lb. bag) with 3 lb. of alkali-resistant glass fibers (Cem-Fil Corp., 120 Spence Lane, Nashville, Tenn. 37210) added. The glass fibers replace the horsehair that was originally used. Brown-coat and finish-coat as with any three-coat work.

If preserving the lath isn't important to you, you can replace it with Rocklath plaster base (U.S. Gypsum), which requires only a two-coat system. Attach the Rocklath with nails or buglehead screws to the studs and joists, and plaster as usual.

Removing plaster from brick

What is the best way to remove 60-year-old plaster that was applied directly over an exterior brick wall? *—Richard L. Riemer II, Santa Ana, Calif.*

F. Neale Quenzel, a restoration architect in West Chester, Pa., replies: The best way to remove plaster from a brick wall is to chip it off with a 3-in. to 4-in. wide flat metal chisel, such as a brick chisel. Cut away a small area down to the face of the brick substrate. Once you have determined the depth of the face of the brick, the chisel can be held nearly flat across the brick. Power chisels can be used, but only with great care, as it is easy to go too deep and gouge the brick.

Try a small area first by cleaning it thoroughly to make sure that the reclaimed brick is going to give you the appearance you want. After you've finished chipping away the plaster, a weak solution of muriatic acid should remove the plaster stain from the brick face. Wear rubber gloves and goggles while using the

acid, and protect all adjacent finished surfaces. The best way to keep the inevitable plaster dust out of the rest of the house is to seal off the area where you are working by draping plastic sheets taped to the ceiling, walls and floors. If you have forced-air heating, cover any return-air ducts with several layers of cheesecloth, and change the cloth daily through the course of the job.

Reproduction plaster

The walls in my house, which was built in 1925, are finished with Swedish putty plaster. It has an irregular, craterlike texture. How can I reproduce this finish? *—Bernadette A. Burke, Pittsburgh, Pa.*

Dan Desmond, a specialist in restoration and energy retrofits in Lancaster, Pa., replies: Plaster is generally applied in three stages— the scratch coat, the brown coat and the finish or skim coat. The putty coat is generally equivalent to the finish coat. If you have completely stripped the walls of plaster, you might want to use veneer plasterboard as a base for the finish coat. This gypsum product, sometimes referred to as blueboard, takes the place of the scratch coat and brown coat. If you only need to reapply a finish coat to the original plaster base, keep the old plaster damp with a spray bottle of water, or it will suck much of the moisture out of your finish coat before you have time to texture it to your liking.

Finish-coat plaster usually consists of equal portions of lime putty and washed sand. Plaster of paris and marble dust were occasionally added to plaster, but this material is noticeably harder than the usual plaster of that era.

The cratering in the finish coat is done most often with a steel trowel, which can be used simply to imprint a pattern or pulled quickly from the surface, creating a suction that will leave a characteristic texture. You can also trowel the plaster as it hardens to create a layered effect. I have used sponges, brushes and even wadded newspaper to match old plaster textures. It takes some patience and a lot of experimentation to get the effect you need.

The more you work the plaster with a trowel, the harder it will get. The best plasterers use a brush to fling water at the wall, and work the moisture in with the trowel to extend the working time before the plaster sets. Even so, they have to work quickly. When it's cured, the new plaster should be sealed with shellac or a similar commercial product to prevent the lime in it from burning through the finish coat of paint.

Cutting plaster

I use a variable-speed reciprocating saw in my renovation work. My special plaster-cutting blades dull so fast that I spend more time changing blades than cutting. What kind of sawblade is best for cutting lath and plaster, and on what speed should I operate the saw? —*David Roberts, Wilmette, Ill.*

Tom Law, a builder in the Washington, D. C., area, replies: Although plaster varies considerably in its composition because it's an earth material, I find a silicon-carbide masonry blade in a circular saw most effective. I use this blade frequently in remodeling to make new openings or to let in new drywall. Be sure to seal off the room where you are working and wear a mask, because a masonry blade generates large amounts of gritty dust. Chipping by hammer and chisel is the most dust-free method, but it sometimes causes unwanted breaks, and is slow. If you continue to use a reciprocating saw with plaster, use a good metal-cutting blade with as few teeth as possible per inch, and operate the saw at a low speed.

Dean Russell, of Mattituck, N. Y., also replies: I specialize in restorations of historic and ornamental plaster interiors. I have found that chisels and hammers definitely should not be used, especially around delicate ornamental work. Power tools with rotary blades of any kind make entirely too much dust. The best tool for cutting plaster precisely with very little dust or vibration is the lowly utility knife. You will destroy lots of blades quickly but you get a clean, gentle cut. Just score the white coat through with one or two passes with the blade, and then run down this scoreline repeatedly using increasingly heavy pressure on the knife until you have cut through the brown coat to the lath.

Sagging plaster ceiling

I have an 1820 house in which the ceiling plaster has come loose from the wood lath. There is about ½-in. of play between the plaster and lath. I'd like to save this plaster if at all possible. How can I repair the ceiling? —*William Fildes, Baltimore, Md.*

Gregory Schipa, a restoration specialist in Randolph, Vt., replies: In our restorations we deal with this problem in one of three ways:

1. If the separation of the lath and plaster covers much of the ceiling, we consider only the complete removal of all plaster down to the lath—cleaning it carefully—and then a replastering job. This is a messy and time-consuming job, but it definitely saves future headaches.

2. If the ½-in. separation is observed in a limited area, it can be repaired rather than replaced. We sometimes cut along the perimeter of the separation, and remove all loose plaster. We then repair the holes (using rock-hard water putty or taper's quick-set for small ones, and real plaster, two coats, for anything bigger than a tennis ball).

3. Only in a case where we have very definite reason to save the plaster (plaster detail, stenciling, etc.) do we ever try to save loose old plaster. Where there are solid nailers, we use screws with wooden washers, spaced about every 6 in. Where there are no nailers, we use toggle bolts instead of screws. Screws or bolts must be set slightly and covered (as in taping drywall). Rock-hard water putty works well here. For all our care, though, cracks and separations often recur.

Plaster cornice

I plan to remove a partition between my living room and a bedroom. The living room has a 6-in. radius cove between walls and ceiling. I want to continue this detail into the bedroom, which now has a 90° wall-ceiling juncture. All surfaces are ⅜-in. gypsum lath with ½ in. of plaster. How should I make and finish the cove?
—*Gary Grubin, Edgewater, Colo.*

Dean Russell, restoration and ornamental-plaster specialist in Suffolk County, N. Y., replies: Running or drawing a cornice molding in plaster requires a good deal of practice. The process itself is simple—a mold is taken, the plaster is mixed and then the molding is run. But plaster setting times and running techniques are not very forgiving, and they do require experienced hands to get what you need on the first try. I recommend having an ornamental plasterer do the actual running of the molding in his or her shop, and then installing the pieces yourself.

First determine whether the living-room and bedroom ceilings are the same height. Also check to see if the wall and ceiling meet at 90°. The original cornice was run in place, requiring the wall and ceiling to be perfectly straight and true. It is likely that the plasterers did not take as much care in the room without the cove.

If the two ceilings are within ¼ in. of each other in height, patch the area where you removed the partition, and feather with several coats of drywall compound and a 4-ft. straightedge. If they differ by more than ¼ in., plaster may have to be removed from a portion of the lower ceiling and feathered back in over a much larger area to create a more straight-line transition.

The partition you are going to demolish should yield a piece of cornice 4 in. to 5 in. long with a complete wall-to-ceiling profile to use as a pattern. Most urban areas still have practicing ornamental plasterers. If this service is not available in your area, mail your cornice section to the nearest shop, tell them how many lineal feet you will need, and ask them to telephone you with an estimate.

After receiving the finished cove sections, measure them for length and lay out what you'll need for an entire wall. If a short section is required, don't end a wall with it, but use it near the center of the run. Measure the sections for height and establish a horizontal chalkline on the wall as an index for the bottom edge of the molding. Tack finish nails into the wall along the chalkline so that each section will be supported, as shown in the drawing below.

Begin the run with a corner miter, which you can cut with a fine-toothed handsaw. Drill several small holes in the top and bottom lip of the cornice for finish nails, staying back 4 in. from the ends. These nails will hold the cornice in place while the drywall compound or adhesive dries.

Next, butter the top and bottom surfaces of the back of the molding. Use drywall compound for this if the molding is still slightly damp from the shop. If the pieces are really bone dry, they will draw all the moisture out of the mud before it

has a chance to bond; so you should either dampen the molding slightly or use tile adhesive. In either case, spread drywall compound on the end of the molding that will butt the previously installed piece.

Set the buttered molding in place, and wiggle it around to bed it firmly in the compound. Let the mud squeeze out and then trim it off while wet to check that you've kept to the chalkline. If the line of the ceiling isn't straight, you may need to use thin wood wedges between it and the top of the molding to keep true to the chalkline. Place each section in the same manner, and adjust the joint before nailing the previous section tight. Use drywall compound to fill nail holes and to point joint gaps. If there are large gaps, use plaster of paris. After the installation dries thoroughly, usually a couple of weeks, seal the area with a good penetrating primer/sealer, and paint the room as usual.

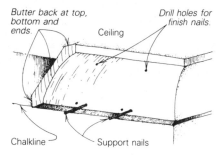

Butter back at top, bottom and ends.

Drill holes for finish nails.

Ceiling

Chalkline

Support nails

Chapter 11:

Logs, Timbers and Earth

Sawdust bricks

Do you have any information on using sawdust as a building material? —*Alton C. Thompson, Greendale, Wis.*

Pliny Fisk III, director of the Center for Maximum Potential Building Systems in Austin, Tex., replies: Our earth-materials specialist, Steve Musick, has come up with a rough formula for making insulating sawdust bricks from mesquite, a local hardwood. The sawdust is a byproduct of cutting the mesquite into floor tiles. This mix is still in the experimental stages, but has worked well on our demonstration building so far.

To make the bricks, first mix water and lime (or caliche, a kind of clay) to the color and consistency of milk. Add as much sawdust to the liquid as it will take, stirring to make sure all of the sawdust gets wet. This mixture should sit for a day and be allowed to dry until it is slightly damp.

In another container, mix equal amounts of cement and water, and then add the treated sawdust to the slurry. For every part of cement, add six to eight parts of sawdust. Stir thoroughly, pour into a mold and tamp lightly.

After the brick has set, paint it with latex paint so that it's waterproof. The first coat should be heavy; let it soak through the brick as much as it can. The two additional coats should remain on the surface of the brick.

Rammed-earth in Illinois

How successful would a rammed-earth building be in northern Illinois, where the temperatures range from over 100°F in the summer to −25°F in the winter? I am also curious about interior partitions. I'm assuming that they can be made load-bearing, but can they also be made thinner than the exterior walls? —*Daniel Levit, McHenry, Ill.*

Magnus Berglund, of Rammed Earth Works in Wilseyville, Calif., replies: Rammed-earth buildings are found all over the world in a variety of climates, and many have survived centuries of bad weather. In the U. S., you'll find rammed-earth houses in the West, the Northwest, the Southwest, the Midwest and the East.

Although you might feel a bit like a pioneer in Illinois, rammed earth does have a history in the Midwest. Much of the definitive research in this country was done by R. L. Patty in the 1930s at the South Dakota Agricultural Experiment Stations, where extreme temperatures are common. Prof. Menefee of the University of Michigan built a six-room, two-story rammed-earth residence in Ann Arbor in the 1920s. John Sukup built a five-room rammed-earth house in Milwaukee in 1947, and he still lives in it. There's probably a rammed-earth house within a day's drive of most people in the U. S. The trouble is that most of these were built during the 1930s and 1940s, and they were stuccoed to look like all of the other houses on the block. Window casements 14 in. to 20 in. deep are the giveaway.

David Easton, the architect-builder I work with, has built some houses where all the interior walls are rammed earth, and others, like mine, with stud and gypboard interior walls. You can also mix them — the stud walls for hiding vents, plumbing, fuse boxes and recessed electric heaters, and the earth walls for mass. Easton's approach is to put the bearing walls on the outside and keep all the interior walls just above head height to allow for a free circulation of inside air. His interior earth walls are the same as the exterior walls — 14 in. thick and topped with a concrete bond beam. If you still want interior bearing walls, you have an engineering problem that can be easily solved. You'll need the figures from compressive-strength tests of your soil mix, your roof-loading figures, and an engineer who will put his stamp on your plans.

Cooling a rammed-earth house

I bought a lot in Fountain Hills, Ariz., and hope to build a house in about a year. I am interested in rammed-earth construction. What is the calculated effect of rammed-earth construction, compared to conventional, on cooling in the hot season? I expect that it would be more effective because of the mass of the walls. —*Clair D. Siple, Lakefield, Minn.*

Architect Brian Lockhart replies: In order to answer your question, I consulted Tom Schmidt of Schmidt Builders in St. David, Ariz., and Tom Wuelpern of Rammed Earth Solar Homes in Tucson, Ariz. Both have extensive experience with earth building in a range of different climates. Schmidt and Wuelpern build rammed-earth walls in superinsulated homes, generally passive solar in design. While the cost is more than frame construction, it is cheaper than other mass-wall constructions. The temperature in these homes varies only slightly, depending on the time of the year, to give a very even comfort level.

Conventional construction without storage capacity needs a more constant input of heating or cooling, depending, of course, on many variables. Having survived a number of summers in the Phoenix area, I can attest that mechanical cooling becomes a major concern for functioning on any level. With radiant heat on one side and cold air on the other, the tug-of-war exacts a high price on body and pocketbook.

A home with rammed-earth walls can be comfortable in summer and winter if it is designed for its environment. The Phoenix area, where Fountain Hills is located, has a far greater cooling requirement than heating (3,500 cooling degree days, 1,550 heating degree days). The house must be well insulated, with the mass walls protected on the outside to isolate them from the high temperatures. This permits the storage to interact with the interior. Windows must be good quality, at least dual pane. Window openings, unless protected, should be minimized on the north, east and west, as these are the directions of major summer solar gain, besides directly overhead. Direct gain in the summer through south-facing windows is usually minimal.

With the average day and night temperature above 80°F from May to September (91°F in July), the home will eventually not be able to rid itself of excess heat through simple ventilation. The house temperature will gradually rise toward that average temperature. Because of high humidity, evaporative cooling often does not bring temperatures into the comfort range.

The best solution seems to be to use air conditioning at night, when the rates are lower. The unit is not working in the extreme heat of the day, and the stored cooling can carry the house through the daytime with a minimal heat rise.

Sandy soil for rammed earth?

I am interested in building a rammed-earth house, but the soil where I live is almost entirely sand. I tried my hand at rammed earth on a cabin floor with this same sandy soil and a small amount of cement a few years ago, but had no success. Can I make my soil work at all, and if so, how much cement will I need?
—P. Silverman,
Faro, Yukon Territories

Magnus Berglund of Rammed Earth Works in Wilseyville, Calif., replies: None of us is a soils engineer, and our approach to this science is somewhat simplistic, but here is some of what we have learned building 25 rammed-earth structures using widely varied soils. With especially sandy soil, or soil that has an abundance of decomposed rock, the amount of cement required can go as high as 15%. This mixture can best be described as rich soil-cement.

Soil scientists around the world classify soils into three basic types: sand, clay and silt. Particles larger than sand are called gravel. Microscopic clay particles are called colloids. To compact properly, a soil should be a mixture of particles of various sizes—fine particles for binding and coarse particles to prevent shrinking and cracking. Clay's colloidal make-up acts as a binder that cements the sand and silt together. Clay, then, provides the plasticity and cohesiveness for wall construction. When it is absent, a binder like cement must be added.

To determine how much binder, stabilizer, sand or clay you need to add to your soil, you have to run some tests. Start with the jar test. Remember that the ideal soil for ramming has a ratio of 30% clay to 70% sand. Then make some small test blocks using different proportions of soils and moisture. To form these blocks we use a 6-in. piece of 2-in. dia. ABS plastic pipe cut in half lengthwise, and held together with three stainless-steel hose clamps. Fill the cylinder with the prepared mix and pound it with a stick—a short piece of closet rod will do— and a hammer. Tamp it until it won't compact anymore. Remove the clamps and label the pellet.

For your sandy Yukon subsoil, start by adding 6%, 8%, and 10% cement by volume—up to 15%, if you have to. You might also look around for a nearby source of clay to mine and add some—it would save on cement. Let the pellets cure until they are dry and hard. To test their relative strength, use a 2-lb. sledge, and swing with a consistent force as if pounding a nail. See how your pellets resist the impact—you want to see which is strongest. Remember to test for the least amount of stabilizer required. If you or your building department need some real numbers to work from, you can take your pellets to a lab for a test of their unconfined compressive strength.

There is no doubt in my mind that you can make your soil work, but you should probably begin with a test wall. In your severe climate, consider a wall thickness of 24 in.

Best wood for a post

We plan to build a spiral staircase, and want to use a log 8 in. to 10 in. in diameter for the center post. On our woodlot we have straight trees of ash, beech and maple of the proper size. Which would be best, and how should we dry it to minimize checking and splitting?
—*Dave & Virginia Burley, Montpelier, Vt.*

Paul Fuge, a sawyer and architectural woodworker in Shelton, Conn., replies: Most logs develop deep radial splits when they dry because of significant differences in radial and tangential shrinkage rates. The drawing below shows how these conflicting forces stress the wood. Of the species that grow in your area, red and white cedar, butternut and walnut are the least likely to cause problems. The ash, beech and maple growing on your woodlot will all definitely split, although of the three, ash would be the best.

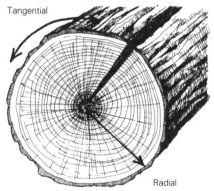

Tangential

Radial

Proceed by cutting several logs a foot or so longer than you need, paint the ends with latex paint, peel the bark, and bring the logs indoors, away from sources of dry heat and sun. Wait as long as you can to use the wood, and then choose the best log of the lot. Cedar can be used the soonest, because its initial moisture content is the lowest.

There are many interesting schemes designed to reduce checking further during the drying stage, but none guarantees complete success. One old Japanese approach is to saw a kerf along the length of the log right into the heart, preferably on the side that will show the least. A chainsaw will do this nicely. With luck, all the movement will manifest itself in the width of the kerf.

Another method of reducing checking by dealing with the heartwood is to bore a 3-in. hole down the center of the log. This was done historically to make water pipe. Plumbers' drill bits, a custom-made extension for the bit and the eye of a Marine sharpshooter are required for this operation. To learn more about drying wood and why shrinkage causes problems, see R. Bruce Hoadley's text on wood technology, *Understanding Wood* (The Taunton Press, 63 S. Main Street, Box 355, Newtown, Conn. 06470).

Interior finish for log walls

We are building a log house in northern Minnesota. The walls will be chinked with quartered logs on the inside, fiberglass between the larger logs and mortar on the outside. Will this arrangement work? I'm looking for a clear finish for the interior of the walls that will also function as a vapor barrier. Any suggestions?
—David R. Warner, Jr., Ada, Ohio

Robert Chambers of Sparwood Log Homes replies: First of all, most log homes do not need a vapor barrier. Water vapor will not go through solid wood in any appreciable amount—especially compared to the amount of vapor that will be transmitted through cracks between your logs (even with caulk). In winter, warm, moist air will migrate through those cracks and condense on the cold fiberglass, accumulating as frost until it melts in the spring. A vapor-barrier finish will do little or nothing for this problem.

Your construction detail, however, adds fiberglass as a potential problem. You need to keep all water (liquid and vapor) out of your fiberglass, which is going to be tough. Some separation between the logs and the mortar chinking is inevitable; the logs and the mortar are going to shrink as they dry (portland cement-based mortar will shrink). As the wood and mortar shrink away from each other, rainwater will be able to drain directly in, wetting the fiberglass. Once wet it may never dry out. You might want to try Perma-Chink (17455 N.E. 67th Ct., Redmond, Wash. 98052) instead. It is far more flexible, and adheres better to wood than mortar does.

If you haven't done the chinking yet, then eliminate the fiberglass. It won't really make your house any warmer, especially if the fiberglass is wet. Instead you could use a closed-cell foam called backer rod, available from Perma-Chink or from large caulking supply outlets. This prevents drafts, adjusts to the shrinking of logs and mortar, and is waterproof. It would also make a vapor-barrier coating inside unnecessary. The interior finish I like is made by Sikkens (1696 Maxwell St., Troy, Mich. 48084), but it isn't a vapor barrier. According to Sikkens, it limits the flow of moisture, but still allows the wood to breathe.

Sealing log joints

To seal the joints of the logs inside my log cabin, I plan to use glue mixed with wood shavings. Can you give me any information on how to fill the cracks?
—*Edward C. John, Oldtown, Md.*

Alasdair Wallace, a builder of log houses in Lakefield, Ont., replies: If your building has been recently completed, I suggest that you allow the logs to settle for at least a year before attempting to seal the cracks between them permanently. Meanwhile, fiberglass or oakum can be used to keep out the drafts. When your building has reached its equilibrium, there are two approaches to sealing the remaining cracks that I recommend over the glue and shavings mix. If the cracks are no more than ¼ in. wide, apply a color-matched rubberized caulking sealer over an oakum backing. If you prefer, or if the cracks are substantial, rip strips of scrap log material on a table saw. Taper the strips front to back and final-fit with a small plane or spokeshave. Apply glue to the cracks and hammer the strips into place, then clean up with a chisel. This takes time and patience, but it will result in a much cleaner, more aesthetically satisfying finish.

Chinking repair

I have a problem that seems to plague many of us who have built log homes—my chinking is separating from the logs. I used fiberglass batts between each round, and nailed hardware cloth to the logs as a backing and reinforcement for the mortar chinking. I know I can remove the chinking and begin again, but this is an alternative I'm trying hard to avoid. Have you ever used fiberglass-reinforced bonding cement as chinking on the exterior of the logs over existing mortar that has separated? Will this create a barrier that prevents the walls from breathing?
—*Steve Stahl, Cabot, Vt.*

Drew Langsner, a log builder who teaches and writes on the subject in Marshall, N. C., replies: The standard practice of waiting to chink until at least a year after placing the last log is a good one. During the first year, much of the log shrinkage and notch settling will take place. Then when you chink, the only movement that your new chinking will have to deal with is the normal expansion and contraction of the logs due to changes in humidity and temperature.

I have not used surface-bonding cement for repairing chinking, but it seems worth a try. It's fairly expensive, so experiment with a small test area first. Fill the cracks between your present chinking and the logs with a flexible caulking before applying the new cement over the top. In places where these gaps are more than ¼ in. wide, use foam wedges or polystyrene rope, which is sometimes sold under the name of backer rod.

Red pine for log building

I am planning to build a log home using half-dovetail notching. The building site is surrounded by a 35-acre plantation of red pines that I own. These trees were planted by the WPA during the 1930s. I am worried about using red pine for this type of structure. I have been told by both a timber framer and a sawyer that I can expect the red pine logs to twist after being sawn flat on two sides.

I have read that twist is caused by what is known as juvenile wood. Presumably the high rate of growth during the first eight to ten years of the tree's life contrasts with the slower growth of later years. The fast-growth wood dries at a different rate from the slow-growth wood, causing tension within the log. This tension results in the twisting that I've been warned about. I have cut down a few of the trees, and this growth pattern appears to be present.

Is twisting a result of my red pine being plantation grown, or is it a problem with all red pine regardless of how it was grown? Is it possible to detect "twisters" before felling the trees? Is there any possible way to prevent twisting from occurring?

—*Frederick J. Bennett,*
Little Falls, N. Y.

Robert Chambers replies: I have no trouble with my logs, which are almost always red pine, either hewn or full-round. But you are correct that there are primary stresses in logs. In general, the inside of a log is in compression, while the outside is in tension. Sawing a log off-center (removing more wood from one side than

from the other) can unbalance these stresses and cause a log to bow. As lumber and timbers lose water there can be secondary (drying) stresses that cause bowing and twisting. Red pine is not especially prone to drying stresses.

Don't hesitate to use plantation red pine, but pick your logs carefully. Perhaps your county forester can help you choose straight trees, with as little taper as possible. Look closely for indications of spiral grain before you fell a tree. To identify spiral grain, look for diagonal striations in the bark. Also, above and below each branch there are slight depressions. These should be in line with the trunk, not diagonal to it.

When the grain curls around the trunk like a barber pole, the wood is liable to twist when it dries. Put your right hand on the tree. If the indications of the grain curl in the direction of your thumb, it is called left-handed spiral and can be especially cantankerous. Right-handed spiral is not as bad, but to be safe I avoid all spiral. Finally, after you peel the logs, look for checks (drying cracks) that spiral around the trunk.

It is also important to saw your logs so as to preserve any existing bow. This seems contrary to first impressions, but it is better to deal with a natural bow than to saw the log straight and have it bow later, as it dries, because of imbalanced stresses. If you are using a circular-saw mill, then put the bow up or down, not to the side. Take equal amounts off each side of the log in order to balance the primary stresses (drawing, facing page), which will also make notching a lot easier because the inside and outside flats will be the same height.

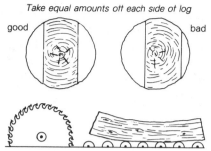

Take equal amounts off each side of log

good

bad

Saw logs to preserve existing bow

I asked wood-technology specialists at the University of Minnesota about your trees, and they told me that plantation-grown pines should work just fine. They predicted no differences in twisting. Juvenile wood can be the cause of bow in lumber and timbers, but it does not often cause twisting or affect whole logs, as long as you follow the precautions I have mentioned.

Sealer to protect logs

We have a log house with cement mortar joints. Is there a sealer on the market, not too expensive, that will weatherproof the logs and mortar? —*John Booker, Shirleysburg, Pa.*

Alasdair Wallace, a designer and builder of log homes in Lakefield, Ont., replies: I suspect that the reason you want to seal your logs and mortar is because you are encountering the perennial problem of wood and mortar parting company as the logs expand and contract with changes in humidity. There is no ready solution, although the problem can be minimized by protecting the logs from the weather. Building location, adequate roof overhang, clearance between the ground and the bottom log are all important factors here. Provision for humidity control within the building, especially during the winter, is essential. All too frequently, a woodstove or oil furnace, unless properly equipped with a humidifier, will reduce the humidity so much that the logs begin to check.

Pentox or Resilacrete are two clear sealers that may be applied to exterior log-mortar surfaces, although old-timers don't use anything. My preference is to spray both interior and exterior log surfaces with an aromatic, nontoxic, hot mixture of 30% boiled linseed oil and 70% turpentine. Heat the oil and remove the mixture from the burner before adding the turpentine. Log ends should never be sealed.

Choosing a log-home kit

I want to buy a log-home package, but the information I'm getting from the different companies seems contradictory. Some manufacturers, usually selling pine or fir kits, promise kiln-dried logs. Another company, which uses cedar, claims their use of green logs is better and make a tighter house based on their allowances for drying. I need some information to balance out the sales pitches.
—*Ray Foster, Girdwood, Alaska*

Rob Ridgway, President of Western Log Homes, Denver, Colo., replies: Contrary to what the salesmen say, there is no "best way" to build a log home. An incompetent carpenter can make a mess of the finest materials, and a fine carpenter can still do an excellent job with inferior materials.

Be wary of "kiln-dried" logs. Unless a moisture content is given, "kiln dried" may simply mean that the lumber was drier when it came out of the kiln than when it went in. Check with the company to see how dry the logs are. If the moisture content is less than 18%, you can expect a good, tight home.

When the moisture content is above 18%, serious problems can result if the shrinkage of the logs isn't anticipated. Once the logs are assembled into a wall, this shrinkage causes the logs to settle. Walls, windows and doors may twist and jam, and cracks that open up between logs will let the cold wind blow through. As a result, using green logs requires much better craftsmanship. Each log must be judged to fit with the adjoining logs and settle properly in relation to the others. Carefully constructed, a green-log house can season to become very strong and tight. However, success depends on the experience of the builder. Improper green log-building techniques will mean having to chink and caulk continually appearing cracks between the logs during the time it takes them to season, which can be three years or more.

I recommend that you select the style of log construction you find most pleasing, whether it is hand-peeled or machined, chinked or chinkless. Do the same with the species of timber. All of them will make a solid, tight home. Your choice of cedar, pine or fir should be based on your personal preference, your budget, and maybe most important, the reputation of the company that supplies or builds the house. Ask for references. Talk to people who have lived in their log homes for several years, and ask them whether they have had problems with the walls, such as maintenance and air infiltration. Was the house delivered and built on schedule? Did they get good service from the company both during and after construction? Would they build another, and if so, what would they do differently?

Notching a log octagon

My husband and I are in the process of drawing plans for an octagonal log home with 20-ft. sides. Are the corner notches more difficult for an octagon than for the typical rectangle? Is there a good source of printed information for questions like this?
—*Elaine A. McPeake, Welch, W. Va.*

Alasdair G. B. Wallace, designer and builder of log homes in Lakefield, Ont., replies: My experience has been primarily with round-log construction. If you choose a different log style and joint type, the methods will differ from mine, but the angle at which the logs intersect remains the same.

As shown in the drawings on the facing page, the procedure for scribing the round notch for conventional 90° inside corners and the 135° inside corners required by an octagonal plan is identical. However, because your logs will intersect at an oblique angle, you will have to hold your scriber so that you can make it work within the confines of the 45° that remains between the portion of the log that protrudes beyond the notch and the exterior wall. Keeping the scriber points vertical is absolutely critical for accurate notching, and I recommend that you purchase

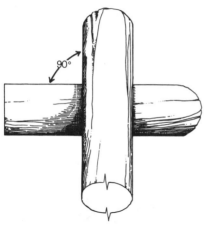

90°

Perpendicular round-log notch

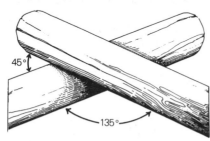

a scriber fitted with spirit-level bubbles so you can be sure you are keeping the tool plumb.

Should you choose to dovetail your logs, the angles of the bearing faces will remain unaltered; however, the angle of the shoulder across the log, will be 45° rather than 90°. A couple of practice notches on scrap material will pay dividends.

While none of the following refer-

45°

135°

Octagonal round-log notch

ences deals specifically with octagonal construction, together they should fill your needs for general reference on all aspects of log construction: *Building with Logs,* by B. Allan Mackie (Charles Scribner's Sons, 597 Fifth Ave., New York, N. Y. 10017); *Notches of All Kinds,* by B. Allan Mackie (The Canadian Log House, Box 1205, Prince George, B.C., V2L 4V3); *The Complete Log House Book,* by Dale Mann and Richard Skinulis (McGraw-Hill Ryerson Ltd., 330 Progress Ave., Scarborough, Ont. M1P 2Z5).

Lifting heavy timbers

I've heard some old-timers say that before the days of power equipment, large beams were raised using some kind of A-frame with which the beam was lifted in increments to the desired height. Do you have any information on this technique?
—*Stephen J. Whiteman,
Idyllwild, Calif.*

Timber-framer Ed Levin, of Canaan, N. H., replies: If your raising can go quickly (in one to three days), your best bet is a crane. Modern rough-terrain cranes can reach sites that are inaccessible to truck-mounted machines. Even if the crane can't drive right to the site, it might be set up well uphill and still reach over the foundation by extending 100 ft. to 150 ft. of telescoping hydraulic boom. This is the fastest, safest and often the cheapest way to erect a timber frame.

However, if your raising requires many days of crane time (at $500 to $800 per day) or your site is completely inaccessible (check with a local crane operator before giving up hope), you will probably have to resort to one of the following old-time raising methods.

Most traditional timber-frame raisings were accomplished by first assembling the beams into walls, or bents, and then pushing these assemblies up into place, using a succession of pike poles of increasing length, powered by a large crew of friends and neighbors. An alternative to this is the pulling and lifting force supplied by tackle rigged to a stout tree, gin pole or homemade derrick. A gin pole (drawing below), is a

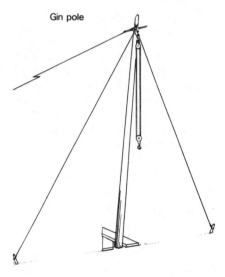

Gin pole

long sapling or beam with a block-and-tackle attached to the top. Since the gin pole is unstable when erect, it must be guyed back to the ground or deck in three directions, making it difficult to raise and inconvenient to move. Thus a gin pole is not useful if the raising requires lifts from many different positions.

The simplest form of derrick is an A-frame with tackle rigged at the apex, and the legs (ranging in size

from 4x4 to 6x6) braced to each other with a 2x at midspan and tied together or firmly bedded at their feet, as shown in the drawing below.

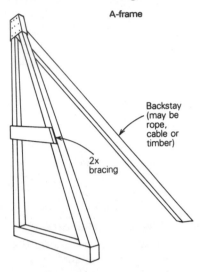

A-frame

Backstay (may be rope, cable or timber)

2x bracing

Since the A-frame is unstable only in one direction, it requires just a single guy opposing the pull of the lift, making it easier to put up and shift around than the gin pole. The A-frame may be stabilized by leaning the top in toward the building so that it is held in place by the guy or backstay (this may be rope, cable or timber).

By keeping the apex clear of the foundation, you can use the A-frame to tilt up exterior walls or bents. Alternatively, if you set it up closer to the building and tilt the top over the deck, the tackle will reach in some distance to lift single timbers as well as interior walls or bents.

Timber-frame hardware

I plan to build a post-and-beam shed with white ash logs. The mortise-and-tenon joints will be held

with ½-in. bolts. Are the bolts and the ash compatible over time?
—*Lawrence A. DeVito, Mason, N. H.*

New Hampshire timber-framer Tedd Benson replies: When iron is used in timber framing, usually the intention is to replace wooden joinery connections with plates and bolts. If you are going to the trouble of making mortises and tenons, don't pin them with metal.

Using hardware on a timber frame can create two problems. First, as the frame dries and settles, the bolt will have a wearing action on the surrounding wood, causing the joint to loosen. Second, the metal bolt will have the effect of drawing moisture, in the form of condensation, into the joint. This will speed the decay of the ash, which has almost no inherent rot resistance. A white oak or locust peg would be much more forgiving of wood movement, and wouldn't begin a process of deterioration that the ash can't handle.

Handling Douglas fir timbers

I plan to build a timber-frame house using Douglas fir trees from my land. These trees are only 12 in. to 17 in. in diameter, so the beams will necessarily include heartwood. How will this affect these beams? I would like to cut the trees this summer and mill them next summer. Will this cause more checking than will milling them just after harvesting?
—*Michael Hildt, Seattle, Wash.*

Timber-framer Tedd Benson replies: Douglas fir heartwood is the least stable and least desirable part of the tree. Regardless of how you treat the wood, you should expect these heart-center timbers to twist and check much more severely than timbers that are free of heart. If you fell the trees this summer and mill the timbers next summer, without retarding the drying process, this checking will be a lot worse. Mills in the West often keep their logs submerged in mill ponds or use sprinklers to keep them wet until they are ready to cut them.

I'd go ahead and mill the timbers and sticker them. Seal the ends with latex paint to slow moisture loss through the end grain. Stack the wood in a shaded area, stickering each new layer. Allow ½ in. of space laterally between timbers to ensure slow and even drying. They will still check and twist, but not as much as if you waited a year to mill them.

Stress-skin subfloors

I am designing a post-and-beam house using stress-skin panels for the exterior siding and insulation. The first floor will be over a crawl space, so the insulation will have to go either under the floor or on the outside of the perimeter foundation walls. The floor joists will be 16 in. o. c. I would like to assemble stress-skin subfloor panels using 1-in. expanded-polystyrene insulation sandwiched between ½-in. CDX plywood top and bottom. The finished floors (carpet, hardwood, linoleum and slate) will be laid on top of the stress-skin subfloor in the usual ways. While the cost will be higher than conventional insulation methods, I feel the floor will be immensely warmer on the feet. Is there any merit to

this method, and are the materials suggested adequate?
— *Timothy A. Lasch, Conesus, N. Y.*

Alex Wade, an architect and author in Mt. Marion, N. Y., replies: A crawl space isn't a good idea for a superinsulated house. It can add to moisture problems if it isn't properly waterproofed and ventilated. Most people don't take the trouble to waterproof properly if the space isn't actually going to be used. If possible, switch the design to a slab, which is easy to insulate around the perimeter. A slab also acts as a heat sink.

If you go ahead with a crawl space, then stress-skin subfloor panels are a convenient way to insulate the floor. However, 1-in. thick expanded polystyrene in a stress-skin panel has little insulation value. Since the rest of the house is post-and-beam, I suggest floor framing on 4-ft. centers with 4½-in. thick expanded-polystyrene panels. RMK Enterprises (Box 337, York Haven, Pa. 17370) can supply the foam, adhesive and laminate panels to your skins for less than $20 per 4x8 panel. If you are fabricating your own, you'll need plenty of space and a method of weighting or clamping the panels. I recommend using Mor-Ad 336 (Morton Chemical Co. 110 N. Wacker Drive, Chicago, Ill. 60606) or 3M 4289 adhesive (3M Center, St. Paul, Minn. 55144-1000). Foam is available quite cheaply from RMK Enterprises and from other panel manufacturers.

Insulating a timber frame

I've torn down an old barn and will be building a house out of the original frame. I want the beams and bracing to be exposed on the interior walls but also want R-30 insulation. I'd hate to resort to building an entire house around this frame to hold insulation and am reluctant to use urea formaldehyde or isocyanurate because of the health hazard. How would you suggest insulating this house?
— *Frank Marrapese, Adamsville, Pa.*

Ed Levin, a post-and-beam builder in Canaan, N. H., replies: There is a product developed specifically to enclose timber-frame buildings without the redundancy of a second frame to hold fiberglass-batt insulation. This is a stress-skin panel consisting of 3½ in. of isocyanurate insulation sandwiched between an interior layer of ½-in. drywall or blueboard (for plaster) and ½-in. exterior plywood or chipboard sheathing. The aged R-value for the 4½-in. thick panel is 26.4. An optional 5-in. thick panel (4 in. of insulation plus the two ½-in. skins) will give a full R-30. The panels span floor to ceiling. They are double-splined together and spiked to the timber frame. Around window and door openings the insulation is routed out to a depth of 1½ in., and studs are fastened in place to increase stiffness and provide nailing strips. An accommodation is made for wiring in and around the panels.

A word about foam insulation. Isocyanurate, unlike urea formaldehyde, emits no toxic or irritating gases, nor is it a significant fire hazard. The material in the panels won't burn except under the most intense heat (such as use of a welding torch). And in any case the insulation meets national building-code fire-protection standards since it is bonded to a thermal barrier of drywall or blueboard and plaster. Finally, in lab tests isocyanurate produced lower smoke densities and a lower level of toxic gases (CO_2, CO, SO_2) than the red oak burned as a control. No measurable amounts of hydrogen cyanide were produced, and the gaseous by-products of red oak combustion proved more toxic to test animals than did those of the isocyanurate.

You can obtain further information on stress-skin panels by writing to Amos Winter, Box 34, Spofford, N. H., 03462; or by calling (603) 363-4271.

Structural potpourri

We want to build a timber-frame house from trees on our property. Unfortunately, of the four species available (fir, hemlock, cedar and spruce), there is not enough of any one to frame the whole house; in fact it would take at least three. Is using mixed species feasible structurally and aesthetically?
—Richard Wasson, Issaquah, Wash.

Tedd Benson, a timber framer and author from Alstead Center, N. H., replies: I don't see any problem at all with a mix of wood species in a timber frame. As a matter of fact, I think it's a terrific idea if a potpourri from the local forest is all that you have available. I mixed three woods in the frame of my own home for nearly the same reasons.

Of the four woods, cedar is the most stable. However, it's also the weakest. But in general, the mix you propose is not difficult because they are all softwoods of similar shrinkage values and strength properties. Still, for aesthetic and structural rea-

sons, it is important to separate the species by making them completely different components of the frame. This type of separation has several purposes: to use the structural properties of the species wisely, to lend symmetry and composition to the frame design, and to keep the effects of drying consistent.

Depending on the quality of your timbers, you might use the strongest wood (probably fir) for the floor system, and the least attractive wood (hemlock, to my way of thinking) for the roof system. This would leave either spruce or cedar for posts and braces. I would pick the cedar. It is adequately strong in compression parallel to the grain, and is the most attractive of the woods.

White pine for a timber frame

I own a timber-frame house that was built in 1740. Although the braces, purlins and ridgepole are hardwood, the heavy timbers are all white pine. These beams seem to have endured well. In fact, the hardwood seems to have suffered the most damage from termites or powderpost beetles. Why is it that white pine is never mentioned as a building material for modern post-and-beam houses?
—Gary Banuk, Hanson, Mass.

New Hampshire author and timber framer Tedd Benson replies: There is no doubt that pine can be used effectively in timber framing, but even historically, it often wasn't the first choice. Pine doesn't compare favorably with most hardwoods in any of the structural categories. Simply put, most hardwoods are stronger. This is the primary reason why the joiners in early America, with so many woods at their disposal, most often chose oak or chestnut. However, if they were in an area where these species weren't growing in abundance or if they wanted to get a building together in a hurry, pine was the logical choice.

In those days, it was easy for builders to find pine that was straight-grained, knot-free and tall enough that the length of most houses could be spanned with a single timber. Stories about those virgin white pine trees are legion. The wood was so perfect that it was used to make ship masts. It was even decreed that the larger trees were the property of the Crown of England, and off limits to the colonists.

But this isn't the same kind of pine that comes out of the sawmills today. The lumber we get from third, fourth and fifth-growth trees can't compare in strength, clarity or straightness of grain. As a result, when I use pine in my structures, which I do, I have to size the timbers carefully, and be willing to discard imperfect pieces or place them so that they don't weaken the frame.

Richard Neroni, the general manager of Timberpeg, in Claremont, N. H., also replies: I'd like to comment on why white pine is not mentioned as a building material for modern post-and-beam homes.

The early emigrés to Massachusetts Bay brought with them the building traditions with which they had grown up. In England during the early 17th century, oak was the material of choice. It was used for framing and for finish trim, doors, partitions and furniture. It would have been highly unusual for the colonists to switch suddenly to another species upon settling in North America when oak was readily available and already familiar to them.

Gradually, other woods such as chestnut and pine began to be used with oak for framing members. The settlers began to use other species more often as they became familiar with them. The massive summer beams of some 17th-century houses are of pine. Abbott Lowell Cummings mentions in *The Framed Houses of Massachusetts Bay, 1625-1725* that the balance shifts in favor of pine for framing during the first half of the 18th century, and pine largely replaces oak in the frame a little later.

Thoreau mentions in his journal in 1845: "I went down to the woods by Walden Pond...and began to cut down some tall, arrowy pines...for timber. I went on for some days cutting and hewing timber, and also studs and rafters." I would suggest that Thoreau chose white pine for the same reasons that others were selecting it. It was familiar, easy to work and light in weight.

The pine that was harvested in 1700 is the same genus and species as that harvested today. The strength of pine today is about the same as that of 100 years ago. The difference is in the proportion of clear lumber that is yielded per tree. Back then it was about 30%. Today it is around 5%. Most of the pine harvested today is third-growth, because the forests were clear-cut 150 years ago to make pasture land. And most of the clear lumber produced in a pine tree is in the first sawlog.

Pine timbers 200 years ago did not come from butt logs, but from top logs. Butt logs produced wide, clear boards that were saved for finish trim, paneling, tabletops and doors. Pine with knots was used where it did not show, such as backboards on furniture, attic flooring and heavy timbers. The pine used in timber today is about as knotty as in the past. Then as now, timbers are usually made from the smallest log that will yield the timber. This means less hewing and waste.

Pine is still used today for heavy timber framing for the same reason that Thoreau chose it. In addition, it is more stable than hardwood, has a higher strength to weight ratio and tends to twist, shrink and check less than other species. Our company manufactures hundreds of post-and-beam buildings a year, and we use white pine for 99% of our timbers. We occasionally use yellow pine or Douglas fir for unusual conditions or spans over 18 ft. If it is properly selected and sized, white pine is an excellent framing material.

Wood for timber framing

I am planning a timber-frame residence. In order of preference, how do you rate these woods in frames you have raised: white oak, red oak, pine and ash? Is it desirable to have all beams center-cut to contain the heart? About how long does it take to produce low moisture content in beams? What moisture content in your frames do you normally work with?
—*Armand E. Picou,*
Baton Rouge, La.

Timber framer Tedd Benson, of Alstead, N. H., replies: For us, the wood of choice in our timber frames is northern red oak. It is quite available in our area and grows well under many different conditions, and it's consistently sound. The quality of some of the other woods, like white oak, isn't as consistent. Some modern lumbering practices, like clearcutting, have caused a decline in the quality of most woods. Clearcutting has not affected red oak.

If I were in another area, I might choose a different wood. In Maine, for instance, I would want to work with pine. On the West Coast, I would look to either fir or cedar. Most of the East Coast woods are more stable as boxed-heart timbers. Fir and redwood, however, tend to have a decayed heart and should be ordered free of heart center (FOHC).

If we could get our timbers dry, we would. It takes about five years to air-dry an 8x8 timber or a couple of months to kiln-dry one. Neither alternative is very practical, so we work the timbers green, use strong joinery, and work toward making a frame in which the strength at the connections is stronger than the effect of the drying process. We want the whole structure to pull in a bit rather than separate at the joints. It remains one of the problems we have to deal with.

Wood characteristics

I am planning to build a timber-frame home, and several questions have come up which aren't adequately answered in the books I've read on the subject. First, in our area, hemlock, poplar, and red oak are readily available. Which species is best for timber framing? Secondly, what will be the effect of the shrinkage of green timber on framing joints? Are there special

joinery techniques to minimize these effects? And finally, how should timber frames be tied to the foundation? *—Dale Royalty, Hampton, Tenn.*

Ed Levine, a timber framer in Canaan, N. H., replies: Red oak would be my first choice for a framing timber, with hemlock and poplar a distant second and third. Oak is superior on all counts save cost and weight, although green oak isn't much heavier than green hemlock. Oak is worth the difference in price.

Wood shrinks considerably in width (across the grain) but not measurably in length (along the grain). The implications for the timber framer are as follows: Mortise-and-tenon joints, girt to post, remain tight in plan. But in section the tenon shrinks while the mortise height remains fixed, leaving a gap at the top, as shown in the drawing below.

Notched lap joints, joist to girt, shrink together in section, apart in plan.

To counter this shrinkage, cut your tenons slightly shorter than the depth of their respective mortises, about ¼ in. for every 4 in. of tenon length. This will allow the mortise to shrink in depth without forcing out its tenon.

Drawboring is another way to prevent tenon withdrawal. By offsetting holes in mortise and tenon so the driven pin pulls the parts together, the joint is spring-loaded against separation. Use dry white oak or black locust pins. Dovetail joints are also less likely to separate as framing timbers shrink.

As for your third question, post-and-beam frames should be bolted to the foundation. Because of the difficulty of accurately locating conventional anchor bolts and lowering heavy timber sills over them, drill ¾-in. holes in the sills at bolt locations. After the first-floor frame is in place on the foundation, extend the holes 3 in. into the cement using the rotary impact hammer. Blow out the cement dust, put expansion shields through the sills and into the concrete and screw in ½-in. bolts or threaded rod, as shown in the drawing below. The holes in the wood

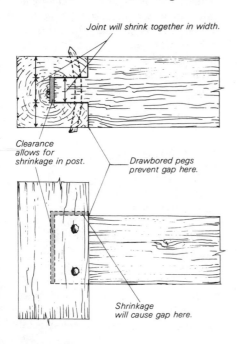

Joint will shrink together in width.

Clearance allows for shrinkage in post.

Drawbored pegs prevent gap here.

Shrinkage will cause gap here.

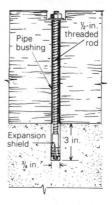

½-in. threaded rod

Pipe bushing

Expansion shield

3 in.

¾ in.

can be bushed with heavy-gauge black plastic water pipe for a tight fit. Counterbore the holes so that the bolt-heads or nuts (over washers) sit below the sill on top.

Shouldered timber joints

Last winter my wife and I took down a 43-ft. by 84-ft. timber-frame barn that was built in the mid-1880s. We found all of the wood to be in excellent condition. All of the beams were taken down with great care and labeled with copper tags.

The first-floor beams are ten-oned into shouldered mortises in the posts. The second-floor beams aren't. They are secured to their posts with simple pegged mortise-and-tenon joints. What type of bracket could we use to get the full strength of the timber when we re-assemble the frame without alter-ing the present joinery?

—*Jeff Hastings, Viroqua, Wis.*

Jeff Arvin of Riverbend Timber Framing Inc., in Blissfield, Mich., replies: If the reassembled frame is to become a barn again, I'd recom-mend deference to past perfor-mance. The original barn put in at least 100 years of good service; the timbers have apparently survived without damage. As they say, "If it ain't broke, don't fix it."

But if you are planning to use the barn frame for a house or an out-building where the loading situation is different, then some careful analy-sis is in order. A timber with should-ered joints is able to carry a greater load because shouldering increases the shear area at the joint. (Two ex-amples of shouldered joints are

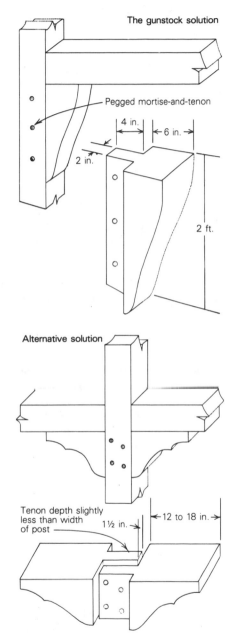

The gunstock solution

Pegged mortise-and-tenon

4 in. ← 6 in. →

2 in.

2 ft.

Alternative solution

Tenon depth slightly less than width of post

1½ in. ←12 to 18 in.→

shown in the drawing above). The entire cross section of the beam is transferring load to the post instead of to the smaller cross section at the tenon.

The final determination should be made by calculating the design load ("How heavily are you going to be loading this system?" and "How much area of this system is the beam in question going to support?"). If that load is greater than the carrying capacity of the weakest part of the beam, probably the simple tenon, then there may be a good reason to create a shoulder for the beam.

Girt-to-post joinery

My timber-frame house will require joining four 8x8 girts to an 8x8 post. Timber framer Tedd Benson has stated: "Three is usually the maximum number of girts that should be received by a post at one location at any cross-sectional plane." I am reasonably certain I've seen designs where four girts were brought into a post. Do you know of a joint design that would permit this? Is there an allowable exception to Benson's "usually?"

—Owen Carr, Huntington, N. Y.

Tedd Benson replies: "Usually" is a safe word, inserted in places where one chooses to be vague. In this case I regret using it. Three *is* the maximum number of girts that should be received by a post at one location. Putting four timbers at one location reduces the strength of the post at the intersection and creates a situation where it's difficult to secure all of the members to the post. A design or construction constraint may force you to have four timbers at an intersection, but you ought to·· explore all other options first.

If you need four girts, consider making the post larger and two of the girts smaller, as shown in the drawing below. This would increase the amount of wood that remains after mortising, and all members

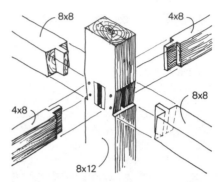

could be pegged, providing that the smaller timbers were raised with the bent, leaving enough room in the post to peg the other two members after the raising.

If you must have all 8x8s, one member could be secured with a wedged half-dovetail (drawing below) and the other three timbers would use typical pegged mortise-and-tenon joinery. Although this joint appears to solve the problem, it forces you to rely on the strength of the tenon to support the timber and

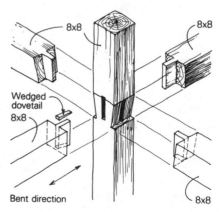

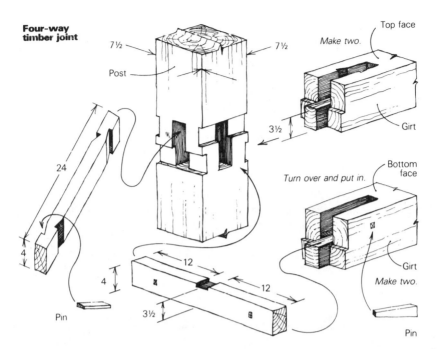

Four-way timber joint

7½ · 7½
Post
Make two.
Top face
3½
Girt
24
4
Turn over and put in.
Bottom face
Girt
Make two.
Pin
12 · 12
4
3½
Pin

its load. Also, the wedge won't remain tight as the timber shrinks and will lose its effectiveness, unless the end of it is exposed and can be snugged up from time to time.

Yoshikuni Shimoi, of Seattle, Wash., also replies: I am a Japanese carpenter living and working in Seattle. The drawing above shows my timber-frame joinery technique. The dimensions have been scaled to American lumber sizes, and it is easy to use power tools. The four girts are the same cut except for the pins.

Using queen posts

I'm designing a 1½-story timber-frame cape. If I add queen posts, I could reduce the size of the rafters, but would have to increase the size of the girt because of the partial roof load it would then be

taking. What is the advantage of using queen posts and how do you determine what load is being transferred to the girt?

Also, I would like to cut the beams out of green logs. I might have to store the finished beams for up to five years. Are there any precautions I can take to prevent them from twisting, warping and checking?   —*Richard A. Strub, Eggertsville, N. Y.*

Tedd Benson, a timber framer in Alstead Center, N. H., replies: Queen posts are generally used to interrupt a rafter span and transfer some of the roof load to other parts of the frame. The most common structural concern that inspires the use of queen posts is outward thrust. Queen posts are very effective at reducing the loads on the exterior posts, but it takes a rather sophisticated structural analysis to determine exactly how much load is transferred through the queen posts. That analysis considers the timber species, size and span, as well as the knee-brace layout, in order to gauge the relative stiffness of the rafters and girts. Without this information, I can't make any specific comments about the load distribution within your proposed frame.

However, in the absence of that analysis (which should be performed by a structural engineer), there is little risk in assuming the worst case—that the queen post might feel the lion's share of the load borne by the rafter. One reasonable way to calculate that load is to multiply the applied loads (live and dead) by the applicable "tributary area" of roof. That area might conservatively be described as being halfway to each of the adjacent rafters in width and the distance from the ridge to a point midway between the queen post and the exterior posts (drawing below) in length. You should certainly assume that the bent girt will have to be enlarged to bear the loads from the queen posts. If the spans and loads are large enough, you

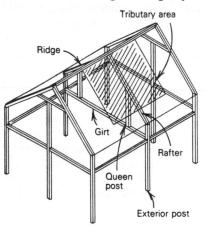

might want to consider adding interior posts to transfer loads to the foundation more directly.

As for the second part of your question, green timbers are notoriously independent rascals and will do as they wish. You can cover them, store them in shady places, seal the exposed end grain, bind and sticker them, but nothing will prevent defects such as twisting, warping and checking. However, if you are working with a five-year schedule, you have the distinct advantage of being able to work the timbers after they have stabilized somewhat. If the beams are softwood, why not do the joinery in the fourth year? If they are hardwood, wait for the third year, before the wood has thoroughly hardened but after it has already spent some of its willfulness.

Timber-frame clerestory

I am planning to build a timber-frame passive-solar home that will include a clerestory. Most of the information on timber framing that I have found covers only traditional design. Can you give me some idea of how to handle the ridge for a clerestory? What joinery should I use with the rafters?
—Stewart Smythe,
Salt Lake City, Utah

Tedd Benson, a timber framer and author in Alstead Center, N. H., replies: The designs for clerestories seem to have evolved from two different approaches. A clerestory is perceived either as two shed roofs of different heights leaning on one another, or as an extension of one plane of rafters above its intersection with the other plane.

In the first approach (top drawing, below), the whole system leans heavily on a post that must fall at the intersection between the sheds. This would call for a post that runs from the sill to the top of the clerestory. It could be difficult to get such a timber, depending on the height of the building. Both sets of rafters should join the posts with a housed mortise-and-tenon joint about 2 in. wide, 4 in. deep and 8 in. long, and pinned with two 1-in. pegs. A housed joint is one that has a shoulder cut into the post on which the rafter bears, as shown in the detail drawing. To tie these rafters to the posts and in-

crease the racking resistance of the structure, frame diagonal braces between the rafters and the posts.

The second approach, also shown in the drawing, makes the function of the clerestory post much less critical to the structure. The roof can be designed using a normal rafter truss, with the clerestory nothing more than an added element. You'd need only to calculate the extra load where the clerestory post joins the rafter. This load is not likely to be significant because most of it would be supported in the cantilever. The joint at the peak of the clerestory could be cut in the same way as the first example, while the connection to the lower rafter could be a simple mortise and tenon. Where the two rafters join, use a housed mortise and tenon.

Whichever approach you use, the rafter-to-post and rafter-to-rafter joints are the most important because they connect and support the truss. The ridge beam and the beam at the base of the clerestory serve to connect the trusses and would act as nailers for the finish work. They should both have mortise-and-tenon joinery, although I'd house the ridge timber because the size would be partially reduced as a result of the roof pitch.

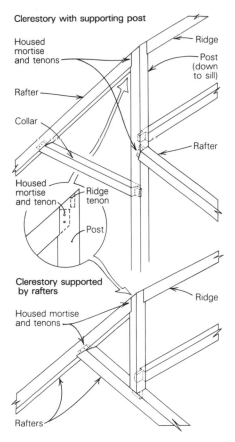

Clerestory with supporting post

Housed mortise and tenons

Ridge

Post (down to sill)

Rafter

Collar

Rafter

Housed mortise and tenon

Ridge tenon

Post

Clerestory supported by rafters

Housed mortise and tenons

Ridge

Rafters

Fixing a sagging floor

The floor in one room of our 200-year-old fieldstone home sags over 1 in. at the center and is very springy. The sag we can live with, but I would like to stiffen up the floor. The handhewn beams, which are exposed in the room below, are about 4 in. wide by 7 in.

deep and span 15 ft. They are spaced about 30 in. on center. According to standard calculations, the beams are undersized to begin with. In addition, several have notches cut in the tops and long cutouts on the bottoms. Lengthwise cracks in at least two of the beams indicate failure in horizontal shear.

Since the distance from the floor to the bottom of the beams is just over 6 ft., deeper beams are out of the question. I am considering filling the notches in the tops with tight-fitting plugs, since this part of the beams is in compression. The cutouts in the bottom of the beams can be filled with matching wood, but the beams would still need to be spanned with some type of strap to take the tension.

Will these methods work? How can I repair the beams that have failed in horizontal shear?
—*William Ailes, Hartsville, Pa.*

Tedd Benson, a timber framer in Alstead, N. H., replies: The methods you suggest will not be effective. The beams are undersized, as you note, and Band-Aids won't do. If you are unwilling to replace the joists, then you are going to have to find another way to reduce the deflection. You could shorten the span by putting in supporting posts or a bearing wall. Or glue (with construction adhesive) and screw 1½ in. tongue-and-groove planking to the flooring above the timbers. The planks should be laid perpendicular to the joists and should be as long as possible. It helps here to plug the cutouts in the top of the timbers.

The best solution, though, would be to hang the joists above the tim-

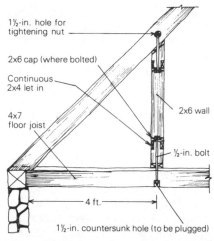

1½-in. hole for tightening nut

2x6 cap (where bolted)

Continuous 2x4 let in

4x7 floor joist

2x6 wall

½-in. bolt

4 ft.

1½-in. countersunk hole (to be plugged)

bers. Since the rafters and the joists would probably not be in line with each other, you should build a wall that would allow you to make a bolt attachment at any point (drawing above). This wall would work in tension, transferring some of the load into the rafter and ultimately to the outside wall. If this "tension wall" can be built at least 4 ft. from the edge of the timber, it should eliminate any noticeable deflection. An added advantage of this solution is that the bolt through the timber would retard what you call horizontal shear (which is probably just a drying check).

Timber/stud-frame marriage

I'd like to build a post-and-beam addition to my house. The house is standard stud-frame construction, resting on an 11-in. poured foundation. I'd like to make the addition 10 ft. wide and 30 ft. long. Can I add a timber-frame room to a stud-frame house? If so, how do I attach the beams to the stud frame? Will the heavy beams of the

addition be too much weight for the house to bear? A sketch of the front elevation of my addition is shown in the top drawing at right. —*Jim Ryan, Putnam Valley, N.Y.*

Ed Levin, a housewright from Canaan, N. H., replies: Standard practice with timber-frame additions is to construct a freestanding new structure adjacent to the old one. In your situation this means running the inside posts in each bent all the way to the floor as shown in the bottom drawing at right. You will probably need additional supports in the garage to pick up the load. This way, the addition will support its own roof load rather than transfer it to the original structure. Beam rafters should end at the juncture between the two buildings, with short 2x rafters making the connection to the existing roof. Make sure they are nailed into rafters and not simply butted against the sheathing. Sheathing and siding will join the old and new walls, and they could also be held together by bolting through the studs and into the timbers.

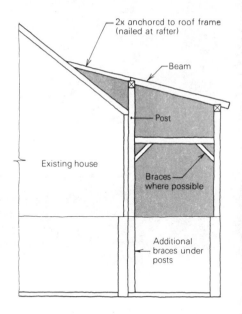

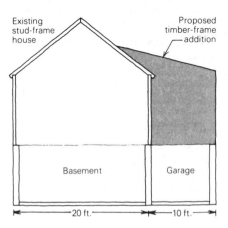

Chapter 12:

Bugs and Mold

Carpenter ants

I recently built a bermed, sod-roofed structure in the Northwest. Carpenter ants have gotten into the exposed T&G 2x6 roof decking, leaving small piles of sawdust on the floor. I have spray-bombed the space (14 ft. by 32 ft.), but it seems to kill only a few ants, leaving the rest to tunnel further. How can I get rid of them permanently?
—*John Liczwinko, Seattle, Wash.*

Phil Pellitteri, senior outreach specialist at the Insect Diagnostic Lab at the Cooperative Extension Program of the University of Wisconsin in Madison, replies: Carpenter ants are unwelcome guests in wood construction. They are the medium-to-large (¼ in. to ½ in. long) black or black and red ants seen crawling both outdoors and in the home. They can be distinguished from oth-

er ants because carpenter ants have only one segmented node between the thorax and the abdomen, while most other ants have two.

The winged forms of carpenter ants are the kings and queens. Except for the queen who founds the nest, they don't appear until a nest is two or three years old. Then a new swarm of winged carpenter ants will emerge, but they move on after a couple of days to form new nests. They seldom settle near the original nest, so you don't have to worry about having 300 new nests if a swarm of flying carpenter ants suddenly appears.

Carpenter ants burrow into wood to make nests, but unlike termites, they do not use wood as a food source. This makes them much more of a nuisance than a structural concern. In ·the United States, the most significant carpenter ant infestations are seen in the Northeast, Great Lakes region and the Pacific Northwest. People sometimes mistake winged carpenter ants for termites. You can distinguish them from each other in several ways (drawing below). Carpenter ants

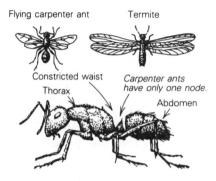

Flying carpenter ant   Termite

Constricted waist
Thorax

Carpenter ants have only one node.

Abdomen

have a constricted waist, termites don't. Carpenter ants have an elbowed antenna, termites have a straight antenna. Both have two pairs of wings, but on carpenter ants the pairs are two different sizes. On termites, the wings are the same size.

It is unusual to have carpenter ants nesting in structures within the first four to five years of construction. Most species start their nest in moist wood that has begun to decay. They will nest in both hardwoods and softwoods, and outdoors they are commonly found nesting in tree stumps and dead limbs. Sometimes the ants will get lazy and nest in existing cavities, such as in hollow-core doors or in the cracks in rough-hewn beams.

The secret to controlling the ants is to find and treat the nest directly. The small piles of coarse sawdust you are finding are a dead giveaway that the ants are nesting indoors, and I suspect that they are in the 2x6

decking, the ½-in. plywood or in any space between the two. Insect bombs and fogs do not penetrate very well, so the treatments you have tried will not solve the problem.

I suggest drilling an ⅛-in. hole into the area where you have seen the activity and spraying an appropriate dust or spray directly into the hole. Where you spray (directly into the nest) is more critical than what you spray. Insecticides such as Diazinon, Dursban and Baygon are labeled for indoor ant control, or boric acid can be dusted into the nest to control it.

Keeping carpenter ants from returning may not be so easy. Because of their fondness for moist or weakened wood, ants are useful in locating moisture problems, which are far more serious to the structural integrity of the home than the ant nests are. But with new construction, that may or may not be the cause of the problem. I would not suggest a preventive treatment, as the expense and the large amount of pesticide used are not justified for routine carpenter-ant problems. If the ants find the environment to their liking, they will move in. On the other hand, if things remain sound and dry, ants should not be a problem.

There is some hope for the future. A very effective antibiotic-type bait should come on the market within the next 18 months. It is very safe to use, and as few as two traps placed in a home will take care of the ants without having to use a messy spray treatment. It will take about two weeks for enough bait to be taken back to the nest and poison the queen and young, but it will eliminate the often difficult task of locating the nest and make carpenter ant control much easier.

Molly Cook-Field, of Putney, Vt., also replies: Here's another solution to the carpenter-ant problem. The ants around here do not discriminate about what types of wood they like. They go for new construction as well as old and have moved into several well-built and rot-free new homes—including ours.

Mix a solution of 2 cups water, ¼ cup sugar and ⅛ cup powdered boric acid (boric acid is available from drugstores). These are approximate measurements. The idea is not to make the solution so strong that it kills the ants on contact. You want them to carry it back and feed it to the queen and the rest of the nest. The ants are attracted to the sugar, so pour the solution into shallow dishes, sardine cans, or ideally, plastic containers with lids. Punch holes in the sides (above the liquid level) and in the lid, large enough to let the ants travel freely. I put little sticks of wood inside to act as bridges and ladders. The container should be placed in the ants' path. Once they find it, it will take two to three weeks to kill the entire colony.

Our cats were not interested in drinking the stuff, but be mindful of pets and children because the solution is toxic if swallowed.

Our house is now, happily, ant-free, and we can finally appreciate ants out in the garden and forest.

Carpenter bees

I am having a problem with carpenter bees. For years they have been boring into the fascia on the eaves of the house. They bore in on the edge of the 1x10 cypress. To remedy things, I drill out the hole with a ⅜-in. bit and fill it with a dowel. But the bees return, and now their horizontal tunnels are breaking through the surface of the fascia.

Someone mentioned that replacing the fascia with redwood might stop the problem, but that's too costly. Are there additives to stains that stop bees? I've heard of some additives that kill insects but I'm not sure they kill bees. Any suggestions?   —*L. Poindexter, Hilton Head Island, S. C.*

Phil Pellitteri, a specialist in entomology at the University of Wisconsin Extension program at Madison, replies: There are at least twelve species of carpenter bees in the United States, but by far the most common is *Xylocopa virginica virginica,* which ranges from Maine to Florida and westward to Nebraska and Texas. Adult carpenter bees are ¾ in. to 1 in. long, and they look much like bumblebees.

The adults hibernate in abandoned nest tunnels, and in areas that have low winter temperatures they may be killed off. If they survive (they often don't here in Wisconsin), they emerge in the spring to mate and begin nest construction.

Fertilized females often clean out and reuse an old nest without further burrowing, or may bore an entire new gallery into various wooden structures. Carpenter bees prefer softwoods such as redwood, cypress, cedar and pine for nesting sites. Hardwoods are used by the bees only if the wood has been softened by exposure or decay. The entrance/exit hole is round, and ½ in. in diameter. Once inside the wood, the female turns and burrows with the wood grain to a depth of 4 in. to 8 in. She then goes out and collects pollen, and mixes this with regurgitated nectar to make "bee bread." After placing this bread at the bottom of the tunnel, she lays one egg and seals the gallery with a disc of chewed wood pulp. This procedure is repeated until a linear series of six cells is made. Eggs hatch in a few days, the larvae feed on the pollen mass, grow, pupate and emerge as new adults within 35 to 70 days. For most of the United States there is only one generation per year, but in very warm southern states two or more generations can take place in one year.

Damage to structures is usually slight and amounts to cosmetic defacement. It takes several years of neglect for serious structural failure to occur. Unfinished wood and weathered wood—shingles, eaves, window and door sills, fences and porch ceilings—are the preferred areas of attack. Damage can also be caused by woodpeckers that feed on the larvae.

If you don't want to use chemicals, you can remove the infested wood and replace it with pressure-treated wood. Maintaining a good coat of paint on all exposed wood will help. Plugging newly excavated nests with dowels will discourage further activity but will not kill the bees already inside, so before plugging the hole, kill the bees by running a stiff wire all the way to the end of each tunnel.

Several chemicals can be used, but regulations differ in each state, so it's good to check with your County Extension Agent for up-to-date information. In Wisconsin sprays or dusts of carbaryl (Sevin), propoxur (Baygon) and Resmethrin

can be used. Place the treatment inside the nest and on the wood surface around the entrance (take precautions to avoid being stung). Wait 12 to 24 hours before plugging the hole to be sure all bees are affected. Spraying without sealing the entrance is a temporary measure and may have to be repeated yearly.

There used to be insecticides that could kill insects for two to three years if added to paints or stains, but these products are no longer sold. The new insecticides have too short a residual life for effective long-term control.

Blue stain on white pine

We have been using northern white pine for timber frames, and some of the finished timbers grow a blue mold. Once started, it spreads to adjoining timbers. We sand and oil the wood with Watco. What is the best way to prevent this? Is there a fungicide that could be added safely to the finish? For timbers already infected, what is an effective treatment?

—Philip Payson, Freeport, Maine

William Feist, project leader of the Wood Surface Chemistry and Property Enhancement department at the Forest Products Laboratory in Madison, Wis., replies: The blue mold on your northern white pine could be ordinary mildew, which is a common cause of wood discoloration. The most common species of fungi are black to blue. They grow mostly in warm, humid climates, but are also found in northern states.

Mildew can be removed by using liquid household bleach. The chemical in household bleach (sodium hypochlorite) will kill the mildew but will not prevent its re-occurrence. Such mildewcides are often present in water-repellent preservatives. Some new materials with manufacturer's claims of low toxicity will contain one or more of the following chemicals: 3-iodo-2-propynyl butyl carbamate; copper-8-quinolinolate; 2-(thiocyanomethylthio) benzothiazole, plus methylene-bis thiocyanate.

The culprit could also be blue stain, which is caused by fungi that commonly infect sapwood. Blue stain does not weaken wood structurally, but the conditions that favor its development are also ideal for wood decay and paint failure.

While wood may contain blue stain, there will probably be no detrimental effect so long as the moisture content is kept below 20%. Wood in properly designed and well-maintained houses usually has a moisture content of 8% to 13%. However, if the wood is exposed to heavy moisture, the blue-stain fungi will develop.

To prevent blue stain from discoloring wood, follow good construction and finishing practices. Keep the wood dry by providing adequate roof overhangs and by properly maintaining the shingles, gutters and downspouts. Window and door casings should slope out from the house to drain water away rapidly. Untreated wood should be treated with a water-repellent preservative, then with a non-porous mildew-resistant primer and finally with at least one top coat also containing a mildewcide. Ordinary household bleach may sometimes remove blue-stain discoloration, but it is not a permanent cure. Be sure to use fresh bleach, since its effectiveness can di-minish with age. The moisture problem must be corrected if a permanent cure is expected.

Though blue stain itself is benign, the "blue mold" on your pine could also indicate rot or decay. The most effective way to control decay is to keep water out and the wood dry. If this is impossible, the wood exposed above ground must be treated regularly with a fungicide. Wood in contact with the ground must be pressure treated with preservatives. A water repellent with the fungicide would also be beneficial.

Removing mildew

All of the rooms in our recently purchased 40-year-old house in north Florida have ¾-in. tongue-and-groove magnolia boards on walls and ceilings. The varnished wood has acquired a beautiful dark patina over the years. The trouble is, there are numerous places where knotholes are ringed with the grey-green "glow" of mildew. What is the best way to remove the mildew and prevent its immediate return? I don't want to destroy or alter the finish.
—*John McDevitt, Crawfordville, Fla.*

Don Newell, a chemist, replies: Your first job is to determine the cause of the mildew. Is moisture getting in behind the boards as a result of water leakage or inadequate venting? If so, then no treatment of the interior sides of the boards will help. Mildew requires moisture to live, and you'll have to deal with this unwanted moisture before proceeding further. I hate to suggest it, but you might carefully remove one or two of the mold-damaged boards and check the condition of their back sides.

It could be that the problem on your walls and ceiling is strictly a surface phenomenon resulting from the high humidity in your part of the country. I don't know of any way to remove mildew and prevent its return without removing the covering layer of varnish. What I would do is carefully scrape or sand down the mildewed spots until the bare wood is exposed. At the edges of the sanded areas, feather the varnish so that the transition from bare wood to untouched varnish is gradual. This will make your spot refinishing job less conspicuous.

Take some Clorox or other household bleach, dilute it according to the instructions on the label (about one tablespoon of bleach to a quart of water) and wash the affected areas well with a sponge soaked in this solution. Protect the surrounding furniture with plastic dropcloths; otherwise you may get bleach spots. The bleach will kill the mildew. After a few minutes, rinse the treated spot with fresh water and a clean cloth. Get the surface as dry as you can, then just let it air dry. If the mildew appears to be gone after the wood has dried, clean the spot with denatured alcohol (shellac solvent) to kill any remaining mold or mildew. Repeat the bleaching operation, this time with a slightly stronger solution.

Let the surface of the wood dry completely before you proceed. The area you sanded and bleached will be lighter that the surrounding untouched surface. You'll have to refinish the bare wood to match the patina by applying some varnish. Check the samples of colored varnish at your hardware or paint-supply store;

pick the finish that most closely matches the tone of your walls. If you can't find a colored varnish, make one by mixing an oil-base stain with some clear varnish.

Use a clean, soft brush to apply a thin first coat of varnish, and allow it to dry overnight. Then rub with some medium-grade steel wool to cut off dust particles that may have settled onto the face as it dried. The second coat should be heavier and wetter. Brush it all the way up to the feathered edges of the repaired spots. What you're trying to do now is to lay down a substantial coating of varnish, blending it in with the tapered edges of the old finish. If the refinished area still stands out, brush a very thin third coat over the entire board to make the surface of the wall uniform.

There's no guarantee that all this will prevent the mildew from returning. If spores are left in the wood and growth conditions are favorable, it's probably inevitable that you'll get a repeat performance.

Bleaching out mold

My new home has exposed rough-sawn Douglas fir 6x10 beams on 4-ft. centers. The beams had some dark blackish areas on them when they arrived. I thought it was dirt, but they are getting larger and are appearing on other beams. What is it, and how do I get rid of it?
—*Mark Price, New Berlin, Ill.*

R. Bruce Hoadley, a professor of wood technology, replies: The blackish areas sound like some type of mold. I'd try a cleaning with a solution of chlorine bleach and TSP (trisodium phosphate). This will kill the mold spores and bleach out the black stain. This cleaner also works well on white painted surfaces.

To mix the solution, add about a cup or two of bleach and a handful of TSP to a pail of warm water. The proportions aren't critical, and your local paint dealer may have a more precise recipe. Using rubber gloves and eye protection, sponge the liquid lightly onto the darkened surfaces, scrub briskly with a bristle scrub brush, and then sponge with clear water. Remove excess moisture quickly with a barely damp sponge, and allow to dry. Once the beams season fully in place, and as long as their moisture content remains below 15% to 18%, there should be no additional bloom of mold.

Finish for a cypress deck

Here in southern Louisiana mildew is a constant and persistent antagonist. Last fall I removed the mildew from the deck behind my house with 2,000-psi water pressure and gallons of bleach (the same way I remove it from the siding). The bleached look is nice, and I am fairly happy with it, but it is definitely not what I want for the floor of the screened-in front porch I'm about to build. I would like your advice on how to preserve the beauty of natural cypress with a clear finish that would have the durability of a painted finish.

The other problem I face is trapped moisture. Rainwater that blows through the screen on my porch walls will be blocked by the sole plate (or bottom screen rail). I don't like the idea of drilling weep holes. I think sawing kerfs in the bottom of the plate would be a better idea. What do you think?
—*Robert Duane Dyer,
Ponchatoula, La.*

Terry Amburgey, of the Forest Products Utilitization Laboratory at Mississippi State University, replies: First of all, both Koppers Co. (Wolman Protection Products, Koppers Building, 436 Seventh Ave., Pittsburgh, Pa. 15219) and Osmose Wood Preserving (P. O. Drawer O, Griffin, Ga. 30224) have deck "brighteners" on the market that do a good job of brightening discolored exterior decking. These products oxidize the top, discolored layer of the wood and restore its natural look. They are usually available in building-supply outlets.

The cleaned deck surfaces should then be treated with a product that contains both a water repellent and a wood preservative. Several clear water-repellent preservatives (WRP) are on the market, including Wolman Clear Wood Preservative (Koppers Co.). Whatever you use on your deck should be reapplied annually. And because clear finishes offer little or no protection from the ultraviolet rays of the sun, you'll probably still see some fading of the cypress. So you might want to use the deck brighters annually, too.

These same products—deck brighteners and WRPs—could be used to treat the decking boards on your screened-in porch. I recommend soaking the end grain of all flooring pieces in a WRP for three to five minutes before installation. As with your deck, it probably would be a good idea to retreat the porch floor every year.

The saw kerfs in the bottom of the screen rail are essential. All lower rails should also be treated liberally with a WRP once a year.

Powder-post beetles

How serious a problem is the presence of powder-post beetles in an old house? The exterminating company that inspected the two-story house I now own reported the presence of beetles in some sill timbers and the attic space. Should I go to the expense of fumigating or just ignore them, as another exterminator suggested?
—*Cecil E. Smith, Augusta, Ga.*

R. Bruce Hoadley, a professor of wood technology at the University of Massachusetts, replies: Powder-post beetles most commonly infest the sapwood of coarse-textured hardwoods. In the United States, ring-porous hardwoods such as oak and ash are common host timbers. The adult beetles lay eggs in the large open vessels (pores) of the wood and the hatching larvae burrow through the wood, feeding on the carbohydrate residues found in the parenchyma cells of the sapwood. It's not unusual to find powder-post beetles in old houses. Large timbers of oak or chestnut that have been squared up from logs are common sites, especially in the sapwood portions along the edges of the beams.

When evidence of powder-post beetles is discovered, a couple of things should be investigated. First, the host timbers should be carefully monitored to determine how heavy the infestation is and how active the insects are. (Many times people dis-

cover very old damage in which there are no longer any active insects.) If possible, mark every existing hole in a few test areas with a marker or crayon to see whether any new ones are appearing. Next, vacuum away all frass (powdered wood and insect excrement) and check at regular intervals for new frass, which would indicate newly emerging adults. You may find the activity is far less—or far more serious—than you imagined.

Second, decide whether the damage is, or could be, critical if allowed to continue. If the infestation is merely in the narrow sapwood edges of heavy timbers, even total eventual destruction of the sapwood may have no consequence. On the other hand, if the continued activity would result in structural weakening, cosmetic damage, or in the buildup of an epidemic population that could spread, corrective procedures are in order.

In certain cases where infestation is limited and open to view, liberal surface spraying with a contact insecticide may help hold the situation in check by reducing the reinfestation of emerging adults. However, in more serious cases the only really effective approach is professional fumigation, which can be quite expensive. Your assessment of the magnitude of the problem and the consequences of allowing it to continue should guide you in deciding whether to invest in fumigation.

Termite proofing

How do you install termite proofing on an earth-bermed home where the roof is conventional

wood construction with superinsulation? What non-heat-conducting material would you use for the shield? —*J. Kaye, Uniondale, N. Y.*

Charles Lane, an underground-construction consultant in St. Paul, Minn., replies: Termite protection for an earth-covered roof and earth-bermed walls is identical to conventional termite protection for foundation walls. Since most earth-sheltered walls are made of concrete, a termite shield is placed on top of the concrete and under the wood construction. Any conventional termite shields available in your area are acceptable.

Don't be concerned about using a metal shield. The area of the shield material is so small that it is negligible in heat loss. The ability of the material to stop termites is the primary goal.

In addition to the termite shield, soil poisoning is used. The type and concentration of soil poisoning should be appropriate to your location. Your area is classified as slight to moderate with respect to termite-protection needs. Typical soil poisons used are Aldrin, Benzene Hexachloride (BHC), Chlordane, Dieldrin and Heptachlor. Do not use any poison that contains DDT. All of these chemicals (except DDT) are used in low-concentration water emulsions and must be applied by professionals. These chemicals are enormously toxic, and it just isn't the kind of task even the careful home owner ought to attempt.

Termites in air-core floors

A termite inspector has told me that air-core floors are a pest-control nightmare. He was referring to the prospect of drilling into the slab in various places in order to inject poisonous chemicals to combat subterranean termites. He said that because of the risk of accidentally contaminating the air-flow system with long-lasting chemicals, he would never touch the job. Has this problem ever been addressed with respect to this emerging technology? —*Don Bradshaw, Irvine, Calif.*

Bion Howard, an energy engineer for the National Concrete Masonry Association in Herndon, Va., replies: Several methods can be used to relieve concern about termites in air-core floors. In new construction, the air-core system requires vapor retarders (at least 8 mil thick) and is typically placed on top of sand and plastic foam insulation. Thus the builder can first treat the soil in the air-core slab area with termiticide, then construct the heat-storage system above the treated soil.

With strong pesticide applications comes concern for long-term indoor air quality. The use of 24-mil poly vapor retarders (recommended for high radon areas), heat-seamed or solvent-welded in the field and caulked and sealed at all penetrations, provides superior resistance to pesticide penetration into the home at only slightly higher cost. This would be even better than the 8-mil poly vapor retarder normally used in air-core floors.

I think most new construction in infested areas uses soil applications of pesticide strong enough to last the life of the building. Since such pesticides are "persistent" and do not break down, retreatment is rarely necessary. However, new EPA controls may affect what termiticides are currently available.

With the standard construction methods used today, an unknown amount of persistent pesticide leaks into our termite-proofed buildings through cracks and openings in foundation walls from treated soils. I suspect that an insulated, vapor-proof and waterproof air-core system would reduce entry of pesticide and/or radon better than standard foundation designs without such protections. The air-core system can even be adapted to enhance indoor air quality by providing ventilation of the slab and foundations, preventing pollutants from soils from entering the building in the first place.

Concrete-block air-core slab systems have been proposed as radon control systems for Florida's phosphate lands, where soil radon is a serious issue. More frequently the air-core floor system is used in colder climates. Data from simula-tions have shown that air-core floor designs provide superior thermal performance and cost-effectiveness in heating.

Using all-masonry construction, particularly in foundations and exterior walls, should significantly reduce the threat of long-term pest damage in infested areas, compared to wood-frame construction. This has been well known for years, and is one reason why all-masonry homes are so widely constructed in Florida and throughout the Sun Belt.

If the need for retreatment is a genuine concern, a sub-slab network of metal tubing could be laid in the soil, and the heat-storage system would then be built above it. This would add to system cost, but would provide a retreatment option superior to drilling into and through the air-core slab, which is not recommended. Frequent drilling of holes might cause the concrete to crack if the underlaying soil/gravel base has subsided.

Index

P

Paints:
bonding agents for, 102
epoxy, 116
failures in, 78
latex acrylic vs. oil-base, 79
removal of, 95-96, 182
removers, toxicity of, 73
surface for, 78
vapor-barrier, sources for, 130
woods for, 177
Paneling, sealers for, 187
Patios, on garage roofs, 63
Pee-Vee, for pulling plates to line, 33
Penetrating-oil finishes, for teak, 160
Pentachlorophenol, toxicity of, 75
Pine *(Pinus spp.)*:
for log building, 202
for timber framing, 209-211
Plaster:
bonding agents for, 188-189
coves in, matching, 194
cratered, reproducing, 102
cutting techniques, 193
dust from, minimizing, 192
finish for, 188
glass fibers for, 191
insulation over, 129
joint compound over, 188
liquid bonding agent for, 191
loose, dealing with, 103
moldings of, 186
relath for, 191
removing, 192
repairing, 189-191
sealing, for paint, 102
Swedish putty, reproducing, 102
Plastic laminate, seam problems with, 166
Plates, persuading to line, 33
Plywood, T-111 siding, 123
Polybutylene pipe, for warm floors, 156-157
Polyethylene, 40-mil membrane of, 88
Polystyrene:
expanded, 26, 123
extruded, 26
Polyurethane foam:
as exterior spray, 130
as slab insulation, 26
on stone masonry, 131
Polyurethane insulation board, 123
Polyurethane varnish:
for floors, disadvised, 149
and sanding sealer, 162
over teak, 160
Poplar, yellow *(Liriodendron tulipifera)*:
for framing, 170, 211
qualities of, 170
Porches:
for sun moderation, 178
timber-framed, 218-219

R

Radiant barriers, and heat buildup, 127
Radiant-floor heating systems, 155-159
Rafters:
fire blocking for, 121
jack, compound cuts for, 45
for octagonal bay, 42
strength of, 49
superinsulated gusseted, 121-122
trussed, 122
Raising, of timber frame, 205
Rammed earth, 196-198
Reciprocating saws, plaster-cutting blades for, 193
Redwood *(Sequoia sempervirens)*:
construction grades of, 38
for timber framing, 211
Renovation, condensation problems and, 187
Resorcinol glue, exterior use, 30, 80
Respirators, source for, 73

Restoration:
molding fitting for, 168
plaster repair in, 188
Ridge vents, commercial, source for, 125
Rise (roof), finding, 43
Rock beds, heat distribution in, 21
Roofing:
adjoining, flashing for, 56
asphalted sheeting, 123
association for, 63
bowed, methods for, 44
cheap insulated, 123
as decks, 62
dormers in, adding, 42
gable end in, 46, 85
galvanized, 123
life of, and ventilation, 121
membranes for, 62
metal, over stress-skin panels, 61
mineral-felt roll, 67
nailers in, 123
for octagonal bay, 42
radiant barriers for, 127
radiational losses from, 120
removing, tool for, 66
rubber-membrane, single-ply, 63
standing-seam, flashing for, 59
ventilation for, 120
and vertical-wall abutment, flashing for, 55-56
Routers:
tongue-and-groove bit sets for, 142
trammel jig for, 171

S

Safety, with masonry blades, 64
Sanding sealer, 162
Saunas, woods for, 35
Sawdust, bricks from, 196
Sawhorses, folding, 34
Sealers:
exterior, homemade, 75
for flooring, 148
for logs, 203
oil-based, 187
shellac based, 187
over wallpaper, 187
against water-soluble stains, 187
Septic-tank systems, and tree roots in, 5
Sheathing:
insulated, 136
solid vs. let-in, 28
Shingles:
cutting of, 67
felt strips with, 70
fire danger of, 69
grades of, 71
pilot holes in, 67
removing, tool for, 66
seasoning of, 67
solid vs. open sheathing for, 70
woods for, 67, 69, 71
Showers, tile, repairing, 88
Shutters, louvered, wood for, 176
Siding:
board and batten, 86
finishes for, 75, 78
mildewcide for, 76
stains on, dealing with, 77
Sinks, recessed, below tile, 89
Sites, drainage for, 6
Skylights:
curbless, 57, 59-60
glass for, 175
insulating systems for, 174
R-value in, increasing, 173
Slabs:
and superinsulated houses, 207-208
vapor-barrier retrofit for, 22
Soffits, vents in, and fire blocking, 121
Softwoods, sealers for, 187

Fine Homebuilding
For more information...

We hope you enjoy this book and find it useful in your work. If you would like to know more about Taunton Press magazines, books, and videos, just fill out this card and return it to us.

Name

Address

City   *State*   *Zip*

I'm interested in:
- [ ] *Building and remodeling*
- [ ] *Gardening and landscaping*
- [ ] *Woodworking and cabinetmaking*
- [ ] *Sewing, knitting, and needlecrafts*

FHAA

Fine Homebuilding
To subscribe...

All the useful advice in *Tips & Techniques for Builders* comes from *Fine Homebuilding* magazine. If you would like a subscription, just fill out this card.

1 year (7 issues) for just $24—over 23% off the newsstand price. Outside the U.S. $28/year (U.S. funds please).

Name

Address

City   *State*   *Zip*

- [ ] *My payment is enclosed.*
- [ ] *Please bill me.*
- [ ] *Please send me information about other*
  Taunton Press magazines, books, and videos.

FHAB

BUSINESS REPLY MAIL
FIRST CLASS PERMIT No. 19 NEWTOWN, CT

POSTAGE WILL BE PAID BY ADDRESSEE

The Taunton Press
63 South Main Street
Box 355
Newtown, CT 06470-9989

NO POSTAGE
NECESSARY
IF MAILED
IN THE
UNITED STATES

BUSINESS REPLY MAIL
FIRST CLASS PERMIT No. 19 NEWTOWN, CT

POSTAGE WILL BE PAID BY ADDRESSEE

The Taunton Press
63 South Main Street
Box 355
Newtown, CT 06470-9989